Qualitative Data Analysis with ATLAS.ti

SAGE has been part of the global academic community since 1965, supporting high quality research and learning that transforms society and our understanding of individuals, groups, and cultures. SAGE is the independent, innovative, natural home for authors, editors and societies who share our commitment and passion for the social sciences.

Find out more at: **www.sagepublications.com**

Connect, Debate, Engage on Methodspace

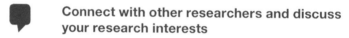 **Connect with other researchers and discuss your research interests**

 **Keep up with announcements in the field, for example calls for papers and jobs**

 **Discover and review resources**

 **Engage with featured content such as key articles, podcasts and videos**

 **Find out about relevant conferences and events**

Connecting the Research Community

www.methodspace.com

brought to you by

⑤SAGE

Qualitative Data Analysis with ATLAS.ti Susanne Friese

Second Edition

Los Angeles | London | New Delhi
Singapore | Washington DC

Los Angeles | London | New Delhi
Singapore | Washington DC

SAGE Publications Ltd
1 Oliver's Yard
55 City Road
London EC1Y 1SP

SAGE Publications Inc.
2455 Teller Road
Thousand Oaks, California 91320

SAGE Publications India Pvt Ltd
B 1/I 1 Mohan Cooperative Industrial Area
Mathura Road
New Delhi 110 044

SAGE Publications Asia-Pacific Pte Ltd
3 Church Street
#10-04 Samsung Hub
Singapore 049483

Editor: Katie Metzler
Assistant editor: Lily Mehrbod
Production editor: Ian Antcliff
Copyeditor: Nevill Hankins
Proofreader: Louise Harnby
Indexer: David Rudeforth
Marketing manager: Ben Griffin-Sherwood
Cover design: Shaun Mercier
Typeset by: C&M Digitals (P) Ltd, Chennai, India
Printed in Great Britain by Henry Ling Limited at
The Dorset Press, Dorchester, DT1 1HD

Library of Congress Control Number: Available

British Library Cataloguing in Publication data

A catalogue record for this book is available from
the British Library

MIX
Paper from
responsible sources
FSC™ C013985

ISBN 978-1-44628-203-8
ISBN 978-1-44628-204-5 (pbk)

What does ATLAS.ti stand for? Atlas was the Greek Hero, who held up the sphere of heaven and brought astronomy and navigation to mankind. Today, an atlas is a collection of maps – models of the world – which helps us to orientate ourselves and find the right way to our destination. Besides that, in German ATLAS.ti is the acronym for *Archiv für Technik, Lebenswelt, AlltagsSprache* [Archive of Technology, Lifeworld and Everyday Language]. ATLAS bears on the idea of mapping the world by an archive of meaningful documents. The abbreviation *ti* in the software name means *text interpretation*.

Contents

About the author

Susanne Friese started working with computer software for qualitative data analysis in 1992. She was introduced to CAQDAS tools during her time at QualisResearch in the USA, between 1992 and 1994. In subsequent years, she worked with the CAQDAS Project in England (1994–6), where she taught classes on The Ethnograph and Nud*ist. Two additional computer programs, MAXQDA and ATLAS.ti, followed shortly thereafter as the respective Microsoft Windows versions of these programs. During her dissertation and later as an Assistant Professor at the Copenhagen Business School in Denmark, she carried out a variety of research projects using both qualitative and quantitative methods. Dr Friese used SPSS software to analyze quantitative data and the ATLAS.ti program to support her work with qualitative material. She has taught qualitative and quantitative research methods at both undergraduate and graduate level at various universities. Currently she is a Research Fellow at the Max Planck Institute for the Study of Religious and Ethnic Diversity in Göttingen, Germany, working on methodological issues around computer-assisted qualitative data analysis. She runs courses in ATLAS.ti and computer-assisted qualitative data analysis (see http://www.quarc.de). In addition, she has assisted on numerous projects around the world in a consulting capacity and has authored didactic materials and works for ATLAS.ti at the intersection of developers and users.

Preface to second edition

Since software development is an ongoing process, after two years it was time to update the first edition of this book to encompass the new features and functionalities of ATLAS.ti 7. One major change that was introduced with version 7 is related to project management. The basic idea behind this change is to make it easier for users to manage their projects, thus having to think less about how the software is handling the data and spending more time on the main task of analyzing the data. To support the latter, the available analysis tools have been improved and new ones have been added. Further, it has become much easier, nicer and more efficient to work with audio and video data. They are now also displayed with a margin area on the right hand side, where you can see your coding, and can be handled very similarly to text data. The interface has been augmented with a number of new features such as the display of documents side by side, side panels and fly-out windows to optionally show additional objects and improved visualizations. I spent about a year working with all these new functions and features and would now like to share with you what I have learned and how I have adapted my way of working with the software. The general procedure has not changed but some steps are easier to handle, for example due to the new side panels. The new and improved analysis options are excellent. They also allow you to ask different types of questions and in different ways. To reflect these changes, I have completely rewritten the chapter on project and data management (Chapter 3). I have added a section that concentrates solely on team project management, as was suggested by one of the reviewers. In addition, you will find a description of how to prepare and set up a project when working with survey data, synchronized audio/video and text documents, and for special situations such as working with large-sized documents.

Throughout the book, I work with a new sample data set on children and happiness, which I have already used quite successfully in my workshops over the past year. The major issues discussed in the data are whether children add to happiness or not; what the reasons are for having children or for not having children; and what the effects are of either. As almost every person at some point in their life has to think about the issue of having or not having children, this data set works well around the globe. Besides, it is quite entertaining to code. In addition to this data set, I provide three more sample projects on the companion website that cover different topic areas and data types. All sample projects are described in the introductory chapter.

In Chapter 2 I have added a description of the new interface features. Chapter 4 on the technical aspects of coding includes a revised section on working with audio and video data. Further, I have made some slight changes reflecting the technical enhancements of the coding procedures. As in the first edition, Chapters 5 to 7 cover the core of the analysis method that I describe in the book. The basic idea behind the various steps and procedures has not changed, but due to the new functions and features offered by ATLAS.ti 7, a few mouse clicks have. Different to the first edition, I describe issues on data organization first in Chapter 5 and then introduce the memo function (previously Chapter 6). Both aspects are better placed here in the workflow of the overall data analysis process. Since I use a different sample data set for this book, all the examples and the analysis questions posed in Chapters 5 to 7 are different. Further, in Chapter 7 I have added a new section where I describe different applications of the network view function.

The previous Chapter 8 on the NCT method is now Chapter 1. It provides the reader with an overview of the whole process and gives some idea about what is to come. The placement of the NCT method at the end of the first edition was related to its genesis. I have been teaching the various steps and procedures for some time, but it was not until I began to write the book that I began to formalize it. This was also the time when I came up with the name 'computer-assisted NCT method of analysis'.

I end this second edition with some thoughts about how to bring together the various threads of your work in ATLAS.ti so that you can complete your analysis with a shining written report.

In terms of usability for teaching, I have labeled all practical hands-on sessions as 'skills training' and at the beginning of each chapter you will find a box that lists all the skills training sessions. As before, to test your knowledge or the knowledge of your students you will find a list of review questions at the end of each chapter and a glossary of terms.

In preparing the second edition, I am thankful for the continuous support of the team at SAGE publications. Special thanks go to my editor, Katie Metzler, who prepared the way for writing this edition, asked reviewers to provide feedback, and continuously encouraged and supported me throughout the writing process. Further, I am grateful for the work done by the production team, Ian Antcliff and Laura Gil Lasheras, be it in terms of copyediting or laying out the final book. Last but not least, a big 'thank you' to the five anonymous reviewers who provided valuable feedback.

Introduction

ATLAS.ti belongs to the genre of CAQDAS programs. CAQDAS stands for Computer-Aided Qualitative Data Analysis Software. It is a somewhat lengthy acronym as compared to 'QDA software', which can also be found in the literature. The latter stands for Qualitative Data Analysis software and the apparent similarity may be responsible for some of the misunderstandings and misperceptions related to CAQDAS.[1] ATLAS.ti – like any other CAQDAS program – does not actually analyze data; it is simply a tool for supporting the process of qualitative data analysis. Computers are generally very good at finding things like strings of characters or coded data segments in a large variety of combinations, but the researcher first needs to tell the computer, by way of coding, which data segment has what kind of meaning (see also Konopásek, 2007). This prerequisite is used by some people as an argument against using software, who ask: 'if the computer doesn't do the coding, then what it is good for?' And without 'test driving' a CAQDAS package, they judge the software to be inadequate in a qualitative research context and return to their manual methods of colored pencils and filing cabinets. Welsh (2002) describes two camps of researchers: those who see software as central to their way of analyzing data and those who feel that it is peripheral and fear that using it leads to a 'wrong' way of analyzing data. Smith and Hesse-Biber (1996) found that software is used mainly as an organizing tool. However, technology has advanced considerably since 1996 and I suggest that software can be used for much more than just organizing data.

Software frees you from all those tasks that a machine can do much more effectively, like modifying code words and coded segments, retrieving data based on various criteria, searching for words, integrating material in one place, attaching notes and finding them again, counting the numbers of coded incidences, offering overviews at various stages of a project, and so on. By using ATLAS.ti, it becomes much easier to analyze data systematically and to ask questions that you otherwise would not ask because the manual tasks involved would be too time consuming. Even large volumes of data and those of different media types can be structured and integrated very quickly with the aid of software (Saillard, 2011). In addition, a carefully conducted, computer-assisted qualitative data analysis also increases the validity of research results, especially at the conceptual stage of an analysis. When using manual methods, it is easy to 'forget' the raw data behind the concepts as it is quite laborious to get back

---

1 The acronym CAQDAS was developed by the directors of the CAQDAS networking project at the University of Surrey, Guildford, UK (http://caqdas.soc.surrey.ac.uk/).

into the data. In a software-supported analysis, the raw data are only a few mouse clicks away and it is much easier to remind yourself about the data and to verify or falsify your developing theoretical thoughts.

Your ideas about the data are likely to be different three or six months into the analysis as compared to the very early stages, and modification of codes and concepts is an innate part of qualitative data analysis. With the aid of computers, this process can also easily be documented. The steps of analysis can be traced and the entire process is open to view. For a more extensive discussion on the advantages as well as the disadvantages of using computers for qualitative data analysis, see Fielding and Lee (1998).

Even if some of the information in this book applies to all CAQDAS packages, you will learn in particular how to carry out a project with ATLAS.ti. Like a lot of other software, ATLAS.ti offers many functions and options but it does not explain what you actually need do to in order to conduct your analysis. Looking back at my own experience, when I started to use software to analyze qualitative data in 1992, I did what most novices probably do: I looked at the features, played around a bit, muddled my way through the software and the data, gained some insights and wrote a report. It worked – somehow. But it wasn't very orderly or systematic.

Since then, my way of working with ATLAS.ti has gradually become much more systematic and – to a certain point – even standardized. This did not happen overnight: it took many years of working with the software and teaching it, as well as involvement in many project consultations. As each qualitative research project is to an extent unique, this allowed me to test my ideas in different contexts and to develop a method of computer-assisted analysis.[2] I often see users struggling instead to find their own way of working with a particular software package. They are overwhelmed by its many functions and sometimes don't even know where to start. They appreciate very much having someone to guide them through the analytical process, advising them which function to use when and at what stage.

What is fundamentally lacking in the literature is a data analysis method for computer-assisted data (see also chapter 1). A number of books and articles have been written on the general use and usefulness of software for qualitative data analysis, the early ones often expressing concern as well as enthusiasm about how software can help (Alexa and Zuell, 2000; Barry, 1998; Hinchliffe et al., 1997; Morrison and Moir, 1998; Richards and Richards, 1994; Seidel, 1991). Occasionally, a chapter on computer-assisted analysis is included at the end of qualitative data analysis books (e.g. Silverman, 2000; Mayring, 2010), or there are short descriptions and screenshots showing how certain analysis steps could be implemented (Corbin and Strauss, 2008). I was very surprised,

---

2 The term 'method' is used here in an epistemological sense as a set of steps and procedures by which to acquire knowledge, as distinct from the more encompassing term 'methodology', which includes the entire research process starting with ontological considerations of what there is that can be studied (Blumer, 1969; Hug, 2001; Strübing and Schnettler, 2004).

however, to read descriptions of pile sorting and other manual methods of data analysis in a book first published in 2010 (Bernard and Ryan, 2010). The authors point out that the various procedures they describe can also be accomplished using a software package, but they do not explain how. Maybe the assumption is that it goes without saying: you simply load the software and it is immediately obvious how to adapt your old manual procedures.

I argue that this is not the case. Today, with the new possibilities available, we can approach data analysis in different ways. Therefore the methodology of analysis needs to be rewritten to exploit the benefits of a software-supported approach. Software changes the way we build up coding systems. The process becomes much more exploratory due to the ease of renaming and modifying codes. Computers also change the ways we ask questions about the data. Data analysis procedures have become much more sophisticated because, for a computer, it is much easier to find things in the data and to output results. Also, CAQDAS makes it easier to combine qualitative and quantitative methods, which of course does not preclude a purely qualitative approach. It allows qualitative researchers to move out of black box analysis and to make the entire analytic process more transparent. And it allows them to work in teams, even across geographical boundaries. This creates new opportunities and also new challenges.

This book, in addition to teaching you how to work with ATLAS.ti, proposes a method for computer-assisted data analysis. The method is called 'computer-assisted NCT analysis', where NCT stands for Noticing, Collecting and Thinking. As the name indicates, the focus of the method is on data analysis and not on the entire research process. Thus it is possible to integrate it into various methodologies; you don't need to subscribe to a particular world view in order to use it, and it doesn't prescribe how you should tackle your analysis. If the overall methodological approach or the research questions require an inductive approach, you can work inductively; if it makes more sense to work deductively, you can do that as well, or use a mixed approach. You can work purely qualitatively or, if applicable, quantify some of the findings. Whether you come from an ethnographic, a phenomenological or a grounded theory tradition, whether you have conducted action research, narrative interviews, focus groups or biographical research, whether you have structured or unstructured data, observational data or audio-visual material, I am interested in teaching you how to approach the analysis of your data in a systematic computer-assisted way.

Computer-assisted analysis is like exploring a data landscape

Computer-assisted analysis can be thought of as a journey. Think of your ATLAS.ti project as an excursion into unknown territory. The data material is the terrain that you want to study; the chosen analytic approach is your pathway through it. The tools and functions provided by ATLAS.ti are your equipment to examine what there is to discover. In Chapters 1 to 3 we prepare for the journey. The preparation of the data material can be compared to selecting the right time of the year for the excursion. Ice and snow may hinder the success of our excursion; so can a careless transcription or wrongly chosen data file formats. A well-thought-out project setup is like planning your excursion carefully and not just running off up the first dirt track you see: that might turn out to be a dead end. Learning the technical aspects of coding in Chapter 4 is essential before you can make progress. With that knowledge, you will be well prepared to embark on the journey. Along the way you will improve your coding skills and learn further skills, like developing a system for all the interesting things you observe; how to write notes on them (writing comments); how to write a diary that documents the excursion and your major insights and findings on the way (writing memos); and how to examine specific characteristics of certain objects and their relations to other objects in depth, using the query tool, the cooccurrence explorer and other helpful functions.

Let's think of our data as a landscape that we want to explore (Figure I.1). The nature trail that I will take you on will take a couple of days and we will naturally take some breaks (e.g. to rest, to play games or to listen to a story around the campfire in the evening), and I have more metaphors in store that will help you to understand better why some paths are dead ends or detours and why some tools should be used in particular ways to best achieve what we are aiming for – that is, a meaningful and comprehensible representation of the terrain we are examining.

Figure I.1   Looking at data like a landscape to be explored

As your tour guide, I provide some tips on how to get ready and how to prepare for the journey. When it is time to gain your first hands-on experience, you will begin by observing the terrain, spotting things that might be interesting, collecting them and putting your coding skills into practice. The aim of this first day of the journey is to become familiar with the terrain, to observe and then to write down notes and first coding ideas. We will meet up later to discuss what you have found. You may already be starting to structure your thoughts about the things you have noticed, or at least wondering how to do so. I will explain it using the terrain of the example data provided, but I will also draw on other examples to show how their investigators managed to add more structure to their enquiries.

This calls for some more skills training and some storytelling, where you will learn first how best to describe surface observations (developing subcategories) and secondly how to pull together very detailed observations by recognizing common characteristics (developing categories). Most people are likely to find examples of both when they look at their coding after the first day of the journey. A few will find that they have so far paid attention only to surface characteristics or the smallest details. Equipped with some new skills, you can move on to explore more of the data landscape until you feel that it is mapped out well and that you can describe what the terrain looks like. At this stage, the development of the coding system is more or less finished.

For some the journey will end here, as this is all they want to achieve. Maybe it was a first excursion into qualitative data analysis as part of a qualitative methodology course or a first independent project in the form of an undergraduate thesis. Others will want to continue the journey, to dig a bit deeper and find out how all the different observations relate to each other and whether some causal relations can be discovered – perhaps to develop a theory about what was discovered in the field. In order to do this, we will need to learn to handle new tools like the query tool, the cooccurrence explorer and the network views. Thus, the journey needs to be halted for a few days to acquire some new knowledge. With these new skills, you will no longer need a tour guide to accompany you on your journey. You can take it from there, gaining your own experiences and maybe becoming a tour guide yourself one day.

For whom did I write the book?

I wrote this book for new users as well as for more experienced users of ATLAS.ti who would like some guidance on how to work with the software. In it, I have answered a lot of questions that are frequently asked at the ATLAS.ti help desk or during my courses. These are often questions that cannot be answered by a technically oriented software manual. They relate to project management issues, how to organize team work, methodological issues on how to build up a good coding system and what to do with the data once coded.

I also wrote the book for teachers of qualitative data analysis. My personal conviction is that, in the twenty-first century, qualitative data should be analyzed with the support of software. It is time that what has long been standard practice in quantitative statistical research is applied to qualitative data analysis as well.

As methodological training is quite diverse, the book can be used for undergraduate as well as postgraduate courses. It is suitable for undergraduates where method training comprises a large part of their study program. My aim for those students is to teach them descriptive-level analysis and thus they could work productively up to Chapter 5 in this book. At this stage, students have learned how to set up and manage projects (Chapter 3), how to code data (Chapter 4) and how to build up a coding system (Chapter 5). While working through the chapters and coding their own data material, they are likely to have learned a lot about their data and gained some insights. They will have mapped out their data landscape (see Figure 5.16). At this level, you can also teach them how to write various types of memos, including research question memos (in the first half of Chapter 6). They have not yet learned the various, more complex retrieval options, but queries can also be based on simple retrievals (i.e. querying single codes). From my experience, students by this time are motivated enough to take a look at the network view function on their own and begin to visualize their findings.

For advanced, Master's and PhD courses, you can take the students one step further and teach them how to analyze data on the conceptual level. This means teaching them about the various analysis tools described in Chapter 6, talking more extensively about writing memos, inserting a lecture or two on issues of reliability and validity in qualitative research, and showing the students how this can be achieved with the support of software. All this can be rounded off by providing more details about the network view function, including the possibilities of working inter-textually using hyperlinks (see Chapter 7).

From the book's companion website, lecturers can download presentations and sample data for use in tutorials etc. The samples contain raw as well as coded data and projects which follow up the skills training sessions in the book.

Chapter overview

In Chapter 1, I provide an overview of the analysis steps I am suggesting in this book and introduce you to the NCT method of computer-assisted qualitative data analysis. In Chapter 2, I take you on a tour through the ATLAS.ti interface and the terminology used by the software. There is unfortunately no common language among the different CAQDAS packages. What is called a variable in one software package is an attribute in another. Codes might be referred to as keywords or as nodes. In ATLAS.ti, however, a node is a nodal point in a network view, and so on. Thus, it is first necessary to learn the language of the software. With time, this will enable you to sound like a pro, to become a member of the ATLAS.ti community where talk is all about HUs, families, managers, P-Docs, and the like. If you already have some experience of working with ATLAS.ti, you will probably be familiar with the terminology and can skip Chapter 3 on getting to know the interface.

In Chapter 3, we are ready to rock – and to begin an ATLAS.ti project. It is a very important chapter: data management issues are often dismissed as boring and thus get neglected, and this frequently leads to difficulties, time wasting and sometimes data loss further down the line. You learn about the data file formats that ATLAS.ti supports, when and for what purpose to choose which file format and how to prepare data transcripts so that you can best utilize software features later on. Miscellaneous settings like language support are also discussed, as ATLAS.ti users are spread around the globe and speak and use a variety of languages. Further, I explain the basic principles of data management in ATLAS.ti – they are not difficult to understand but you need to know them – followed by a description of various project setup scenarios for single user and team situations. Here you can choose any scenario that applies to you. There is no need to read through all of them.

In Chapter 4 I explain the technical aspects of coding. You will find out about all the options for the variety of data file formats available. This is followed by a chapter on the methodological aspects of coding. Coding on its simplest level refers to the process of assigning a label to a data segment that the analyst deems to be relevant for some reason. Whether the code is merely a description, a paraphrase of the text, or a concept or category on an abstract level makes no difference to the software. Software offers the option to code; what users do with this option is up to them. In Chapter 5 you will learn everything that you need to know about building a well-structured project, including an efficient coding system. This is the prerequisite for the continuing conceptual level analysis, the topic of Chapters 6 and 7.

In Chapter 6 the idea of second-level conceptual analysis is introduced. This chapter combines an explanation of the memo function with a description of the analysis tools offered by ATLAS.ti. The two topics are discussed side by side, because querying data and writing memos are related analytic procedures. Describing them as separate entities would not adequately reflect the methodological process of this stage of the analysis.

Chapter 7 is about visualizing ideas and findings in the form of network views and hyperlinks. These are tools that enable you to create links within and across data. If you don't yet know what network views look like, think of them as concept maps. As in previous chapters, there is a mix of technical explanations and methodological considerations.

In Chapter 8, I provide some ideas on how to prepare and write your research report. As recently examined by Paulus et al. (2014), often little is written in published papers how ATLAS.ti or other software packages have been used throughout the analysis process. In this chapter, I provide some ideas on how the work already done in the software can help you to prepare and write your report.

Sample projects

On the companion website you will find a number of sample projects that you can use in class or if you teach a workshop. If you work through this book on your own, it is best to work with the Children & Happiness project that I use as an example throughout the book, plus your own data material. In the following, each project is briefly described in order to give you a general idea about the content and data file formats that are included. You can find more detail on each project on the companion website.

- Children & Happiness, various stages of the project, used as the main sample throughout the book.
- Schwarzenegger election 2003, various stages of the project, main sample project for the first edition of this book (now adapted to version 7).
- Jack the Ripper, various stages of the project, official version 6 sample project.
- News coverage of the financial crisis of 2008–9.

Children & Happiness

When looking for example data I came across an article on children and happiness written by Nattavudh Powdthavee in the journal *The Psychologist*. Nattavudh reports on a number of academic studies that repeatedly found a negative correlation between having children and levels of happiness, life satisfaction, marital satisfaction and mental well-being. Since having children or not having them is an issue that most people, regardless of their cultural backgrounds, religions or geographic locations, have to deal with, this promised to be a topic that a lot of ATLAS.ti or potential ATLAS.ti users might be interested in.

In addition to the journal article, two blog posts and the comments from readers are included in the sample material. Furthermore, the data contain a short video that allows you to explore the new video functionality in ATLAS.ti 7. The video contains quotes on happiness and how to reach it. The video is associated with a 'transcript' as an example of the synchronized document option. The sample project also includes two image files that were generated as snapshots from the video file.

Furthermore, the sample contains some fictional survey data imported via an Excel spreadsheet. The survey data contain answers from 24 respondents to two open-ended questions: the reasons for having and for not having children. The socio-demographic characteristics of the respondents plus two answers to yes/no questions can be seen in the PD Family Manager (children bring fulfillment & purpose/children bring happiness). This sample project is suitable to demonstrate and practice the full range of functions including coding, analysis, linking and building network views.

Schwarzenegger election 2003 (newspaper analysis)

This project is about the news coverage of the election of Arnold Schwarzenegger as Governor of California in 2003. If you can read and understand German and English, you can use the sample data that compare the coverage of four German and two US newspapers. A second sample project on this topic includes US papers only, seven text files and two images. The question that can be examined is whether the reporting in the various newspapers about the same event – the election of Schwarzenegger as Governor – is the same, similar or completely different. As in the Children & Happiness project, this sample can also be used to practice the full range of functions.

Jack the Ripper

The main aim in preparing this sample project was to cover all the file formats that are supported by ATLAS.ti (text files, PDF files, image data, audio and video files, transcripts based on associated audio files, and locative data, i.e. Google Earth). Further, the sample was designed to experiment with different features and functions. For instance, one of the transcripts (Primary Document 14) has been left incomplete. At the bottom of the transcript you will find instructions on how to continue transcribing the associated audio file. The main themes of the project are the murders by Jack the Ripper and the investigation of the case. Depending on your subject area, you may find it interesting to code and to work with the data. If you don't like to read about murders and how they are committed, this may not be the project of your choice – I just thought I'd warn you.

News coverage of the financial crisis of 2008-9

The data set originates from the KWALON experiment (Evers et al., 2011) and consisted of a large number of html, PDF, audio and video documents downloaded from the Internet in June 2008 and June 2009. The common theme was 'reports on and around the financial crisis'. The sample of 11 documents that are provided on the companion website represents a subset of the data. It includes data from the two years 2008 and 2009, from various countries (USA, UK and Germany), and different media types: html files converted to rich text or PDF, audio and video files. The purpose of this selection was to be able to compare the views and arguments over time and across countries and media types. In addition to the two stages of the project, a full paper describing the analysis process is available (Friese, 2011).

Background reading

Bong, Sharon A. (2002, May). Debunking myths in qualitative data analysis. *Forum Qualitative Sozialforschung/Forum: Qualitative Social Research*, 3(2), www.qualitative-research.net/fqs-texte/2-02/2-02bong-e.htm.

Bourdon, Sylvain (2002). The integration of qualitative data analysis software in research strategies: resistances and possibilities. *Forum Qualitative Sozialforschung/Forum: Qualitative Social Research*, 3(2), Art. 11, http://nbn-resolving.de/urn:nbn:de:0114-fqs0202118.

Fielding, Nigel G. and Lee, Raymond M. (1998). *Computer Analysis and Qualitative Research*. London: Sage.

Friese, Susanne (2005). Software and fieldwork, in R. Wright and D. Hobbs (eds), Part Nine: Fieldwork, Science and Technology, *Handbook of Fieldwork*. London: Sage.

Gibbs, Graham R., Friese, Susanne and Mangabeira, Wilma C. (2002). The use of new technology in qualitative research. Introduction to Issue 3(2) of FQS. *Forum Qualitative Sozialforschung/Forum: Qualitative Social Research*, 3(2), Art. 8, http://nbn-resolving.de/urn:nbn:de:0114-fqs020287.

Hahn, Christopher (2008). *Doing Qualitative Research Using Your Computer*. London: Sage.

Hesse-Biber, Sharlene (2003). Unleashing Frankenstein's monster? The use of computers in qualitative research, in S.N. Hesse-Biber and P. Leavy (eds), *Approaches to Qualitative Research: A Reader on Theory and Practice*. Oxford: Oxford University Press. Chapter 25.

Hinchliffe, Steve, Crang, Mike, Reimer, S.M. and Hudson, Alan (1997). Software for qualitative research: 2. Some thought on 'aiding' analysis. *Environment and Planning A*, 29, 1109–24.

Legewie, Heiner (2014). ATLAS.ti – How it all began (A grandfather's perspective), in Friese, Susanne and Ringmayr, Thomas (eds.), *ATLAS.ti User Conference 2013: Fostering Dialog on Qualitative Methods*. University Press, Technical University Berlin. http://nbn-resolving.de/urn:nbn:de:kobv: 83-opus4-44140.

Mangabeira, Wilma C., Lee, Raymond M. and Fielding, Nigel G. (2004). Computers and qualitative research: adoption, use and representation. *Social Science Computer Review*, 22(2), 167–78.

Morrison, Moya and Moir, Jim (1998). The role of computer software in the analysis of qualitative data: efficient clerk, research assistant or Trojan horse? *Journal of Advanced Nursing*, 28(1), 106–16.

Muhr, Thomas and Friese, Susanne (2001). Computerunterstütze qualitative Datenanalyse, in *Wie kommt die Wissenschaft zu ihrem Wissen. Band 2: Einführung in die Forschungsmethodik und Forschungspraxis*. Hohengehrenpp: Schneider Verlag. S.380–99.

Richards, Lyn (2009). *Handling Qualitative Data: A Practical Guide*, 2nd edn. London: Sage.

Seidel, John (1991). Methods and madness in the application of computer technology to qualitative data analysis, in Nigel G. Fielding and Raymond M. Lee (eds), *Using Computers in Qualitative Research*. London: Sage. pp. 107–116.

Silver, Christina and Lewins, Ann (2010). Computer Assisted Qualitative Data Analysis, in Barry McGaw, Penelope Peterson and Eva Baker, (eds.) *The International Encyclopedia of Education*, 3rd edn. Oxford: Elsevier.

Silver, Christina and Fielding, Nigel G. (2008). Using computer packages in qualitative research, in C. Willig and W. Stainton-Rogers (eds), *The Sage Handbook of Qualitative Research in Psychology*. London: Sage.

Tesch, Renata (1990). *Qualitative Research: Analysis Types & Software Tools*. New York: Falmer Press.

ONE

NCT – A method for computer-assisted qualitative data analysis

Introduction

The model underlying the method is originally based on a paper by Seidel (1998). The model was first presented to me in 1992 and since then I have developed it further, adapting it for computer-assisted analysis procedures. As the three basic components of the model are Noticing things, Collecting things and Thinking about things (see Figure 1.1), I named the analytic approach 'Computer-assisted NCT analysis'. The three thin arrows indicate that the process of analysis can be linear – starting with noticing interesting things in the data, collecting these things and thinking about them, and then coming up with insightful results. This direct sequential process is, however, rather rare. More often, analysis means moving back and forth between noticing, collecting and thinking, as shown by the heavy arrows in the middle of the figure.

Below I explain the three components in more detail. Although there is a large range of analytic practices in qualitative research, the three components of noticing, collecting and thinking can be regarded as basic elements common to all of them. For example, if you take a look at the book by Creswell (1998), you will find these three elements in each of the five research traditions he describes. Let's take a closer look at them now.

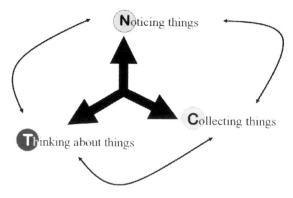

Figure 1.1   The NCT model of qualitative data analysis adapted from Seidel (1998)

Noticing things

Noticing refers to the process of finding interesting things in the data when reading through transcripts, field notes, documents, reports, newspaper articles, etc., or when viewing video material or images, or when listening to audio files. In order to capture these things, the researcher may write down notes, mark the segments or attach preliminary codes. Codes may be derived inductively or deductively. At this point, the level of a code does not play a role. Codes may be descriptive or already conceptual. The important point is to mark those things that are interesting in the data and to name them.

Collecting things

Reading further, you will very likely notice a few things that are similar to some you may have noticed before. They may even fit under the same code name. If a similar issue does not quite fit under the same heading as the first issue you noticed, you can simply rename the code to subsume the two. Even if the term is not yet the perfect code label, it doesn't matter. You can continue to collect more similar data segments and later, when you review them, it will be easier to think of better and more fitting code names to cover the substance of the material you have collected. The intellectual work that needs to be done at this stage is the same as has been described in the past for manual ways of coding. As Strauss and Corbin wrote in 1998:

> As the researcher moves along with analysis, each incident in the data is compared with other incidents for similarities and differences. Incidents found to be conceptually similar are grouped together under a higher-level descriptive concept. (p. 73)

Differently from grounded theory, the NCT analysis does not prescribe any particular way of coding. The initial process of collecting (i.e. coding) can be manifold depending on the underlying research questions, research aim and overall methodology you are using. To name just a few of the various procedures that you will find in the literature:

- descriptive or topic coding (Miles and Huberman, 1994; Saldaña, 2003; Wolcott, 1994)
- process coding (Bodgan and Biklen, 2007; Charmaz, 2002; Corbin and Strauss, 2008)
- initial or open coding (Charmaz, 2006; Corbin and Strauss, 2008; Glaser, 1978)
- emotion coding (Goleman, 1995; Prus, 1996)
- values coding (Gable and Wolf, 1993; LeCompte and Preissle, 1993)
- narrative coding (Cortazzi, 1993; Riessman, 2008)
- provisional coding (Dey, 1993; Miles and Huberman, 1994).

The NCT method of analysis suggests computer-assisted procedures for how to deal with them. Researchers may choose to follow just one of the suggested procedures or combine them. The things you collect in your data may include themes, emotions and values at the same time. You may approach the process with a deductive framework in mind, as used in provisional coding, or you may develop codes inductively, as suggested by initial or open coding, or use a mix of deductively and inductively developed codes. Some researchers develop about 40 codes, others a few hundred or even a few thousand. The NCT method of analysis provides answers for what to do with your codes within a software environment. Often there is a lack of methodological understanding of what a code is. The software does not explain it; it just offers functions to create new codes, to delete, to rename or to merge them. The metaphor of collecting helps to understand better that a properly developed code is more than just a descriptive label for a data segment and that it does not make sense to attach a new label to everything one notices. Developing too many codes is clearly an adverse effect of using software – no one would ever come close to 1000 codes or more when using old-style paper and pencil techniques. Although computer programs can easily handle 1000 codes, too many codes lead to a dead end. There might be exceptions, but in most cases this hinders further analysis. Chapter 5 explains the methodological components of coding.

Thinking about things

We need to use our brains from the very beginning of the analytic process, even though I have left the thinking aspect of the model until last. We need to think when noticing things, when coming up with good names for codes, or when developing subcategories. We need to do some more thinking when it comes to finding patterns and relations in the data. This mostly takes place after coding when asking: 'How do the various parts of the puzzle fit together? How can we integrate the various aspects of the findings in order to develop a comprehensive picture of the phenomenon studied?' At this later stage we need different ATLAS.ti tools like the **query tool** (see Chapter 6) or the **cooccurrence explorer**. When we begin to see how it all might fit together, we can use the **network view** function to visualize these ideas and to explore them further (see Chapter 7). According to Konopásek (2007), ATLAS.ti is especially suited to making the thinking part of qualitative data analysis visible.

The basic steps of the NCT method of analysis can be understood very easily. It enables novices to work in a systematic manner instead of declaring the software to be the method in itself. With more experience, the cyclical nature of the basic steps becomes more apparent and one learns to apply the method in a more sophisticated manner. In this book, I explain the application of the method within the context of ATLAS.ti. However, it is not an approach that just fits one software package. I also know of MAXQDA and NVivo users who have used it quite successfully in their analysis. Also different in other packages are the mouse clicks and the name of the tools.

Projecting the NCT model onto computer-assisted qualitative data analysis

When looking at the three basic aspects of computer-assisted analysis – preparing data and creating a project file, coding the data, and using the software to sort and structure them with the aim of discovering patterns and relations – the NCT model can be projected as shown in Figure 1.2.

It would be ideal to be able to move in a straight line from the data to noticing, then to collecting, and finally to thinking and discovering wonderful new insights. Unfortunately, it is not as simple as that. Let's take a look at the possible variations in conducting a qualitative data analysis.

Variations of the three notes: noticing, collecting, thinking

One variant is the **sequential** process where you move directly from A to B to C as described above. Unless you have a very structured and simple project like the analysis of an open-ended survey question, then this will seldom be possible.

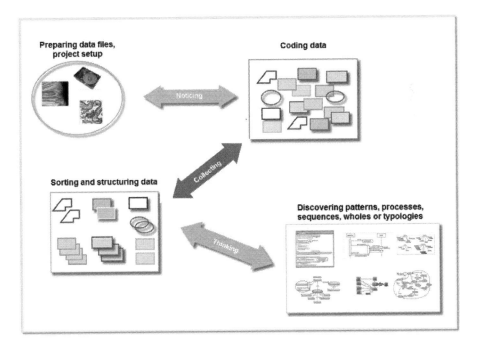

Figure 1.2   A simple projection of the NCT model

More likely is a **recursive** process where you move back and forth between noticing and collecting, for instance when developing subcategories. You may also want to go back to noticing and recoding after already having discovered some relations and created networks. The visualization gives you a different angle on the data: it may be used to talk about your ideas with others and then you may notice you have overlooked something and need to go back, rethink and recode. You may also decide that you need to collect some more data and thus, after further collecting, you begin with noticing again.

A third variation is a **holistic** approach. If you get to a point where you cannot see the wood for the trees or the sheer number of pieces of the puzzle is overwhelming, or if you feel you simply cannot sit in front of a computer screen any longer, then it is time to take a look at the whole again. Take a print-out of one or more transcripts. In summer, look for a nice place outside; in winter, find a cozy spot in front of the fire. Have something to eat and drink and then spend some time reading through your data from beginning to end in a sequential order, reminding yourself of the interview situation or other contexts. Do the same with videos or other types of data you may have. There is no need to sit in front of the computer all the time. Reading the data via a different medium, such as on good old-fashioned paper, is likely to provide further insights. It may help you to see how it all fits together and how the results that you have so far can be integrated.

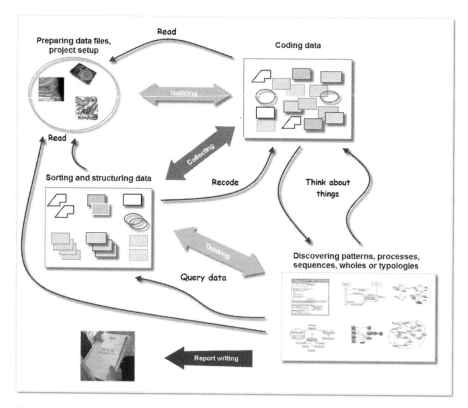

Figure 1.3   The process of computer-aided qualitative data analysis

To sum up, real-life qualitative data analysis looks as shown in Figure 1.3 – a bit messy but fascinating and exciting. Did you note the new element in Figure 1.3, the report? Usually there are deadlines for submitting a research report or your thesis or a paper. Thus, in addition to noticing, collecting and thinking, you need to do some writing. While writing, a lot more thinking occurs. The memo function in ATLAS.ti greatly supports you in this. When used appropriately, it provides you with the building blocks for your results section (see Chapter 8).

You are likely to use memos throughout the entire process of analysis, but they play a major role when it comes to writing and producing a report. We need to talk some more about memos in an analytical sense and memos as a technical function in ATLAS.ti. I often come across projects where the memo function is used very little or not at all, because users either have no idea what to do with it or misuse memos as comments and drown in a large number of what aren't really memos at all. You will learn more about the memo function and how to use it in Chapters 5 and 6.

The two phases of analysis

Descriptive-level analysis

The NCT method consists of a descriptive level and a conceptual level (Figure 1.4). The aim of descriptive-level analysis is to explore the data, to read or to look through them, and to notice interesting things that you begin to collect during initial first-stage coding. Based on these first ideas, the code list is developed further with the aim of describing everything that is in the data, naming it and trying to make sense of it in terms of similarities and differences. This results in a structured code list which can then be applied to the rest of the data during second-stage coding. Very likely the

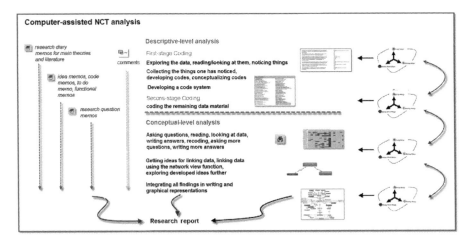

Figure 1.4   The steps of the NCT analytic process and the tools most relevant for each step

code list will need to be refined further and there will be a few more cycles of noticing and collecting until all the data are coded and the coding schema is fully developed. In parallel you can comment on data segments and begin to write memos.

Conceptual-level analysis

At some point, all data will have been coded; then the analyst enters the next phase. Until now, he or she has been immersed in the data, working from the inside out. The aim now is to look at the data from the perspective of the research questions by approaching them from a different angle. This means asking questions using the various analytic tools like the query or cooccurrence tools and the various table outputs that the software provides. Based on this exploration, you will once again begin to notice things in the data but this time, specifically, the relations between them. You move the analysis a step further, dig deeper, look at details and begin to understand how it all fits together. Accompanying the process of querying are what I have labeled *research question memos* (see Chapter 6). The aim of writing research question memos is to find answers to questions, to identify patterns and relations in the data, and to see how various aspects of the findings can be integrated.

When beginning to see how it all fits together, visualization tools like the network view function in ATLAS.ti can be used. Working with network views stimulates a different kind of thinking and allows further explorations in different ways. This can also be used as a means of talking with others about a particular finding or about an idea to be developed. Before you reach the final step of the analysis, a number of network views will probably have been drawn, redrawn, deleted and created anew. The ultimate aim is to integrate all of the findings and to gain a coherent understanding of the phenomenon studied; or, if theory building was your aim, to visualize and to present a theoretical model.

The use of the NCT method in the context of a larger methodological framework

I have been asked by reviewers of the first edition of the book to describe how ATLAS.ti can be used in the context of, for instance, grounded theory, phenomenology or discourse analysis. Further, some reviewers wondered how they could apply the approaches to analysis described by Silverman (2000; 2006) and Miles and Huberman (1994) to ATLAS.ti.

My answer is to use the NCT method within the context of these approaches. If a methodological approach suggests coding, then (1) CAQDAS[1] is well suited and (2) I suggest coding and working with the coded data as described by the

---

1 Computer-Aided Qualitative Data Analysis Software.

NCT method. The NCT method can be understood as a way to manage the data in a computer environment and to prepare them for analysis and interpretation. The various methodological approaches – whether by grounded theory, case study research, a certain type of discourse analysis, action research, narrative research, or more self-reflective approaches like ethnomethodology or phenomenology – complement it by prescribing the kinds of data to collect and how to approach their interpretation within a given epistemological framework.

Silverman and Miles and Huberman belong to the early adopters of computer-assisted analysis (see e.g. Silverman, 1993); however, in their writings they do not link analytic steps and software application. Other approaches follow a tradition that goes back to long before there were computers and software to aid the analytic process. Grounded theory for instance was developed in the 1960s and then further in the 1990s. The step-by-step instructions provided by Strauss and Corbin (1998) made the approach popular around the globe. Nowadays, with the advent of CAQDAS, it might, however, be appropriate to question whether the described ways of going about developing a grounded theory still apply, or whether one needs to adapt them. When coding on paper, it is not feasible to go through all the data again (and again) to recode if one notices something interesting in interview 10 or 12. In the process of conceptualizing codes, new data get coded with the further developed codes but the previous coding is not changed because it would be too much work. In software-supported analysis, you can rename a code in interview 20 and all instances that are coded with this code are renamed. If built up properly, the coding system is consistent across the entire data set and options like looking at frequencies become a feasible choice of analysis.

Properties and dimensions of categories were also not necessarily translated into actual codes and applied to the data in form of codes. In the third edition of *Basics of Qualitative Research*, Corbin presents a memo in which she developed the properties and dimensions for the category pain (Corbin and Strauss, 2008: 133). On the page next to it, she shows how this could be translated into a code tree in MAXQDA. The code tree starts with the category name 'Codesystem-JC (Juliet Corbin)', and underneath various aspects of the experience of pain are listed; further subcodes are types and management of pain, and the dimensions of pain. Building the tree this way renders it quite useless for further software-supported analysis. A main category name should never be a coder's name unless you want to base your analysis on a comparison of coders rather than on content. Also, if you want to relate various pain types, management and possibly the dimensions, these aspects need to be sorted in branches at the same level and not as subcodes. I could continue commenting on further screenshots in the book. They have little to do with how to conduct a good computer-assisted analysis. This is not to say that Corbin's ideas on how to go about analysis are not valuable; methodologically speaking, I grew up with grounded theory. However, the screenshots in the book to my mind are only placed there to say: 'Hey, you can also apply software when using GT as your methodological approach.' Corbin never really used software for her analyses, but sees the value of it for future generations of researchers (Corbin and Strauss, 2008). Today terms like 'axial and selective coding' are rather confusing since they imply that some form of coding should be done (see e.g. Boeije, 2010). This might also be the reason why Corbin and Strauss move away from the term in the third edition of the book and write that what they actually meant by axial coding was when they began to relate two concepts to each other in writing a memo (2008: 1995). Within the NCT method, this is part of conceptual-level analysis when making use of the analysis tools provided by software in combination with writing research question memos (see Chapter 6). Similar to axial coding, selective coding is also not a form of applying codes to data. It is the process of integrating all categories and deciding on a core category. If this is the aim of your analysis, then Chapter 7 provides some answers on how to utilize ATLAS.ti and its network view function for this process.

Thus, the ideas about how to move the analysis forward are still valid, but the implementation is different. The latter is a problem that lots of software users struggle with. The literature provides little help and so the users go through a process of trial and error in attempting to translate manual ways of going about analysis. Basically, this is how I started myself. In Chapter 5 I show you the code list I developed for my dissertation research in 1999. This was after I had already worked with software for seven years. Today I use it as an example of how *not* to code your data. By reading this book, you can cut a few corners and benefit from the mistakes I was making. Today my position is that you need to build up software-supported analysis in a particular way as described by the NCT method and fit your methodological approach (i.e. the way of interpreting the data) around it. This is supported by the writings of Bazeley and Richards (2000) and Richards (2009), two seasoned researchers and users of CAQDAS who describe the process of analysis in very similar ways. They have, however, not formalized their approach. Lewins and Silver (2007) in their book on using software in qualitative research express concern that the use of software conventionalizes data analysis and leads to expectations and assumptions about how the data should be analyzed (p. 57). I do not share their concern as I think it no longer applies as soon as you differentiate between method and methodology (Friese, 2014).

Regarding the writings of Silverman, and Miles and Huberman, they provide the larger context for conducting a qualitative research project. You can learn from them about how to design a research study, how to choose a methodology, how to become a good observer, how to pay attention to deviant cases, how to make comparisons, how to begin your analysis and develop it further, how to add rigor to your data collection and analysis process, and the like (Silverman, 2000). Miles and Huberman (1994) provide valuable tips on coding similar to what I will show you in Chapter 5; they also provide an example of a poorly structured code list, suggest procedures for further analysis and how to make sense of your data. However, these ideas are not linked to tools in computer software. In 1995, Miles and Huberman wrote the landmark book on qualitative data analysis software, but this text is not linked to their methodological ideas.

The NCT method links analytic ideas to software application. Based on my experience, I argue that you need to use it if you want to use the full functionality of computer software to analyze your data – regardless of the *methodological* approach you are using.

Further reading

Araujo, Luis (1995). Designing and refining hierarchical coding frames, in Udo Kelle (ed.), *Computer-Aided Qualitative Data Analysis*. London: Sage. Chapter 7.

Bong, Sharon A. (2002, May). Debunking myths in qualitative data analysis. *Forum Qualitative Sozialforschung/Forum: Qualitative Social Research*, 3(2), www.qualitative-research.net/fqs-texte/2-02/2-02bong-e.htm.

Bourdon, Sylvain (2002, May). The Integration of Qualitative Data Analysis Software in Research Strategies: Resistances and Possibilities [30 paragraphs]. *Forum Qualitative Sozialforschung/Forum: Qualitative Social Research*, 3(2), Art. 11, http://nbn-resolving.de/urn:nbn:de:0114- fqs0202118.

Breuer, Franz (2009). *Reflexive Grounded Theory: Ein Einführung in die Forschungspraxis*. Wiesbaden: VS Verlag.

Charmaz, Kathy (2006). *Constructing Grounded Theory: A Practical Guide Through Qualitative Analysis*. London: Sage.

Dey, Ian (1993). *Qualitative Data Analysis: A User-friendly Guide for Social Scientists*. London: Routledge.

Friese, Susanne (2014). On methods and methodologies and other observations, in Friese, Susanne and Ringmayr, Thomas (eds.), *ATLAS.ti User Conference 2013: Fostering Dialog on Qualitative Methods*. University Press, Technical University Berlin. http://opus4.kobv.de/opus4-tuberlin/frontdoor/index/index/docId/4413.

Gibbs, Graham (2007). *Analysing Qualitative Data (Qualitative Research Kit)*. London: Sage.

Kelle, Udo (2004). Computer-assisted qualitative data analysis, in C. Seale et al. (eds), *Qualitative Research Practice*. London: Sage. pp. 473–89.

Kelle, Udo and Kluge, Susann (2010). *Vom Einzelfall zum Typus: Fallvergleich und Fallkontrastierung in der qualitativen Sozialforschung*. Wiesbaden: VS Verlag.

Kluge, Susann (2000, January). Empirically grounded construction of types and typologies in qualitative social research. *Forum Qualitative Sozialforschung/Forum: Qualitative Social Research*, 1(1), www.qualitative-research.net/fqs-texte/1-00/1-00kluge-e.htm.

Lewins, Ann and Silver, Christine (2007/2014). *Using Software in Qualitative Research: A Step-by-step Guide*. London: Sage. Chapter 7.

Miles, Matthew B. and Huberman, Michael (1994). *Qualitative Data Analysis*, 2nd edn. Thousand Oaks, CA: Sage.

Morse, Janice M. (1994). Emerging from the data: the cognitive process of analysis in qualitative inquiry, in Janice M. Morse (ed.), *Critical Issues in Qualitative Research Methods*. Thousand Oaks, CA: Sage. pp. 22–43.

Richards, Tom and Richards, Lyn (1995). Using hierarchical categories in qualitative data analysis, in Udo Kelle (ed.), *Computer-Aided Qualitative Data Analysis*. London: Sage.

Saldaña, Jonny (2009). *The Coding Manual for Qualitative Researchers*. London: Sage.

Seidel, John V., (1998). Qualitative Data Analysis, http://www.qualisresearch.com/qda_paper.htm (originally published as Qualitative Data Analysis, in *The Ethnograph v5.0: A User's Guide*, Appendix E, 1998, Colorado Springs, Colorado: Qualis Research).

Silvers, Christine and Rivers, Christine (2014). Learning from the Learners: the role of technology acceptance and adoption theories in understanding researchers' early experiences with CAQDAS packages, in Friese, Susanne and Ringmayr, Thomas (eds.), *ATLAS.ti User Conference 2013: Fostering Dialog on Qualitative Methods*. University Press, Technical University Berlin. http://nbn-resolving.de/urn:nbn:de:kobv:83-opus4-44300.

Starks, Helene and Brown Trinidad, Susan (2007). Choose your method: A comparison of phenomenology, discourse analysis, and Grounded Theory. *Qualitative Health Research*, 17 (10), pp. 1372-1380.

Woolf, Nick (2014). Analytic strategies and analytic tactics, http://nbn-resolving.de/urn:nbn:de:kobv:83-opus4-44159.

TWO

Getting to know ATLAS.ti

For this chapter, we will work with the 'Children & Happiness' sample project that was copied to your computer when you installed ATLAS.ti. You can play around with the project material and explore as many functions and possibilities as you like – you don't have to be afraid of causing any serious damage. It is just 'dummy' material!

Within this sample project you will get to know the main features of the user interface and the structure of the program as a whole. Please do not expect to learn about all the features and functions of the program at once. The aim is to give you a quick and easy insight into the possibilities of the software; to show you what a coded text or a network looks like; or how to use the context menus. The operational parts of the architecture are the same for all sorts of different functions, so having seen a few you will easily recognize others and find your way through the program.

This chapter also functions as an overview of what is to come. All subsequent chapters go into further detail regarding the various aspects and functions previewed here.

Skills trainings

Skills training 2.1: getting to know the user interface

Skills training 2.2: handling the code list

Skills training 2.3: previewing the network view function and the query tool

Skills training 2.4: finding your way around the main menu

Some basic terms and concepts

To understand how ATLAS.ti handles data, think of your entire project as an intelligent 'container' that keeps track of all of your data. This container is the ATLAS.ti project file, called the **hermeneutic unit** or HU for short. The HU contains the analysis you carry out in ATLAS.ti. The term follows the tradition of hermeneutic sciences. It reminds us of Hermes, the divine messenger in Greek mythology and the god of fortune-tellers (and thieves!). Derived from it is the term 'hermeneutics', referring to the art of fortune-telling and text interpretation.

The ATLAS.ti HU, technically speaking, contains the link to your primary documents or the documents themselves, quotes, code words, notes, memos, links, code families, stored query results, i.e. supercodes, etc. You will learn more about these object types below and throughout this book. Opening an HU automatically activates all associated materials, thus streamlining your data and enabling you to work with a single entity.

Your source data can comprise text documents (such as interviews, articles, reports), images (photos, screenshots, diagrams), audio recordings (interviews, broadcasts, music), video clips (audio-visual material), PDF files (papers, brochures, reports) and geo data (locative data using Google Earth). Once you add a data file to your project, it becomes a primary document which represents and contains additional information about its source counterpart (i.e. the assigned data file). Once your various documents are added and organized, your real work can begin.

Creating quotations and coding them is the basic activity you engage in when using ATLAS.ti and is the basis of everything else you will do. In practical terms, coding refers to the process of assigning categories, concepts or 'codes' (more generally speaking) to segments of information that are of interest to your research objectives. This function corresponds to the time-honored manual practice of marking (underlining or highlighting) and annotating text passages in a book or other documents.

In its conceptual underpinnings, ATLAS.ti has drawn from what might be called an earlier 'paper and pencil paradigm'. The user interface is designed accordingly and many of its processes are based on this analogy and thus can be better understood by it.

Because of this highly intuitive design principle, you will quickly come to appreciate the margin area as one of your most central and preferred workspaces – even though ATLAS.ti usually offers a variety of ways to accomplish any given task.

Starting the program

When you open ATLAS.ti for the first time, click on the start button (if you have one) and select ALL PROGRAMS / SCIENTIFIC SOFTWARE / ATLAS.TI. If you use Windows 8, you will find the ATLAS.ti app on your Windows 8 start screen.

When the program opens, the welcome project is loaded. The start image provides an overview of some of the basic features to help you get started. If you have worked with ATLAS.ti on your computer before, the most recently used project is opened. Let's now open the sample project.

Opening the sample project

The sample project was copied to your computer during the installation process of ATLAS.ti.

- From the main menu select **Help / Quick Tour / Load "Children & Happiness stage II"**. This opens the coded version of the sample project.
- Look at the title bar. The name of the project is displayed there.

Skills training 2.1: getting to know the user interface

At the top of the user interface (Figure 2.1) there is a title bar which displays the file name. Underneath you will find the main menu, the toolbar and a number of drop-down menus. In addition, there is a vertical toolbar at the left margin. The rest of the screen is dedicated to displaying project data. Around the editor space, you will find some new interface features in version 7. If you click on the three arrows on the left hand side, a fly-out window opens allowing you to access various object types. On the right hand side, you will see a plus sign. If you click on it, you can open up to three more regions for displaying documents. Thus, given a large enough screen, you can display up to four documents next to each other. Therefore another feature has been added, the PD bar.

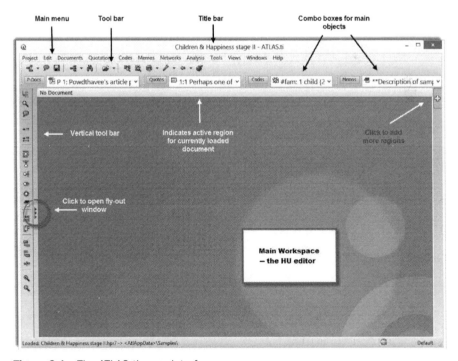

Figure 2.1   The ATLAS.ti. user interface

The yellow color indicates the currently active region. Both new features are explained in more detail below.

All materials for analysis must be available in digital format. In ATLAS.ti these become primary documents (P-Docs).

With progressive analysis, you code your primary documents; attach memos to data segments, link codes and other objects to each other, and so on. In contrast to manual ways of analyzing qualitative data, ATLAS.ti does not alter the original material, so the document files are not affected by your analysis. Instead you work with a virtual copy of a document (e.g. a transcribed interview). It is displayed on the left hand side of your workspace. When you load another document, only the copy is removed from the screen. All notes, code words, memos, etc., are stored in the HU. The HU thus holds all materials and the results of your analysis in an 'electronic container'.

Unlike confusing piles of paper with notes and references, the HU keeps growing but remains clearly arranged. Every step is documented according to strict rules so that the electronic HU means not only a tidier desk, but also a change from the art of fortune-telling to an understandable, verifiable technique of text interpretation. Keeping this background information in mind, let's now begin to work with the software.

The drop-down menus and object managers

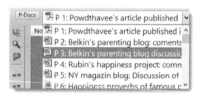

Figure 2.2 Drop-down menus

After opening the sample project file you will find a number of new entries on the screen but you cannot see the data yet. First, we want to take a look at the four drop-down lists (Figure 2.2).

On the left hand side is the list of all documents added or imported to an ATLAS.ti project. As mentioned, they are called primary documents or P-Docs. Next to it is the list of all coded segments, or quotations, followed by the list of codes and the list of memos.

- The four drop-down menus can be moved by 'dragging and dropping' and their size can be adjusted by dragging the dotted line from right to left with the mouse. Try it!
- If you click on the down arrow to the right of a list, the list of objects is displayed. Open the list for all four object types and take a look.
- Open the list of documents (P-Docs) and select one document with a left click (e.g. **P3: Belkin's parenting blog discussion**). The selected primary document will be loaded and displayed on the screen with all related codings, hyperlinks and memos.

The object lists are convenient for some tasks but not for others. Therefore ATLAS.ti offers the possibility of opening all objects in a separate browser called the Object Manager.

- Open all four Object Managers by clicking on the icon to the left of the drop-down menu (see Figure 2.3).

Figure 2.3   The four Object Manager buttons

- Arrange them on your screen so that you can view them next to each other (Figures 2.4 and 2.5).

In your everyday work with ATLAS.ti, you will probably not open all four managers at once. The purpose of this exercise is to show the commonalities of ATLAS.ti browsers that you will see throughout the program. Besides a simple list, the Object Managers also provide further information like author name, creation date or date of last modification. The different kinds of objects can be recognized by a specific symbol, as shown in Figures 2.4 and 2.5.

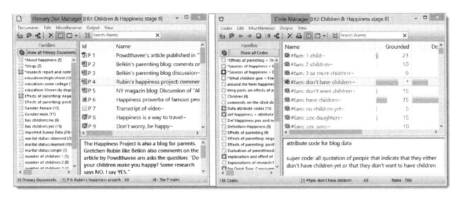

Figure 2.4   Primary documents and the Code Manager

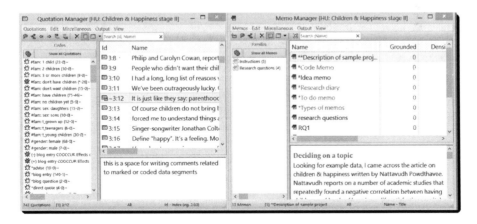

Figure 2.5   Quotation and Memo Manager

The first primary document P1 is a PDF file. P2 to P5 are Word documents, P6 is a video file, P7 is the transcript for this file added as an internal text document, P7 and P8 are image files, and all others are imported survey data. The symbols may vary depending on the multimedia software you have installed. Quotations also show the respective media format. Codes use a yellow diamond symbol and show a Post-it note when a definition has been entered. The memo symbol resembles a note booklet with a red cover.

Each Object Manager offers a **menu** and a **toolbar**. The menu options are the same as in the main menu and submenus. To spare you long treks with your mouse you can access them directly from here. In the space underneath the toolbar of the Object Manager you will find the objects and additional information in table format. The handling of this table is similar to other Microsoft Windows programs such as Excel: every column has a header and the table can be sorted by a click on the column head; the width of the column can be adjusted by dragging the border.

Underneath the object list there are a **screen splitter** and a white area. The white area is a text editor in which you can write. By grabbing the splitter with your mouse you can adjust the size of the object list or editor respectively.

Apart from the Quotation Manager, the other three have a side panel for families. In the Quotation Manager, the codes are listed in the side panel. Families will be discussed in greater detail in Chapter 5. For now, it is sufficient to know that families are a device in ATLAS.ti to group objects and that their purpose is to serve as filters. As a memory hook, remember that both words start with the letter *F*: family = filter. There are no families for quotations, as codes already fulfill the function to group quotations. While coding, you group all those quotations whose content is similar under one common label.

To train yourself in the use of the Object Manager, carry out the following exercises:

- Sort the entries in the table with a click on the column header.
- Adjust the width of a column.
- Grab the splitter and move it up and down.
- Select an object from the list and write a comment about this object in the text editor (i.e. the white space). To save this new entry, click on another object in the list or open the context menu (right click) and click on **Accept**. Every entry for which you have created a comment carries a tilde symbol (~).

- For more comfort, the comment editor can be opened in a separate window. To do this, click on the third icon from the left in the toolbar of the manager (the speech bubble).
- In the P-Docs Manager, click on a family in the side panel (e.g. *blogs). The list of documents will be filtered showing only the two blog discussions. Try another family (e.g. Gender::female). You will see the case documents for all female respondents from the survey.
- Experiment with the side panel in the Code Manager as well. Click on some code families. Notice how this facilitates navigation of the code list and allows easy access to smaller groups of codes.

Multi-region

ATLAS.ti 7 allows you to display up to four documents side by side. On the right hand side of the screen you will see a button with a plus sign.

- Click on the plus sign to open a new region. It will be empty. The active region is indicated by the yellow document bar (see Figure 2.6).
- To add a document to the new region, one way is to click on the drop-down menu for P-Docs and to select a document with a left click from the list. I present an alternative way below (see the section on the fly-out window).

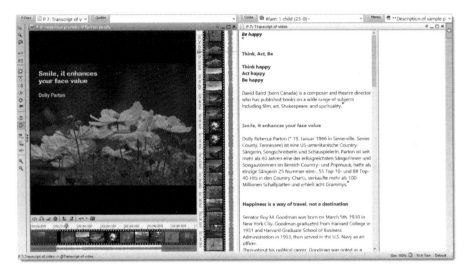

Figure 2.6   HU editor with two open documents displayed side-by-side (a video file and its transcript)

- You can change the position of the documents by dragging the yellow document bar over to the other region (see Figure 2.7).

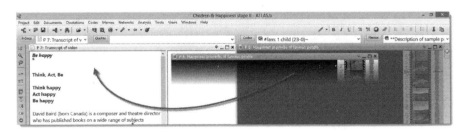

Figure 2.7   Changing document positions

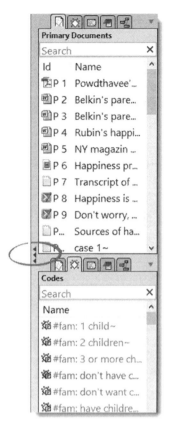

Figure 2.8   Fly-out window

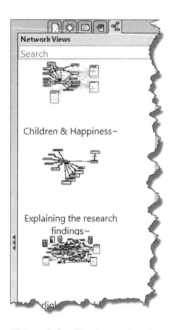

Figure 2.9   Preview network view images

Fly-out window

On the right hand side of the screen you will see three black arrows. If you click on them a so-called fly-out window opens (Figure 2.8). It displays five object types: primary documents, codes, quotations, memos and networks. You are already familiar with four of the icons that symbolize each of these objects from the drop-down lists. The one you don't yet know is the icon for network views.

- Click on each icon to move from one object list to the next. If you want to see a long list of one object type only, you can also close the second pane by clicking on the minimize button.

For documents and network views, you can display preview images (Figure 2.9). This is a useful option if you work with images, for instance:

- Click on the primary document tab. Right click on a document and select the option **SHOW PREVIEW**.
- Now let's take a look at the network previews. Click on the network view tab, right click on a network view and select the option **SHOW PREVIEW**.

As a last exercise, I want to show you how you to load a document into an existing or new region from the fly-out window:

- Click on the primary document tab again. Select a document and drag it onto one of the document bars (can be an active or an inactive region). This replaces the document that was loaded in this region.
- Select a document and drag it onto the plus button on the left hand side of the window to open a document in a new region.

Skills training 2.2: handling the code list

For a regular project it is quite common to have between 120 and 200 codes. This is an average number based on experience that you can use as a rule of thumb. It can vary depending on the type of project and the type of analysis. This is discussed in more detail in Chapter 5, where I discuss the methodological aspects of coding. In this section, I explain what you need to know about handling codes in the Code Manager and how you can easily deal with a long list of codes.

To prepare the screen for the next exercise:

- Close the fly-out window. Close all but one document so that only one region remains open. Load P10: Sources of happiness.
- Open the Code Manager.

As in the Windows file manager, you can select different types of views. This applies to all Object Managers, but, right now, just have a look at the Code Manager:

- Select **VIEW / SINGLE COLUMN**. If you want, you can also try out the other options. Return to the single column view to finish this exercise.

In single column view, you only see the code word followed by two numbers in braces: for example, #fam: have children {75–46}. This is all you need to know when coding the data. This view allows you to resize the Code Manager to save space on your screen. The numbers in braces are explained below.

Resize the Code Manager as shown in Figure 2.10, so that you see a long, narrow list of codes on the right hand side of your screen next to the loaded text document. Your screen should be divided into three areas: the text of the loaded document on the left; the attached codes and possible other objects in the middle; and the Code Manager to the right.

ATLAS.ti remembers the views and position of its windows. This means that when you close and reopen a window or close and reopen ATLAS.ti, the Code Manager will be shown in the current view and in its current position.

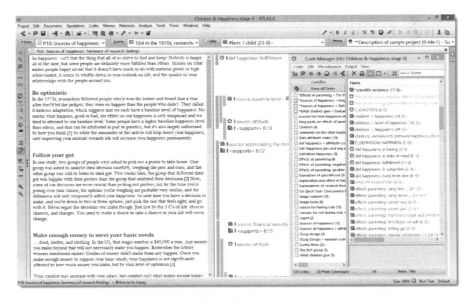

Figure 2.10 Preparing your screen for coding

Code lists can become quite long and you won't see all the codes on your screen at once. Thus, you either need to scroll through the list or, easier, jump to a specific code by typing the first letter(s) of a code word. Try it out:

- The mouse pointer should be located somewhere within the Code Manager. Click on the letter **r** on your keyboard. The focus of the code list moves to the code REASONS FOR HC. Type the letters **reg**; you will then jump to the code word REGRET. Type the letter **e**; this brings you to the code word EFFECTS OF PARENTING, and so on.
- In the search field next to the toolbar, type the word **child**. Only code words containing the five letters **child** remain in the list.
- Empty the search field. Click on a code family to reduce the list of codes to the ones included in the family (e.g. Effects of parenting).
- Click on **SHOW ALL CODES** to see all the codes again.

You may already be wondering what the numbers in braces after the code words mean.

- Click on the code **children:=level of happiness {18–2}**.

The first figure shows how many times the respective code has been used; in this case, 18 times. It gives you some information on the **groundedness** of a code (i.e. how relevant this code is in the data). The second figure displays the so-called **density**, which is the number of links to other codes. The code has been linked to two other codes.

First, we want to take a look at the frequency of usage:

- Double click on the code. This opens a window showing the list of the 18 coded segments, the quotations (Figure 2.11).
- By left clicking on each quotation, it will be displayed in context. Click through some of the quotations; do not double click, otherwise the list will be closed. You can also use the down arrow to move from one quotation to the next.

Next, we want to explore the second number and the term 'density'.

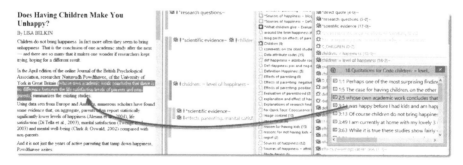

Figure 2.11   Retrieving coded segments

Skills training 2.3: previewing the network view function and the query tool

A preview of the network view function

- Close the list of quotations. Then click on the network button in the Code Manager toolbar (or right click and select **OPEN NETWORK VIEW**). The network view for this code opens, showing the two links with other codes that have been created.
- Play around with the codes in the network view by dragging them to different positions (Figure 2.12).

The network view 'tells' you that there is no difference between those reporting negative or positive effects of parenting with regard to their perception of the relationship between children and happiness. Compare this to the network view for the code 'children: < happiness' (= children make you unhappier) by opening the network view on this code.

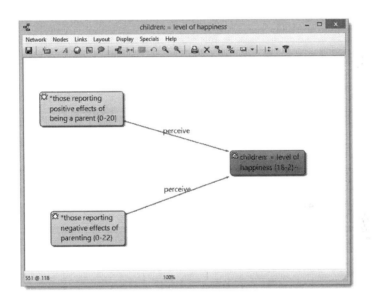

Figure 2.12 Focused network view on code 'Children:=level of happiness'

By the way, the network views are not automatically created by the software; they are a result of the interpretation process and need to be created manually.

- Close the network view window(s). When you are asked whether you want to save the network view, select **No**.

A preview of the query tool

Here's what we have done so far. We learned about the four object types in ATLAS.ti and how they can be accessed via the four drop-down lists or via a manager window. We took a closer look at the Code Manager and learned what the terms 'groundedness' and 'density' mean. Double clicking on a code opens the list of all segments that have been coded with it. This is also referred to as **simple retrieval**, simple because it is based on just one code. We can, however, also ask more complex questions based on multiple codes. This is done using the query tool.

- To open the query tool (Figure 2.13), select the main menu option **ANALYSIS / QUERY TOOL** or click on the binoculars symbol in the main toolbar.

At this point we do not actually want to click on a query, just note that there are 14 operators, organized into three groups (Boolean, semantic and proximity operators), which you can use to combine codes and groups of codes in order to ask questions about your data. In addition, you can use the query tool to restrict searches to particular subsets of data via the scope button. This allows you to set tasks such as: 'Find all data segments coded with "reasons for not having children" that have also been coded with "effects of parenting: negative".' You can compare the blog data to the survey data, or within the survey data compare male and female respondents. Thus, retrievals can become quite complex. The **query tool** along with other analysis tools will be discussed in detail in Chapter 6.

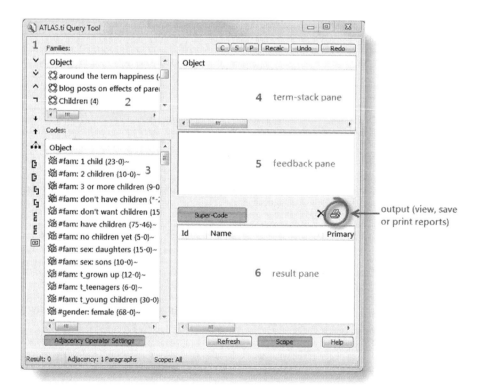

Figure 2.13 Previewing the query tool

Skills training 2.4: finding your way around the main menu

The main menu

There are 12 main menus (Figure 2.14) and each of them has submenus and further options. At the time of writing, the total number of menus and submenus amounts to more than 400! This sounds frightening and you may think that you will never be able to learn each option. But there's no reason to panic: some menus are repetitive and you can find the same option in different places. Furthermore, here is an easy rule to help you to find your way around.

Figure 2.14   The main menu

We have already learned about the four main object types: P-Docs, quotes, codes and memos. Take a look at the main menu bar. You will find a main menu option for each of these object types. When you need an option related to primary documents like renaming, closing or removing, or when you want to create document-related output, click on the main menu **Documents** and your choices are already reduced. When you want to do something related to codes, click on the main menu **Codes** and then you will find the options related to coding with various suboptions. When you want to edit or rename a memo, click on the menu **Memos**. And so on.

Further, you will find one menu for all project-related functions, one menu for networks and one for accessing the analysis tools. To practice, find the following options. The solutions are provided at the end of this chapter.

- You want to add documents to your project? Which menu do you need to access? (a)
- Next, let's assume you want to filter some codes. Where do you find the option? (b)
- You want to output a document with all the codes as you see them on the screen in the margin area. Which main menu and submenus do you need to select? (c)
- You want to create a new network view. Where do you find the option? (d)

Do you get the point? It's not as difficult as it appears at first. Did you notice that within each submenu for documents, codes and memos there is a sort option, a filter option, a miscellaneous option and an output option?

The toolbars

Many of the menu options can also be launched via the icons on the horizontal and vertical toolbars. When you move your mouse over the icon you will see a tool tip displaying a useful keyword or explanation (Figure 2.15).

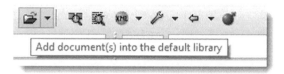

Figure 2.15   Tool tip for icon 'add documents'

Of course, all these options can be launched via the text and context menus as well. Over time, you will develop your individual preferences about which ones to choose.

Summary

In this chapter you have learned about important terms and concepts used in ATLAS.ti, like the four main object types: primary documents, quotations, codes and memos. Then you previewed some of the major tools needed for a qualitative data analysis, like the Code Manager, the query tool and the network view function, and you received some guidance on how to find menu options, even though you do not yet know all of them by heart.

REVIEW QUESTIONS

1   What are the four main object types in ATLAS.ti?
2   What are Object Managers and what are they useful for?
3   Which objects are contained in the side panel of the four Object Managers?
4   If you are familiar with version 6 of ATLAS.ti, what has changed? What type of new elements and interface features have been added in version 7?
5   What is the optimal position of the Code Manager to allow for maximum space and to have a free view of all relevant areas of the screen when coding or reviewing coding?
6   How can you navigate through a long list of codes?
7   What do the numbers mean that you see in braces after the codes in the 'single column' view?
8   What is the query tool useful for?
9   How do you find your way around the many menu options?

GLOSSARY OF TERMS

Analysis tools: The tools offered by ATLAS.ti are the word cruncher, the code cooccurrence tree and table explorer, the query tool and the Codes-Primary Documents Table. See Chapter 6 for more details.

Codes: Keywords that are generally linked to quotations, but do not have to be. You can also create free codes. When you link free codes to a number of different codes, then they are called abstract codes.

Hermeneutic unit (HU): A data file that stores everything you do to the data, but not the data themselves. An exception is when you work with internal text documents. Then the HU also contains your data. The HU data file has the file extension .hpr7 for version 7 files or .hpr6 for version 6 files. The file type is 'Hermeneutic Unit'. The file does not have to be stored at a specific location; you can store it wherever you want. As the HU file is just a regular file, you can copy it, move it, delete it or rename it in the file manager, just like any other file.

Memos: From a purely functional perspective, memos in ATLAS.ti consist of a title, a type and some text. They can be free or linked to other memos, to codes and to quotations. In Chapters 5 and 6, I suggest various way of using memos in ATLAS.ti. Memos are places to write down all sorts of ideas and thoughts. You can use them to remind you of things like what to do next week, what you wanted to ask your supervisor about, what you wanted to discuss with your team members; thus for project planning. And you can use memos as a place to write up your analysis and as building blocks for a later research report.

Network views: Network views offer a place for visualizing relations within your data. You can link almost all objects to each other; visualize your codings; and visualize relationships between codes, relationships between quotations, relationships between memos and memos, relationships between memos and quotations, relationships between memos and codes, and relationships between object families and their members. Network views can also contain thumbnail images of primary documents (for more details, see Chapter 7).

Object Managers: The four main objects in ATLAS.ti are the primary documents, the quotations, the codes and the memos. The list of objects can be viewed in the fly-out panel (version 7), by clicking on the down arrow to open the list field, or you can open a separate window for each object. These separate windows are called 'Object Manager'. The Object Managers have their own main menu and a toolbar. The options available are repetitions from the main menu, but with one slight difference. When selecting an object in the Object Manager and then one of the menu options, the option only applies to the selected object. Selecting the same option from the main menu has a global effect.

Primary documents (P-Docs or PDs): When you add or import a document to your project file, the HU, ATLAS.ti creates a primary document. Each primary document has a name and stores information about the author and when it was created and last modified. In addition, it has some information about where to access the source file. Only when the source is available can the primary document display the content. In version 7 projects, the source files are usually stored in the library. The name of the primary document can be changed within ATLAS.ti without affecting document access. The default name is the name of the source file. Think of the primary document as being like an office assistant who knows all kinds of information about your source files and also where to find them. If the source files are *not* stored at the expected location, the assistant comes back empty handed. This means that you see a blank screen instead of the document content. See also Chapter 3 on project management.

Query tool: The query tool allows you to retrieve quotations based on a combination of codes. It offers four Boolean operators, three semantic operators and seven proximity operators. Further, it allows you to combine code queries with variables; that is, you can ask for information such as: 'Find me all quotations that I have coded with code A and code B, but only for women between the age of 31 and 40.'

(Continued)

(Continued)

Quotations: Marked data segments that have a clearly defined start and end point. Often quotations are coded, but they don't have to be. You can also create so-called free quotations. Free or coded quotations can be used as a source or target to link data segments to each other. Linked quotations are called hyperlinks.

A quotation has an ID and a name. The ID consists of the primary document number that it belongs to and a number that indicates the sequence of when it was created. The position where a quotation can be found within a primary document is indicated after the name.

The quotation name is based on either the first 30 characters of a text quotation or the name of the primary document. This automatically generated name can be modified. If the default number of characters is not sufficient, it can be increased under Tools / Preferences / General Preferences, Tab: General: List Name Size for Quotes.

Solutions to the 'survival' exercise

(a) Project / Add Document(s)
(b) Codes / Filter
(c) Documents / Output / Print With Margin...
(d) Networks / New Network View

THREE

Data and project management

The first part of this chapter provides an overview of the data file formats supported by ATLAS.ti and a few things you need to pay attention to. The recommendations and suggestions are derived from everyday user problems and questions that I have come across in the past. In addition, I include some transcription guidelines relating to the technicalities of the software. Following these guidelines will facilitate your work with ATLAS.ti at later stages of your analysis. In the second part of this chapter you will learn how to set up projects for single users and teams, how to set up a project with synchronized audio or video files and how to treat survey data. Further, you will find some information on how to work with large-sized projects.

Skills trainings

Skills training 3.1: auto coding

Skills training 3.2: setting up a single user project

Skills training 3.3: working with transcripts and synchronized media files

Skills training 3.4: working with survey data

Skills training 3.5: creating user accounts

Skills training 3.6: merging projects

Skills training 3.7: creating backups and transferring a project

Skills training 3.8: creating partial bundle files

Data preparation

Supported file formats

In principle, most textual, graphical and multimedia formats are supported by ATLAS.ti (see Table 3.1)

Table 3.1   Supported file formats

Type of data	Format	Specific features/considerations
Text	txt (plain text); rtf (rich text) doc(x): converted to rich text by ATLAS.ti. In version 7, ATLAS.ti stores a copy of the rich text version so that restrictions to editing no longer apply	Can be modified within ATLAS.ti[1]
PDF	Image and text format	Pay attention, when scanning documents, that they are scanned with character recognition. If the scan is an image rather than a text PDF, you cannot retrieve text. ATLAS.ti treats it just like an image document
Image	Over 20 different image file formats are supported. The most common ones are jpg, jpeg, bmp, tif(f), giv, png, jif(f), emf+ graphic PDF	Multi-page tiff images can also be used
Audio	The most commonly used formats are aif, mp3, wma, midi, au, wav	When there is a problem in playing audio or video files, it is most likely due to a missing codec. You can find complete codec packages online that you can install on your computer
Video	The most commonly used formats are mpeg, mpeg2, mp4, mv4, wmv, avi, mov	
Geo data	Google Earth as data source	Google Earth needs to be installed on your computer
Survey data (Excel)	Results from an online survey can be imported as case-based primary documents (commonly used for the analysis of open-ended questions)[2] Variables from surveys are imported in the form of primary document families (= document attributes in ATLAS.ti)	

[1] Modification of documents is only possible if you add them to the library. Externally linked documents cannot be edited (see below).

[2] For more information see the section on working with survey data on p. 60.

Preparing documents

Text documents

For some formats, their suitability depends on your version of Windows, particularly in regard to what other software is already installed. Doc and docx files, for example, are converted to rich text. For this process a doc(x) to rich text converter needs to be installed on your system. These are usually installed on your computer if you use an Office package; if, however, you get a project that contains Word 2007 or 2010 files and you still use Word 2003, then you may need to go online and download the latest compatibility pack from the Microsoft website, or else store the file in rich text format before adding it to an ATLAS.ti project. The OpenOffice odt format is not supported. Save OpenOffice files in rich text format before adding them to a project.

When you work on a Mac having installed ATLAS.ti in a virtual Windows environment, it is best to work with rich text files. By the way, a native Mac version will be released in the second half of 2014.

PDF files

ATLAS.ti displays PDF files in their original layout – no formatting is lost. Misunderstandings sometimes arise in distinguishing between textual and image PDFs. When you scan a document, activate the character recognition option to turn the document into a text rather than an image PDF. Image PDF files are treated like all other image documents by ATLAS.ti. Further, you also need to be aware that all retrieved text from textual PDF files is rich text. You will lose the original layout when creating an output of coded PDF segments.

Choosing between different text formats

As shown in Table 3.1, you can choose between four different text file formats: plain text, rich text, doc or docx files, and textual PDF documents. **Plain text** does not include any formatting such as different font types and sizes, bold or italic characters, or colors. As the name says, these text files are plain. You still find them today in emails or online texts like blogs and in forums. If your primary data are in this format, there is no need to save them in a different one. You can assign them just as they are to an ATLAS.ti project. As soon as you go into edit mode to modify some file content, the texts are enriched and saved in rich text format by ATLAS.ti.

When preparing your own data (e.g. transcribing recorded data), my recommendation is to store the files as **rich text in order to avoid conversion**. This assures the greatest compatibility across platforms and various versions of Word and Windows. You will find this file type option in any word processing program. The advantage over doc and docx files is that rich text is the standard format used by ATLAS.ti.

PDF files are bit more difficult to code than Word files. Therefore don't make them your standard, catch-all format to use. **PDF files** are a choice when the original layout is important for analysis purposes or when the documents are already available as PDFs. ATLAS.ti supports native PDF; this means the files are displayed within ATLAS.ti just as they look in their native PDF environment. The content is not converted. Thus, nothing is lost and the full information is available to you when coding the data.

If Word files contain lots of pictures or images, they can become quite sizable and you may experience long loading times. In such cases, save the Word file in PDF format as it reduces file size quite considerably.

Audio and video files

A common problem with audio and video files is a missing codec. Audio and video files are usually compressed to use up less storage space, and for this process a codec is used. In order to read the files, the same codec that was used to 'pack' the files is needed to 'unpack' them. Today you can find free codec packages online that you can download and install in case your video file cannot be played in ATLAS.it.

Another video file-related problem I have come across was where the camcorder software installed on a computer was blocking everything else and not allowing the files to be played in ATLAS.ti. After uninstalling this software, everything worked fine. I generally advise that before you prepare all of your video files, create a short trial file for testing in ATLAS.ti. After you have figured out the settings and appropriate format and file type, you can prepare the rest of the material.

Image files

When working with images, there is no point in adding the full-quality image taken with a 14 million pixel camera to ATLAS.ti. The image won't fit on your screen as the resolution is way too high, so you end up resizing the images in ATLAS.ti to make them suitable for analytic purposes. I cannot provide a 'one-size-fits-all' figure regarding the optimal image size because it depends on the resolution and size of the screen. However, a good starting point is 1024 × 768 pixels.

Excel files (survey import, P-Docs Family Table import)

You need to follow a specific syntax when preparing an Excel file for import. Special characters indicate to the software which part of the spreadsheet should be added as document, as variable or as code. How to prepare survey data is explained below.

For Mac users

A native Mac iOS version will be released in 2014. At the time of writing, no testable version was available. However, I do know that the basic concepts and principles will be the same as in the Windows version, but the developers emphasize that the Mac version will look and feel like a Mac version. Therefore the interface is likely to look a bit different. On the one hand, this means that Mac users do not need to get used to how things are done under Windows and will feel 'at home'. On the other hand, it means that some of the described mouse clicks will not be the same and you might need to adapt the descriptions provided in this book.

Size

Theoretically, size restriction is not an issue because of the way ATLAS.ti handles PDs (see below: 'Data handling in ATLAS.ti'). However, you should bear in mind that your computer's processing speed and storage capacity affect its performance. Excessively large documents can be uncomfortable to work with, even if you have an extremely sophisticated computer. The crucial issue is not always the file size, but rather, in the case of multimedia files, the length of playing time. For text documents, the number and size of embedded objects may cause extraordinarily long load times. There is a high likelihood that if a text document loads slowly in ATLAS.ti, it will also load slowly in other applications like Word.

Language support

It is possible to use documents in ATLAS.ti that are not in English or other European languages. For Western languages, usually nothing has to be changed in ATLAS.ti for the characters to be displayed correctly. A basic requirement is that language-specific fonts are installed on the computer. Displaying text in different languages in the HU editor does not require any specific attention. If the text is not displayed correctly in your language, check the default language settings by clicking on the **Default** field at the bottom right hand side of the ATLAS.ti main window. You may also need to change the default if you experience a problem in displaying special characters in Western languages, like the German ä, ü, ö or letters like à, ñ, ŷ, etc.

You do, however, need to configure the font settings and possibly your Windows settings if you want to use Cyrillic, Hebrew, Arabic, Thai, Chinese characters and the like for all other text fields in ATLAS.ti. This applies to code and other object labels, comment fields, memos, quotation IDs and network view entries. For Thai and East Asian language support, you may first of all need to install the appropriate language files on Western European and US Windows systems. Text search and auto coding is not available until the release of ATLAS.ti version 8 for some languages like Hebrew, Greek, Arabic or Cyrillic. If your language is not displayed correctly, check on the button 'Default' at the bottom right of the ATLAS.ti window and select your language.

Font settings

- Select **Tools** / **Preferences** / **General Preferences** and then the **Font** tab.
- Select one or more object types for which you want to change the font.
- Select a font and appearance (bold, italic) for these object types.
- If you use ATLAS.ti in different contexts, you can specify different font themes.

System settings for Thai and Asian language support on Western European and US Windows systems

The prerequisite is that a language pack is installed on your computer.

- Log in to your computer with full administrative rights.

Windows 7 and earlier versions:

- Select START / CONTROL PANELS / REGIONAL AND LANGUAGE OPTIONS
- Select the Languages tab and then the option to install the appropriate language files that you need.
- Under the Advance tab, select the language in the field 'Language for non-Unicode programs'.

Windows 8:

- Select: CLOCK, LANGUAGE, AND REGION, and then REGION AND LANGUAGE.
- Click the Administrative tab.
- Under 'Language for non-Unicode programs', click on Change system locale. If you're prompted for an administrator password or confirmation, type the password or provide confirmation.
- Select the language (e.g. Chinese simplified), and click on OK.
- Restart your computer for the changes to take effect.

User-interface language

You can currently switch between English (default), Spanish and German menus. Other languages will follows. To switch the user interface language, make sure you have updated to version 7.1.

- Select TOOLS / PREFERENCES / SET USER INTERFACE LANGUAGE.

Transcription

A very nice option of ATLAS.ti is the association between transcripts and the original audio or video recording. This allows access to the original recording via the transcript. When you want to make use of this option, a requirement is that you use either ATLAS.ti or the software f4/f5 or Transana to transcribe your data. During transcription you enter timestamps (or, as known in ATLAS.ti, association anchors). It is also possible to enter these anchors later when you have a transcript without timestamps and the recording is still available. In this book I describe the technical aspects of transcribing data in ATLAS.ti briefly in the context of working with video files in Chapter 4. If you want to practice some more, you will find a transcription exercise and some sample files on the companion website. Further, below I describe how to set up a project that contains associated documents (see p. 58).

Transcription guidelines

In this section, I will provide some guidelines for structuring transcriptions of recorded data. In interview transcripts with one interviewee it helps you quickly recognize the different speakers and speaker units in the transcript. In transcriptions of group interviews or focus groups, it lets you automatically code all speaker units by adding attribute codes. This is how you need to prepare the transcript:

- Mark all speakers unambiguously and enter an empty line between each speaker in turn.
- In the sample transcript below, the paragraph marker is visible, indicating when the **Enter** button was pressed. The two speakers in the transcript are marked clearly with unique identifiers: **INT:** is used for the interviewer and **AL:** for Alexander, the interviewee. '**Interviewer**' or '**Alexander**' would be impractical as markers because those words might appear in the text itself, but the character combination INT: and AL: is not likely to be found anywhere else. This is essential for using the auto coding tool.
- If one speaker talks for a long time, break the speech into multiple paragraphs (see sample transcript).

INT: Ok. So how, how, how did you actually um meet him? You met him in class I guess? ¶

¶
AL: In class yeah, and we were in the same form as well so. ¶

¶
INT: How, how do you sort of um ... how do you sort of pass the time with him, you know when you guys are together? ¶

¶
AL: Both, well I suppose we just sat about sometimes, we also sort of played footie as you do and uh um ... he um, after our GCSEs, we um he had a villa in er Minorca um so there was a group of us planning to go out so we basically, we sat in er, during lunchtime planning what we were going to do, and we just sort of went to the pub. ¶

¶
I mean my mum kicked me out at the age of sixteen and told me to go to the pub with the lads, and it's like 'Er yeah cheers mum' [laughs]. Er so you know we went to the pub every Friday and yeah just general stuff, you know just hanging around, meet up with some girls and stuff. ¶

INT: ...

The reason for this is the ATLAS.ti referencing system for quotations. Each quotation has an ID, and paragraph numbers are used to indicate where it starts and finishes – so if you code just one sentence in a longer paragraph, the reference for the resulting quotation might not be precise enough.

This way of organizing the transcript can be used for any documents that include structuring elements, like dates in historical documents, emails or letters. The automatic coding tool can also be useful, and even though you may not know at this point whether you will want to use it, it is sensible to get used to all the above formatting rules as early as possible. Although neglecting these 'best practice rules' will not have a negative effect in the initial phase, you may later regret not having used them from the beginning.

Skills training 3.1: auto coding

In order for you to understand better why these transcription rules are recommended, here is a brief preview of the auto coding procedure:

- On the companion website you will find a project called '**Auto coding example**' in the form of a copy bundle file that contains four transcripts.
- Download the file to your computer and double click the file. The copy bundle install window opens.
- In the field HU Path, select a location for the project file on your computer by clicking on the file loader button. Then click on the **Unbundle** button (for more details see 'Unpacking a copy bundle file' on p. 67).
- Open the auto coding tool via the main menu: CODES / CODING / AUTO CODING.
- Enter one or more codes that you want to use for automatically coding all hits (see Figure 3.1). A search term based on a string of characters or using regular expressions (GREP) is possible.
- Select where you want to search (in the currently selected document/in a selected group of documents based on a document family/in all documents).
- Select the length of the segment to be coded: the entered search term (it must be an exact match), the complete word, the sentence, the paragraph (single hard return), the text up to the next blank line (multiple hard returns) or the entire document (all text).
- Check whether the search should be case sensitive, whether GREP expressions are included in the term, and whether you want to confirm the coding of each hit.

In order to automatically code all of Alexander's speaking parts with his name, gender and student status, 'Al:' is used as the search term. The scope is set to the selected PD and the length of the segment to be coded is the speaker unit.

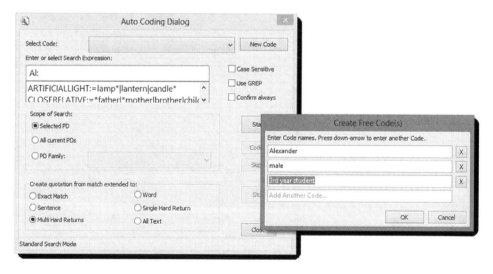

Figure 3.1   The auto coding window

As each speaker unit is separated by a blank line, the option 'Multi Hard Returns' (¶) can be used here.

Best practice rules and solutions in a nutshell

Related to data file formats:

- In case your project includes doc or docx files, make sure that a word processing package is installed on your computer as these files need to be converted to rich text. If this is not possible, download a compatibility pack from the Microsoft website or save the file in rtf format before adding it to your project.
- When considering PDF documents as primary data, pay attention to whether these are image or text PDFs.
- If you experience a problem in playing audio or video files, download and install a complete codec pack. This solves the problem in most cases.

Related to transcription:

- Clearly mark speakers or other text features by using unique identifiers.
- Separate the change of speakers and other divisions with blank lines (= two hard returns).
- Break long paragraphs into smaller units (but keep the units together by not entering a blank line). This facilitates auto coding and results in more exact quotation references.

If you are interested in specific notations for preparing transcripts, see Jefferson (1984) or Kallmeyer and Schütze (1976).

Collecting data with the ATLAS.ti mobile app

With the ATLAS.ti mobile app you can begin to collect and analyze data in the field. Or perhaps you want to work on a document while on a long train journey, flight or boat trip. Email the document to yourself so it is available on your iPad.[1] Then you can add it to an ATLAS.ti mobile project, read it, write comments and perform first coding work. You can later merge the result with your existing ATLAS.ti desktop project. Supported file formats are text, PDF, image, audio and video files. As the app has just been released, I have no real experience in using it in an actual research project. From playing around with it, it currently can best be used as a data collection device. It is easy to take photos and make videos with your mobile applications. If you don't want to use the iPad for this because it is a bit too obtrusive, you can use an iPhone instead.

---

1 At the time of writing, the app was just released as an iPad app, but an Android version is in the making and will be released in early 2014. The app is available free of charge.

Figure 3.2 Impressions of ATLAS.ti mobile

Via the cloud the files can almost immediately be accessed on the iPad. I have used my iPad for recording interviews and it works quite well for this purpose.

Because we are so used to using our mobile devices these days to take pictures and make videos, and having observed people at a recent conference testing the app, my gut feeling is that ATLAS.ti mobile may cause a shift in the types of data researchers will be working with. We see more and more usage of multimedia data in ATLAS.ti, though adoption is slow. Most users still work with text documents. The app may have the power to change this.

The second application – working on documents as a way of using travel time wisely – only works if the document has not yet been added to an ATLAS.ti desktop project. Currently, you can only import data from the iPad to your desktop version. Temporarily checking out documents to work with them on the mobile device to 'return' them later to the desktop version is not yet available. Maybe with some lobbying, this feature will be available at some point. Above I show you some images of the app (Figure 3.2) to give you an impression of how it works. You will find the step-by-step instructions on the ATLAS.ti website in the manual section. As with most apps, using it is quite intuitive and the short explanations that you find in the app may already be sufficient to get you going.

Project management in ATLAS.ti

ATLAS.ti project management entails an understanding of how ATLAS.ti handles and accesses documents. It involves decisions regarding where HUs and documents are to be stored. Most problems can be avoided with a little informed planning about issues such as file locations and paths, and the need to copy, move and transfer ATLAS.ti projects across disks, networks and computers. For more general considerations in designing and conducting qualitative research in a software environment, see di Gregorio and Davidson (2008).

For version 6 projects, the most frequently asked support question was related to project management. It was quite common for users to 'lose' their documents, or at least to have thought so. You can imagine the panic that arises when, after months of coding, a user opens his or her project and cannot see the coded data on the screen: the entries in the drop-down lists are visible but the HU editor is empty. In most cases, this problem could be solved. Nonetheless, the ATLAS.ti development team thought of a new way of handling documents in version 7. The new principle is called 'managed documents', which means that ATLAS.ti takes care of document management – if the user allows it to do so. There are always mysterious ways in which users manage to sidestep the system and end up with unreadable projects.

The aim of this chapter is to help you understand what is happening when you add documents to a project and to introduce you to a few technical issues that happen behind the scenes. Working with ATLAS.ti involves users, files and computers. An ATLAS.ti project can be as simple as a single person working with one HU and a few primary documents (P-Docs) on a stand-alone computer. It can be as complex as large teams working on different computers in a network or at different geographic locations; working on several projects at once; moving files between users, computers and networks; merging partial projects into compiled projects; and many other conceivable scenarios. First, however, you need to know a few basics about how ATLAS.ti handles data and to understand that a well-managed project begins even before you enter any data: that is, when thinking of names for your files. For those readers planning to conduct a team project, I suggest that you still read the description on how to set up a single user project first. This will help you to take the next step in setting up a more complex team project.

What you need to know before setting up a project

Each computer user, I assume, has a preferred way of organizing files and folders. When working with ATLAS.ti, you don't have to get used to a different way of handling or storing them. In that respect, ATLAS.ti is like any other Windows software you know. It may happen that users do not know where they have stored their ATLAS.ti project file simply because they have allowed ATLAS.ti to determine the location for storing the file without paying attention. I then ask them what they do when they save a Word or Excel file. The response is that they normally select a specific location where they want the files to be stored. So, please also do this when saving your ATLAS.ti project file. If you don't specify a location when saving a Word or Excel file, Office saves the files to its default location – the My Documents or My Files folder. This process is no different in ATLAS.ti. The default location for saving project files in ATLAS. ti is the so-called TextBank folder. It can be found under My Documents\ Scientific Software\ATLAS.ti. You can save your project file at this location if you want to, but you don't have to. As in Word or Excel or any other application, you have a choice of where to store your files.

Data handling in ATLAS.ti

Let's assume that you have conducted an interview study with 20 audio-recorded interviews. You transfer the audio files to your computer and begin to transcribe, and save the resulting text files somewhere on the computer, using your own system for organizing and storing them. Next, you want to analyze the data with the help of ATLAS.ti. You open ATLAS.ti and begin to add data to your project. You have several ways to do so, as shown in Figure 3.3.

The standard option is to add documents to either My Library or the Team Library. The **library** is basically a folder on your computer that was created when you installed ATLAS.ti. The default locations of My Library and the Team Library are:

C:\Users\username\AppData\Roaming\Scientific Software\ATLASti\Repository\ Managed Files\

C:\Users\Public\Documents\Scientific Software\ATLASti\Repository\Managed Files\

Thus, the My Library folder is located within the subfolder hierarchy of the currently logged-in user. The Team Library folder is located under public documents. As the names indicate, the idea is to use the My Library folder for individual projects and the Team Library folder for team projects. There are only the two library locations. Often users ask whether there is a special library for each project they work on. The answer currently still is 'No' – in the same way as for

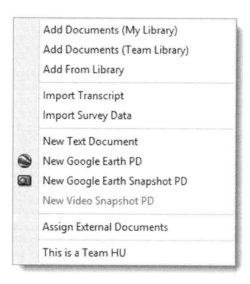

Figure 3.3   The various options to add documents to an ATLAS.ti project

instance your university library stores books for a variety of projects, the ATLAS.ti library stores the data for all of your projects. The reason for offering a second library for team projects concerns the possibility of moving the library folder. In team projects, all team members may want to access the data from one common location, namely a server. Because of popular demand and real project needs, currently a new feature is developed that will allow teams to create a library for each team project. As the solution is not implemented yet, I cannot describe it in detail – but watch out for it. It will be introduced via a service pack.

Similar to version 6, there is still a link between the documents and your ATLAS.ti project file (the HU). The difference in version 7 is that the link is managed by ATLAS.ti. The documents are now stored at a predetermined location (the library) handled by ATLAS.ti, principally out of reach for users to manually make changes, modify, rename or move documents externally.

As there are a number of good reasons for linking rather than importing documents, this basic principle has still been kept:

- When data are not being imported, the size of a document does not affect the size of the HU. This is a prerequisite for working with audio and video files, which are usually quite sizable. It also offers the possibility of working with a large set of data.
- A single data source file can be used by more than one project file. It may even be added to the same project multiple times, to allow for different angles of analysis.
- Team members can share data files. If the project is set up properly, changes to data sources (editing) are broadcast to all subprojects that use the files, keeping everyone up to date.

Incidentally, ATLAS.ti is not the only software that handles data in such a way. It is in fact a procedure common to many professional applications when things get large or complex. Video editing software, for instance, also manages its files in the form of one central project file and a number of dependent subdocuments like snapshots, overlays, music or special effects. The objective is to reduce the overall size of the main document and to make handling easier and faster.

So, what else happens when you add documents to a project?

ATLAS.ti first checks whether the files are compatible. If so, the files are copied and added to the library; doc and docx files are converted to rich text and the rich text version is stored in the library. In addition, each document receives a unique fingerprint; technically this is a 16-digit code. Based on this fingerprint, ATLAS.ti can identify each document. This for example has some implications for team projects. If two members on the team add the same documents to a project, these documents receive different fingerprints and are thus no longer the same for ATLAS.ti.

Let's consider a two-person team. They want to analyze 10 documents. Each person sets up their own project and adds 10 documents to the Team Library. They code the data and then they would like to put it all together. This can be done with the merge option that ATLAS.ti provides (see p. 64). They decide to unify the documents and wonder why they end up with 20 documents after the merge process. Due to the different fingerprints, ATLAS.ti does not recognize the documents as the same and therefore they cannot be unified. As this has happened a few times already, there is now a fix for it. Thus, you can rescue your project in case you started it the wrong way.

This fingerprint identification was not meant to make things more complicated, but rather to facilitate team work. If you have been using version 6, you are probably aware of the fact that the order of the documents in the Primary Document Manager was crucial when merging projects. The documents had to be in the same order in all projects that were to be merged. This is no longer necessary, because documents are no longer identified by their position in the list of documents. Everyone on the team can impose their own order and is free to move documents to a different place in the Primary Document Manager.

About 'good' data file names

After adding documents to your ATLAS.ti project, you will find a shell for each document. The general name for this shell is **primary document**. The primary document has a name which by default is the name of the added data file; it contains the reference where the file is stored and its original location, the file type, date of creation and modification, and the name of the ATLAS.ti user who added it. Also, you have the option to add a comment to each shell (I will return to this later). The important thing to remember is that the shell itself does not contain the added file. It can only load the file into the HU editor, based on the reference it has (e.g. My Library).

Figure 3.4 shows some transcript files that were added. The name of the file comprises the word 'transcript', a consecutive number and the date of transcription: 'transcript 1_ 2013_April 4.docx'. As I will explain further, this is not a very good choice because the name does not include any information that could be helpful for the analysis.

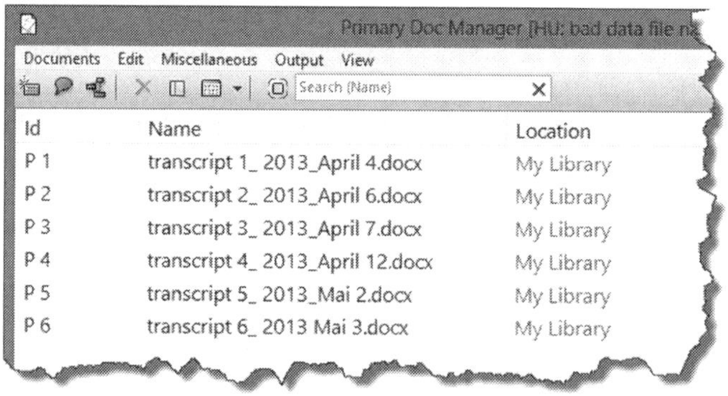

Id	Name	Location
P 1	transcript 1_ 2013_April 4.docx	My Library
P 2	transcript 2_ 2013_April 6.docx	My Library
P 3	transcript 3_ 2013_April 7.docx	My Library
P 4	transcript 4_ 2013_April 12.docx	My Library
P 5	transcript 5_ 2013_Mai 2.docx	My Library
P 6	transcript 6_ 2013 Mai 3.docx	My Library

Figure 3.4   'Bad' data file names

What I mean by 'good' is that the name should assist the analytic process. It won't actually hinder your analysis if you don't do this, but why not do yourself a favor by making it a bit easier? Naming a transcript 'transcript' – as in the example above – is only useful if you're working with other data sources as well. Numbering them consecutively and adding the date of transcription is useful for the process of transcription, but not for your analysis. More informative are names that include criteria which you already know are important for your analysis, like gender, age, profession, location and date of interview. This may not be the case for all studies and for all data analyzed in ATLAS.ti, but it does apply to a large number of projects. To prevent the data file names getting too long by including all this information, my suggestion is to use a code as shown in Figure 3.5:

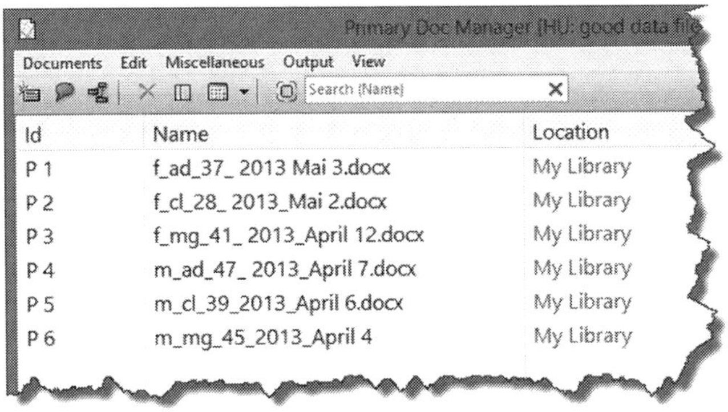

Figure 3.5 'Good' data file names for analytic purposes

Code:
m   : male
f   : female
mg   : manager
cl   : clerk
ad   : administrative stuff
number : age

Naming your files in this way has the advantage that the documents are already sorted by these criteria. This facilitates the creation of subgroups of your documents in ATLAS.ti for analytic purposes (see Chapter 5). In addition, a good analytic name provides valuable information when retrieving data and, overall, adds transparency to your project. If alphabetical order is not useful for your purposes, or if you do not assign all the data at once, you can always drag and drop a document to a different location in the Primary Document Manager.

It may not always be possible to know from the very beginning what might be a good analytic name – or perhaps you have already created a project before reading my suggestions. In that case, you have the option to rename each primary document (right click on a primary document in the Primary Document Manager and select the option **Rename**).

I am often asked how to present and report on a project that has been analyzed with the assistance of ATLAS.ti. Look at the list of document names in the Primary Document Manager. This is where to start – use the Primary Document Manager to explain your sampling. If well chosen, the names will already include some of the major sampling criteria.

Setting up a project

The scenarios are written as hands-on exercises that you can follow either by using your own data or by downloading sample data from the companion website (www.uk/friese2e). If you want to follow the exercises in this and other chapters, I recommend that you set up a project using the provided sample data as 'single user project'.

Description of the sample data set

The data material provided on the companion website consists of seven documents: one PDF file, two rich text files, two docx files, one video file and one image file. In addition, you will find an Excel file to illustrate how the import of survey data works. It is a subset of the data that are included as Quick Tour data with ATLAS.ti 7.

In looking for suitable example data, I came across an article on children and happiness written by Nattavudh Powdthavee. Nattavudh reports on a number of academic studies that repeatedly found a negative correlation between having children and levels of happiness, life satisfaction, marital satisfaction and mental well-being. Since having children (or not having them) is an issue that most people, regardless of their cultural backgrounds, religions or geographic locations, have to deal with, this promised to be a topic that a lot of ATLAS.ti or potential ATLAS.ti users might be interested in.

In addition to the journal article, two documents including comments by parents and non-parents made on two blogs on the issue are included. Furthermore, the data contain a short video that allows you to explore video functionality in ATLAS.ti. The video contains quotes on happiness and how to reach it. You will find a number of supporting or contradictory statements in the comments of the blogs. These can for example be used to practice hyperlinking via drag and drop while multiple documents are open side by side. The video is associated with a 'transcript' as an example of the associated document option (see p. 58). The transcript consists of the quotes plus information about the authors of these quotes. The Abraham Lincoln file is included to show you how to work with images.

For those interested in working with survey data, the sample material contains some fictional survey data that can be imported to ATLAS.ti via an Excel spreadsheet (see 'Working with Survey Data' on p. 60). The survey data comprise answers from 24 respondents to two open-ended questions (reasons for having and for not having children), some socio-demographic data and two answers to yes/no questions.

The main issue to investigate in this project is how parents and non-parents react to the finding that, statistically speaking, happiness and life satisfaction correlate negatively with having children. What is the general reaction? How are the results perceived? Are there differences between parents and those who do not have children (yet)? Let's start setting up this project in ATLAS.ti so that we can find some answers to these questions in later chapters.

Skills training 3.2: setting up a single user project

Project setup

- Download and unzip the sample data set. The name of the unzipped project folder is 'Happiness project'. Store it for instance on your desktop.
- Open ATLAS.ti. Check the title bar. If the last used HU is open and not a new one, select the main menu option **PROJECT / CLOSE**. The text in the title bar should read: New Hermeneutic Unit.
- Select the main menu option **PROJECT / ADD DOCUMENT(S) / ADD DOCUMENTS (MY LIBRARY)**.
- A file loader window will open. Navigate to the desktop and then to the 'Happiness project' folder. Select all documents in the folder.
- Click on the **Open** button (it will appear in the language of your Windows system).
- You will see the File Quality Check window and can follow the process of how documents are checked and added to your project. If there is a problem with one or more documents, you will be notified (see Figure 3.7). If everything works smoothly, you will be informed that seven files were successfully converted and added to your project.

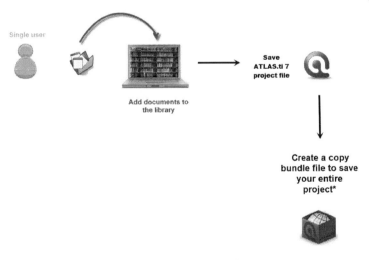

Figure 3.6 Workflow for setting up a single user project

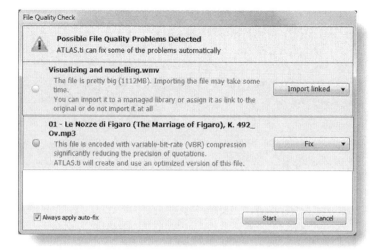

Figure 3.7   Adding primary documents – file quality check

- Open the Primary Document Manager by clicking on the **P-Docs** button. Note that all documents are numbered consecutively. In the column 'Location' you should see the entry My Library. The default author is 'Super' for super user. If you want each entry stamped with your personal name, you need to create a user account. As this is more relevant for team projects, this is explained in the section on how to set up team projects.

Let's save the project before we do anything else, because we do not want to risk losing anything:

- Select the main option **PROJECT / SAVE** (or **SAVE AS…**).

A window will open where you can specify the location of the HU file and its name. The default location is the TextBank folder. You can use the TextBank folder to store your project file(s). However, you can save the HU to any location on your computer.

- Navigate to the folder where you want to save your HU file. I suggest that you create a folder that is called something like 'ATLAS.ti analysis', where you store all HU files for your project. You may end up saving different versions of your HU file, backup files, etc. Therefore, creating a special folder for these files is probably a good idea.
- Enter a name for the HU (e.g. 'My first ATLAS.ti project' or 'Happiness project').
- Click on the **Save** button shown in the language of your Windows system.

You have now saved the HU file that stores all your work *on* the data: your coding, all written comments and memos, families, network views, etc. However, the HU file does not store your data. To save your entire project, you need to create a copy bundle file. The copy bundle file includes your HU file and all documents from the library that are relevant for your project.

- Select the main option **Project / Save Copy Bundle**.

In the copy bundle window you have the option to deselect some documents from the bundle or to work with filters. But for now, we want to create a backup copy of the entire project including all files.

- Click on **Create Bundle**. The default name for the bundle is the name of the HU file. The file extension for copy bundle files is atlcb (atlas copy bundle).
- Select a location for the bundle file, accept the default name or enter a new name, and click on the **Save** button shown in the language of your Windows system. Congratulations. That was probably the biggest hurdle in terms of project management in ATLAS.ti.

It is advisable to save the copy bundle file to a secure location, or store one copy on your computer locally and a second copy on an external drive or server or in the cloud. Dropbox or other cloud services should only be used for storing backup files or for project transfer. If you want to access your project from a different computer, you can store a copy bundle file on a USB stick or an external drive and take it along, or temporarily upload it into a Dropbox, SkyDrive or similar cloud service and download it from there when needed at location B.

Talking about cloud services, never add documents directly from the cloud to an ATLAS.ti project. First download the files, e.g. to a folder on your computer and then add them. The whole idea of the new library principle is that ATLAS.ti is managing your documents for you. ATLAS.ti, however, can only do this if no other application mingles with it. Files stored in the cloud are usually synchronized across the different devices that access them and during this process may destroy the integrity of your ATLAS.ti project. ATLAS.ti detects if you want to store data in clouds like Dropbox or SkyDrive and issues a warning.

To make project management simple and easy for you, allow ATLAS.ti to manage your data files. Then, the only two files you need to be concerned about are your HU file and the copy bundle file. Make it a habit to create a copy bundle file after each work session and store it in a safe place. You may keep a few rolling copies of the copy bundle file or overwrite the old with the new version every time you save. Throughout the book, you will find suggestions on when to save a special backup copy in the form of a copy bundle file.

Next, I explain two further options for adding documents to a project that offer certain functionalities useful for certain types of analytic approaches.

Note that if you add documents to the library, the project can only be transferred using the copy bundle function. If you work with large-sized projects (1 gigabyte or more), creating copy bundle files and transferring projects can become cumbersome. One option is to create partial bundles to keep the file size down. Another option is to set up the project using externally linked files rather than importing all documents to My Library. In this case, it is recommended to use the old HUPATH principle: that is, storing all documents and the HU file in one folder. You will find more details on this special setup on p. 78.

Skills training 3.3: working with transcripts and synchronized media files

Note that you can download an example f4 transcript and audio file from the companion website to follow the instructions.

The advantage of this project setup is that your transcripts remain linked to their original audio or video files. Thus, you can select a quotation or any text segment and play the associated audio or video segment. This is useful for a form of analysis where it is important to analyze not only what was said, but also how it was said or done. When working with video files (see Chapter 4) you may want to transcribe the spoken words only without describing what is going on visually. This allows you to code both the textual level (transcript) and the visual level (video) in different ways without losing the connection between the two.

As mentioned, ATLAS.ti supports the import of transcripts prepared in f4/f5 (Mac) and Transana. An alternative is to transcribe your data directly in ATLAS.ti. When you transcribe your data using f4/f5 or Transana, I suggest that you keep in mind a good analytical name for your document when saving the transcript (see 'About "good" data file names' on p. 52).

- Prepare the transcripts in f4/f5 or Transana. When you save a document, save it under the name that you want to use as the primary document name in ATLAS.ti. A good place for storing the transcripts is in the same folder as the multimedia files.
- Open ATLAS.ti and select **PROJECT / ADD DOCUMENTS / IMPORT TRANSCRIPT**.
- A file loader window opens. Go to the location where your transcripts are stored. Only the rtf files of the transcript(s) will be shown. Select one or more transcripts and click on **OPEN**.

If the multimedia file is stored in the same folder as the transcript, they are automatically recognized and ATLAS.ti will ask you whether you want to add them to My Library, the Team Library or link them as external files. The latter option is useful if you work with large video files. In case the multimedia files are stored elsewhere, you will be asked to locate them before you can specify how ATLAS.ti should handle them. The transcript file will be imported into the HU and turned into an internal document.

- Save the project file: **FILE / SAVE** to any location.
- To save a copy of your entire project, select **FILE / SAVE COPY BUNDLE**.

Let's see what happens to the HU after importing a transcript and its media file:

- Open the Primary Document Manager. It shows the transcript(s) and the multimedia file(s) (Figure 3.8). The data file names tell you that it is an expert interview with a female (me).
- In the column **Location** you will see the entry 'In HU' for the transcripts and the location you have chosen for the multimedia files (e.g. My Library). The column **Origin** shows the location where the files were stored before adding them to a project (applies to files that are not embedded).

Figure 3.8 Primary Document Manager after importing an f4 transcript

Seeing how the association works

- Load the transcript. At the top left you will see a red dot. Click on it to load the associated media file into a second document region (Figure 3.9).

The red dots in the text show the association anchors (timestamps). I usually set them quite frequently – basically every time I stop the recording when transcribing. The closer the anchors are set, the more accurately the associated segments can be played. A standard option in transcription software is to set a timestamp after each paragraph. If paragraphs are long and you want to play just a specific section, the software needs to interpolate between the available anchor points, calculating the start and end positions as best as possible.

- To see the full list of associations (= time marks), open the Association Editor: DOCUMENTS / A-DOCS / OPEN ASSOCIATION EDITOR.
- When you click on an association (Figure 3.9), the associated text segment is high-lighted in the transcript. If it does not work, then the synchro mode is not activated. Press **F3** or select DOCUMENTS / A-DOCS / SYNCHRO MODE.
- Click through the associations to see how you can use them to navigate through your document. Pay attention to the playhead. It jumps to the start position indicated by the time mark.

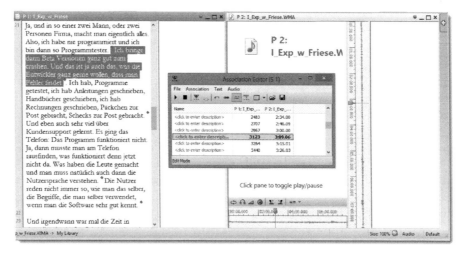

Figure 3.9 Association Editor and associated documents

- If you want to listen to or view an associated multimedia segment, highlight any piece of text in the transcript and press **CTRL+P**. Alternatively, select **DOCUMENTS / A-DOCS / PLAY SELECTED TEXT** from the main menu. Make sure that the sound is turned on.

The two files shown in Figure 3.10 are included in the sample project. If you want to see how you can activate the association between a transcript and a video file:

- Open the sample file 'Children and Happiness Stage I' via **HELP / QUICK TOUR**.
- **LOAD** 'P7: Transcript of video' from the P-Docs drop-down list.
- Open the associated video file by clicking on the red dot in the upper right hand corner. This loads the associated video into the region next to the transcript.

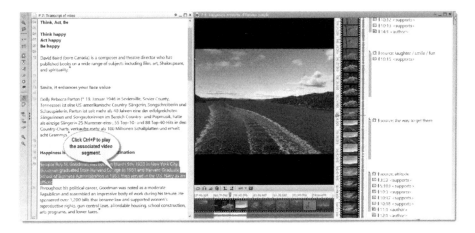

Figure 3.10 Association between a transcript and a video

- Make sure that the synchro mode is active: select **DOCUMENTS / A-DOCS / SYNCHRO MODE**. If the synchro icon is highlighted, then the mode is active.
- As above, highlight a few lines in the transcript and press **CTRL+P**. The video begins to play at the position that you marked in the transcript.

Skills training 3.4: working with survey data

Starting with version 6, ATLAS.ti offers the possibility to import survey data. This makes sense when the survey includes a number of open-ended questions. In paper and pencil surveys, respondents often did not write a lot when asked an open-ended question. This changed with the use of online surveys. Respondents often now write quite a lot and their responses are already in electronic format. Thus, there is no need to retype them. Survey data are imported via an Excel file to ATLAS.ti. Most online survey tools offer an Excel output, which can then be used to prepare the data for ATLAS.ti.

Preparing survey data

Data are imported as case-based. This means each primary document represents the answers to each open-ended question of one respondent. Variables that describe the respondents, like make, type of occupation, age range, education, etc., can be added as primary document families. Whether information is interpreted as content or as variable depends on the syntax you enter into the Excel table. For example, see Table 3.2.

The example is taken from the sample survey file that you will find in ATLAS.ti under HELP / QUICKTOUR / OPEN QUICKTOUR SURVEY DATA.

If you add a colon (:) in front of the variable name, ATLAS.ti creates a document family for each cell value (see Chapter 5 for more details on document families). Thus, the document described in Table 3.2 will be added to the following document families: Gender::male, has children::yes, number of children::1, marital status::divorced, children bring happiness (answer 1 = yes), and education::highschool. As ATLAS.ti can only handle dichotomous variables by way of PD families, a family is created from each value. Thus, female respondents will be added to a document family called Gender::female; those who are married or single in families with the names marital status::married and marital status::single. Note that in ATLAS.ti two colons (::) are used to separate the variable name and the value. This is not a typo.

If you put a period/full stop (.) in front of the variable name, only those cases that contain a 1 or a yes in the cell will be added to a document family. In the above example, survey respondents were asked in one question whether they believe that children contribute to happiness, and in another whether they believe they bring fulfillment and purpose in life. Both questions could be answered with a yes or no. Thus, on a limited scale it is also possible to add quantitative information to your ATLAS.ti project. As families can later be used to compare

Table 3.2 Syntax for preparing survey data

:Gender	:has children	:number of children	:marital status	.bring happiness	.bring fulfillment and purpose	:education
male	yes	1	divorced	1	0	highschool

Table 3.3 Syntax for open-ended questions

SQ1::Reasons for having children	SQ2::Reasons for not having children
Children whittle away your time in ways that are ultimately beneficial: they have an uncanny knack of getting rid of the meaningless hobbies that used to consume you	Responsibility. All of life's prior responsibilities pale in comparison. If you decide to have a child, that new person must absolutely be your top priority. As your child will remind you when he or she is older and something goes wrong, 'I didn't ask to be born.' A child is a lifelong commitment to a person who is innocent of this choice

different groups of respondents, think about the kinds of comparisons you want to make and then decide which quantitative survey questions are useful to bring into ATLAS.ti.

To indicate to ATLAS.ti that an entry is a response to an open-ended question (Table 3.3), no syntax needs to be used in front of the column name. The column name will be used as code to pre-code all open-ended questions. You may, however, not want the entire (long) question to be used as the code name. If so, you can use the question ID as here, SQ1 and SQ2, as the code name, and the full question as a code comment. In order to achieve this, add two colons (::) after the question ID. ATLAS.ti will then add the text after the two colons into the code comment field during import.

Importing survey data

- Download the sample survey file, which you will find under **HELP / QUICKTOUR**. It contains 24 cases, but it is also possible to import files that contain 3000 cases or more.
- To import this file in ATLAS.ti, select **PROJECT / ADD DOCUMENT(S) / IMPORT SURVEY DATA**. The Excel file should not be open in Excel.
- Select the sample Excel file and wait for the import process to be completed. All data will be imported into your ATLAS.ti project file, the HU. This means that if your project only contains survey data, there is no need to create a copy bundle file. Your HU file contains all the data and it will be all you need and to take care of – also in terms of backing it up!
- ATLAS.ti automatically names the HU file after the Excel file. To save your project, select **PROJECT / SAVE**. If you want to save it under a different name, select **SAVE AS…**.

Team project setup

In the following section, a few issues are discussed that are common to all team projects: finding a project administrator, creating user accounts, merging and transferring projects. This is followed by a description of three characteristic team scenarios: a team working on a common set of documents, a team starting out with different documents at each side, a team sharing and working on documents on a server.

In addition, members of a team project need to discuss a number of further issues: how to develop the coding system, how to divide the work, how and when to inform the others about what has been done, how to share the analysis, etc.

Commonalities of team projects

Finding a project administrator

When working in a team, it is best to nominate one person to be the project administrator. If everyone is equally skilled, choose the person with the greatest knowledge of ATLAS.ti and the highest degree of computer literacy. Even though you don't have to be a computer whizz to work with ATLAS.ti, anyone who does not know how to copy files, or has trouble converting doc files to rich text format, or does not know how to search for a file within the system, is not well suited to the task. The job of the administrator is to set up the project, to distribute it to team members, to provide instructions for the team members, and to collect the subprojects from time to time in order to merge them.

> NOTE: The project administrator can be someone from the team who volunteers to take on the task of merging and redistributing.

Skills training 3.5: creating user accounts

You may already have noticed in some of the above figures that my name or 'ATLAS.ti team' is shown in the author field. If no other user account is created first, the *super* user is the default login and all new entries are stamped with the author name 'Super'. When working in a team, it is clearly important to know who has done what, so not all entries should be stamped 'Super'. Creating a user account and logging in with a personal user name allows the steps of the various team members to be traced. It is not a perfect system for every situation, but in most cases it is the best option. For example, modifications to an already existing object like a code are not automatically tracked. The author field only contains the name of the user who created the object and not the name of the person who modified it.

ATLAS.ti recognizes two classes of users: administrators and all others. Administrators have more rights than 'normal' users. The key rights of administrators are the ability to define new users, install service packs or use the more advanced data source management features. Thus, in order to be able to create new user accounts, you need to be logged in as a user with administrative rights. By default, you are logged in as 'Super' user and this user has administrative rights. User accounts are best created by each individual team member and not by the project administrator. Here is what you need to do:

- From the main menu, select **Tools / User Management / User Editor**. A window will open showing the three standard users: admin, guest and super.
- To create a new account, select **Edit / New User**. Four entry fields will pop up, one after the other, asking you to enter an account name, a password, your last name and your first name.

You can enter a password or leave the field blank. When logging in, you are not asked for a password unless you specify this in the user.ini file. Password protecting the user name is only asked for on rare occasions.

- Save the newly created user account by selecting **File / Save** from the User Editor window. A small window will pop up informing you that the user base has been saved to disk.
- Close the User Editor.

To change the user:

- From the main menu select **Tools / User Management / Switch User....** Select your user account (Figure 3.11). Notice that you are not required to enter a password and that the default setting is 'Automatic Login'.

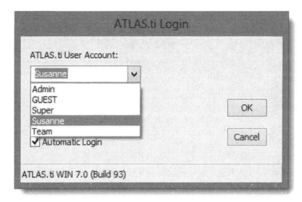

Figure 3.11   Logging in using a personal user account

After logging in, you will be greeted by the software. If you're working late or at weekends, however, the software may not be so friendly; I'll leave it to you to see what happens! ATLAS.ti will remember the setting and there is no need to log in every time. The automatic login can remain activated as long as the same user always works on the same computer. Only when different people use ATLAS.ti on the same computer at different times does this option need to be deactivated; in this case, the login window comes up each time you launch the software.

Skills training 3.6: merging projects

In ATLAS.ti you cannot work simultaneously on the same project file. This means each person works within their individual HU file and these files need to be merged from time to time. When merging you merge a *source HU* into a *target HU*. The target HU has to be loaded into the HU editor first before invoking the merge option.

Three 'strategies' can be chosen for the processing of every object category. These are 'Add', 'Unify' and 'Ignore'. The object categories that can be processed within the HU are PDs, Quotations, Codes, Memos, PD Families, Code Families, Memo Families, and Network Views.

- Load the target HU. It is advisable to save it under a different name so that you don't corrupt the original file in case something goes wrong. Select **Project / Save As....**

- From the HU editor's main menu, select PROJECT / MERGE WITH **HU**. Alternatively you can drag an HU onto the HU editor's caption by holding down the CTRL key.
- The Merge Wizard will open, guiding you through the merge procedure. The first page of the Merge Wizard displays the current target HU, requesting you to enter the source HU's file name. Click on the browse button and select a source HU from the file dialog.
- Click on NEXT. The source HU will be loaded and you can proceed with the next step.

The second step is the selection of *how* the source HU is to be merged into the target HU. Four broad predefined strategies are available that can be customized in a second step, as follows.

Same PDs and Codes: Choose this strategy when PDs and codes are (mostly) the same in the target and source HU. All of the same PDs and codes are then unified. Different PDs and codes will be added.

Same PDs – Different Codes: Choose this strategy when target and source HU contain the same PDs, but different sets of codes. If identical codes are found during the merge procedure, one of them is renamed (e.g. 'effects of parenting' and 'effects of parenting_1').

If there are a number of identical codes, chose the option 'same Codes' to avoid duplication. You do not lose any codes, as all codes that are different or new are added!

Different PDs – Same Codes: Choose this strategy when target and source HUs contain different PDs that have been coded with the same code set. This is a common situation when working in teams and different team members have coded different PDs using a common set of codes. If a few additional codes have been added to the common set, these will be added.

Different PDs and Codes: Choose this strategy when both – PDs and codes – are different. The PDs and codes from the source HU will be added to the ones in the target HU.

> NOTE: If you are unsure which strategy to use, choose 'Same PDs and Codes'. It is the catch-all strategy. It merges all objects that are the same and adds all objects that are different.

Select one of the four stock strategies (Figure 3.12). A short description of the strategy is displayed at the bottom left of the dialog box.

- Fine-tune the strategy so it best suits your needs. For all major object types, you can divert from the predefined stock strategy and manually define how the various object types are to be handled in the merge process.
- Check the option 'Create Merge-Report' to generate an overview of what has been done.
- Click on FINISH to start the merge process.

> NOTE: If you repeatedly merge the same HUs, you might want to deactivate the option 'Merge Comments' as it leads to duplication of entries.

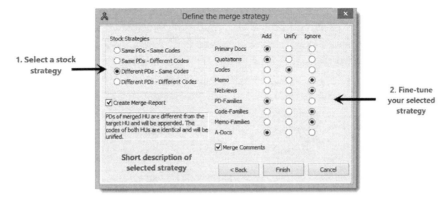

Figure 3.12   Defining your merge strategy

Skills training 3.7: creating backups and transferring a project (also applies to single user projects)

In order to back up your project, transfer a project to a different computer or send it to other team members, you need to create a copy bundle file. Only the copy bundle file contains the project file and the documents. This is also nicely symbolized by the copy bundle file icon: your project in a box (Figure 3.12). Copy bundle files can also be used to preserve a certain stage of your project like the various stages of code system development.

There is no need to always send a copy bundle file when you transfer a project. If all documents already exist on all computers involved, the team administrator or the team members only need to send the HU file. In that case, a new copy bundle file only needs to be created when new documents are added or when data sources are modified. See also 'Data source modification in team projects' on p. 69. All team members should, however, always create a copy bundle file as backup after each work session.

Creating a copy bundle file

- To create a copy bundle file, select **PROJECT / SAVE COPY BUNDLE** from the main menu. The Create Copy Bundle window will open (Figure 3.13).
- Click on **CREATE BUNDLE**.

If you want to exclude documents from the bundle, you can either deselect individual documents or set a PD family as a global filter first and select the option 'Apply current PD filter'. See 'Creating partial bundle files' on p. 77 for further detail.

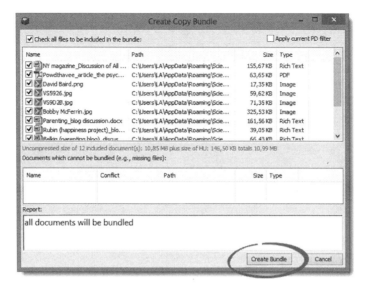

Figure 3.13   Creating a copy bundle file

Unpacking a copy bundle file

- Either double click on the file in Windows Explorer or open ATLAS.ti first and select
  PROJECT / UNPACK COPY BUNDLE and then select a bundle file. The Unpack Copy Bundle
  window will open (Figure 3.14).

The column 'Target Location' indicates where the documents will be stored
when unpacking the file. <Local Managed> means that the documents will be
unpacked into My Library; <Shared Managed> means that the documents will
be unpacked into the Team Library. Other possible locations are <HUPATH>,
<TBPATH> or an absolute path reference. The latter applies to externally
linked files.

- Click on the file loader icon at the end of the field HU Path to select a location for
  storing the HU file.

Figure 3.14   Unpacking a copy bundle file

- Modify the name of the HU, for example by adding your name or initials to the file name (Figure 3.15).
- Click on **UNBUNDLE** at the bottom right of the window.

Figure 3.15   Adjusting the project name while unbundling the file

Frequently asked questions

HU cannot be unbundled: The color of the box behind the field HU Path causes confusion at times (Figure 3.16). As the location for the HU file, ATLAS.ti uses the location where the HU file was stored when the copy bundle file was created. Look at the field HU Path in Figure 3.16. The path shown there is a path under my user name 'Susanne'. If you were to open the bundle on your computer, the colored box at the end of the line would be red, indicating that the path cannot be created. This is also the case if the Master HU was saved to a server location and you want to unpack it to your local drive. In such cases, you will see a read square and the status report will indicate in red letters: 'The HU will not be unbundled'. The solution to the 'problem' is printed right underneath, but often not read.

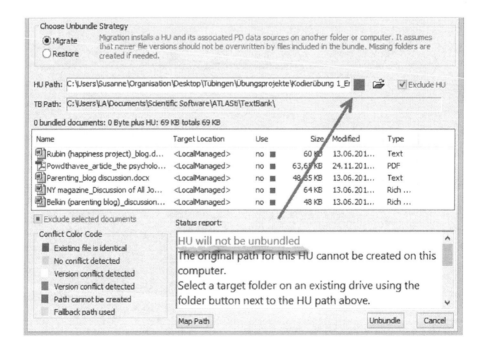

Figure 3.16   Common 'problem' when unpacking a copy bundle file

To solve this issue, click on the file loader icon and select a location that *does exist* on your computer. Then the box will turn green and *voilà* you can click on UNBUNDLE and everything will be fine. :-)

The box remains yellow if the HU file already exists in the selected folder. In Migrate mode, the HU file will be overwritten if the copy bundle file includes a newer version of the HU. In Restore mode, everything will be overwritten.

0 documents will be unbundled: If you unpack a copy bundle multiple times, even if it includes a different version of the HU file, ATLAS.ti checks whether the documents already exist in the library. If this is the case, there is no need to unpack the documents again and therefore the status report will tell you that no documents will be unbundled. This is the same if the HU only contains internal documents, as is the case when importing survey data. There is no need to take any action; there are no documents to be unbundled and thus there is nothing to worry about.

Data source modification in team projects

Modifying a data source (i.e. editing a document) is not difficult, but it is a crucial task as all coded segments need to be adjusted according to the changes that are made within the document. If you work on your own, there is little to pay attention to apart from the fact that you need to create a new copy bundle file after modifying data sources. If you work in a distributed team, data source modification is more critical as you need to coordinate who can make changes where in order not to end up with multiple versions of one document. A server-based team project (see Scenario 3) is easier to handle because all team members access the same data source files. Then ATLAS.ti can ensure that two users do not edit the same document at the same time. This cannot be controlled by the software if multiple users work with the same documents across different sites. This is the case for Scenario 1 and also for Scenario 2 after the first round of merging.

The simplest solution is to leave it up to the project administrator to make changes if necessary and to incorporate the modified documents into a new Master HU and copy bundle file. If individual team members are allowed to modify documents, you need to specify in advance who is allowed to edit which document.

> PREREQUISITE: Only documents that have been saved to any of the two libraries can be edited. Externally linked documents cannot be edited.

Only the project administrator is allowed to edit

With this option, it is best to edit documents after merging the various sub-HUs. All the required changes need to be communicated to the project administrator. He or she will edit the documents after merging all sub-HUs, save the new Master HU file and create a new copy bundle file for distribution to all team members.

Team members are allowed to edit specific subsets of documents

This option requires a strict agreement about who is allowed to edit which subgroup of documents. If the same document is edited at two locations, one version of it will be lost with the next merging procedure. This also refers to the coding done on the document.

If documents are edited by team members, they have to return copy bundle files to the project administrator for the next round of merging. The project administrator will unpack all bundle files and begin to merge the HU files. During this process he or she will be prompted to synchronize the HUs. This needs to be done before all files can be merged. After merging all subprojects, the project administrator will create a new Master HU and copy bundle files for redistribution.

Various team project scenarios

When working in teams, multiple scenarios are possible:

1. A team analyzes a common set of documents across different sites.
2. Initially, the documents at each site are different. Every person analyzes a subset of the data before merging the various project files.
3. A team analyzes a common set of documents, which are stored on a server that everyone has access to.

Below you will find a description of each scenario followed by a step-by-step instruction explaining the tasks of the project administrator and the team members for setting up the project, distributing it and how to proceed with the continuous work.

Scenario 1 – analyzing a common set of documents

This scenario applies if a team wants to analyze a common set of documents. Remember the issue with the unique fingerprint that every document receives once it is added to an ATLAS.ti project (see 'What you need to know before setting up a project' on p. 49). In order for your team not to end up with multiple sets of documents that cannot be unified due to different fingerprints, the project administrator needs to set up the project, adding all documents to the Team Library. If the team wants to start out with a common set of codes, the project administrator can add the codes to the project, save the project as a copy bundle file and distribute it to all team members (see Figure 3.17). The team members unpack the copy bundle file on their computers. During this process, the documents will be copied to the Team Library folder on their computers. At this point the team members can also rename the project file (recommended), for example by adding their name or initials. This is important for the latter merging process. If the project administrator receives HU files for

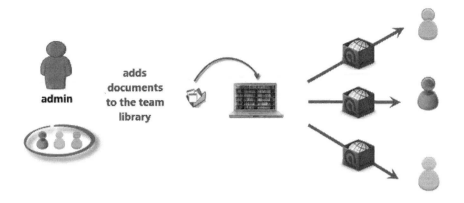

Figure 3.17   Analyzing a common set of documents

merging that all have the same name, there is the danger that one file will overwrite another. Thus, the project administrator would need to rename the files anyway, an additional task that can be avoided.

Project setup

Tasks of the project administrator

- Create a new HU and add documents to the Team Library: **Project / Add Document(s) / Add Documents (Team Library)**, or drag and drop a folder or selected documents from the File Explorer onto the HU.
- Possibly add a list of codes that your team wants to use as a starting point (see Chapter 5, Skills training 5.3).
- Save the project file to any location: **Project / Save**. As a file name I usually use 'Master + project name + date'. I suggest you use the same or a similar naming convention. The purpose is to make it clear by way of the file name where the file is coming from.
- Create a copy bundle file, **Project / Save Copy Bundle**, and distribute it to all team members.

Tasks of the team members

- Create an ATLAS.ti user account on your computer and log in with your user name (see above: 'Creating user accounts').
- Install the copy bundle file that you receive from the project administrator. Double click on the copy bundle file or open ATLAS.ti first and select **Project / Unpack Bundle File**.
- Click on the file loader icon at the end of the field HU Path to select a location for storing the HU file.
- Modify the name of the HU, for example by adding your name or initials to the file name (see Figure 3.15).
- Click on **Unbundle** at the bottom right of the window.
- Begin your work.
- Create your personal copy bundle file after each work session as backup (**Project / Save Copy Bundle**).

Continuous project work

Tasks of the team members

After an agreed-upon interval, each team member should send their work to the project administrator for merging in the following form:

- If no further documents were added or modified (Figure 3.18), it is sufficient to send the HU file.
- If documents were added or modified (Figure 3.19), a copy bundle file needs to be sent. However, it is advisable to leave the task of adding further documents to the project administrator. (See p. 69 on how to deal with document modifications in team projects.)

Tasks of the project administrator

- If team members have sent copy bundle files, unbundle all files.
- Merge the various HU files that you receive from the team members (see above: 'How to merge projects').
- Create a new Master HU and distribute the new Master file to all team members. In case documents were added to the project or modified, a copy bundle file needs to be sent.

Tasks of the team members

- If applicable, unbundle the new copy bundle file you receive from the project administrator, rename the new Master HU by adding your name or initials to the file name, and continue to work.

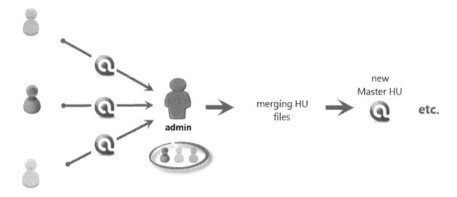

Figure 3.18   Continuous project work if no documents are modified

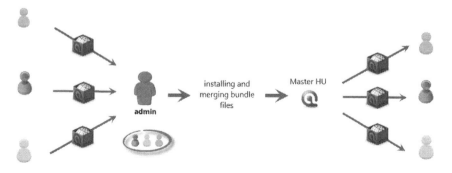

Figure 3.19   Continuous project work if documents are added or modified

Scenario 2 – distributed team work

This scenario applies if a team starts out with different documents at each site. Here, each team member can initially set up their own project similar to a single user project, but adding the documents to the Team Library instead of adding documents to My Library. If all subprojects are combined, a copy bundle file will need to be sent to the project administrator, who will unpack all bundle files, merge them and create a Master HU file (Figure 3.20). To distribute the combined work, he or she needs to create a copy bundle file that can then be distributed to the team members.

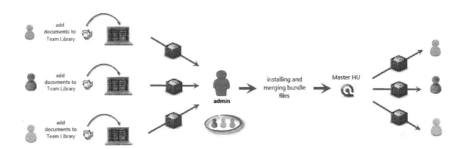

Figure 3.20   Distributed team work

Project setup

Tasks of the team members

- Create an ATLAS.ti user account on your computer and log in under your user name (see above: 'Creating user accounts').
- Set up your subproject by creating a new HU and add documents to the Team Library: **Project / Add Document(s) / Add Documents (Team Library)**.
- Save the project file to any location: **Project / Save**.
- Begin to work on your subproject.
- Create a copy bundle file as backup after each work session (**Project / Save Copy Bundle**).

After an agreed-upon interval, each team member should send their work to the project administrator for merging:

- Create a copy bundle file: **Project / Save Copy Bundle** and send it to the project administrator.

Tasks of the project administrator

- Install all copy bundle files: **Project / Unpack Copy Bundle**.
- Merge all HUs and save the outcome as the new Master HU (see 'Merging projects' on p. 64).
- Create a copy bundle file: **Project / Save Copy Bundle** and distribute it to all team members.

Continuous project work

Tasks of the team members

- Install the copy bundle file that you receive from the project administrator. During the process, rename the HU file by adding your name or initials (see above: Figure 3.15).
- Continue to work on the project.
- Create a copy bundle file as backup after each work session.

Repeat the above cycle as often as necessary to complete the analysis.

Scenario 3 – server-based setup

A team analyzes a common set of documents, which are stored on a server that everyone can access. Server-based in this context does not mean that you share data via a cloud service like SkyDrive, Google Drive or Dropbox. The aim of such services is to allow you to access data from different devices. If you make changes at one location, the documents on other devices will be synchronized. This jeopardizes the principle of managed files in ATLAS.ti and can result in corrupt projects.

The basic procedure is as follows. The project administrator sets up the project, adding all documents to the Team Library (Figure 3.21). Next, the project administrator moves the Team Library to a central location (server) that all team members can access. The Master project file (HU) is best saved in a separate folder on the server as well. Team members make a copy of the Master file and rename it by adding their name or initials. They can store their personal project files at any location. My recommendation is to store the files on the server, for example in a designated folder for HU files where all Master files are stored as well.

In order for the team members to access the documents, they need to redirect their Team Library path to the server location. After an agreed-upon time interval, the project administrator merges all HU files and creates a new Master file, which can be made available via the server as well.

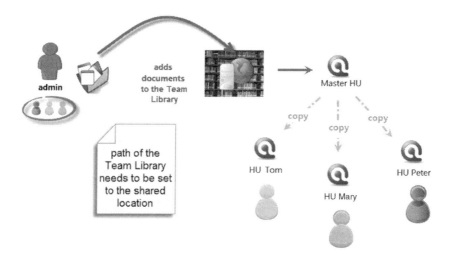

Figure 3.21 Server-based setup

Project setup
Tasks of project administrator

- Create the Master project file by adding documents to the Team Library. Select **PROJECT / ADD DOCUMENT(S) / ADD DOCUMENTS (TEAM LIBRARY)**, or drag them from the File Explorer into the HU editor.
- Save the HU: **PROJECT / SAVE**. The HU can be saved to any location. My suggestion is to create a separate folder for HU files on the server that is shared with all team members.

> NOTE: Whether you actually call the project file 'Master + project name' or something else does not matter. What you need to know is that team members cannot work on one HU file simultaneously. Each person needs to work on a copy of the original 'Master' file and all files should have a unique name. All individual files need to be merged from time to time to create a new, up-to-date Master file.

Next, the Team Library needs to be moved to the shared location (Figure 3.22):

- Move the Team Library to the shared location. Select **DOCUMENTS / DATA SOURCE MANAGEMENT / OPEN LIBRARY MANAGER**.
- In the Library Manager, select **EXTRAS / MANAGE LIBRARY LOCATION**.
- Click on the folder icon to select the shared location for the Team Library and click on **OK**.
- You will be asked to restart ATLAS.ti.
- Inform the team members that the Master project has been created and where to find it. You also need to let them know about the location of the Team Library, as they need to set the path for the Team Library on their computers.

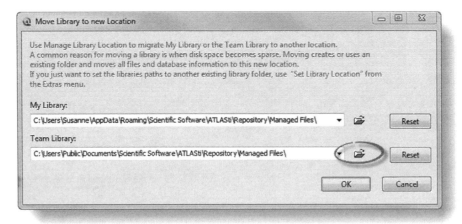

Figure 3.22 Moving the Team Library

Tasks of all team members

- Create an ATLAS.ti user account on your computer and log in with your user name (see above: 'Creating user accounts').

Next, set the location of the Team Library to the shared location as informed by the project administrator:

- Select **Documents / Data Source Management / Open Library Manager**.
- In the Library Manager, select **Extras / Set Library Location**.
- Click on the folder icon to set the location of the Team Library to the shared location and click on the OK button.
- Back in the File Explorer, go to the folder where the Master HU file is stored, make a copy of it and rename the file, for example by adding your name or initials to it. The HU file can be saved to any location. For convenient merging by the project administrator, your team may decide to leave it on the server.

Continuous project work

- After an agreed-upon interval, the project administrator merges all sub-HUs (see above: 'Merging projects') and saves the outcome as the new Master HU in the team's HU folder (Figure 3.23). For the team members to easily find the latest version of the Master file, add the date of merging to the file name.
- The team members grab the new Master file, rename it and continue their work.

Working with the server-based approach allows each team member to edit all primary documents when they see the need to make changes like correcting spelling mistakes, correcting transcripts or adding data. ATLAS.ti tracks all changes and all sub-HUs can be updated. Updating the HU files to the latest revision does not have to occur immediately, but must be done before merging all subprojects.

Working with large-sized data sets

The number of documents that you add to project is not necessarily the limiting factor: data file size is more critical and needs special consideration when setting

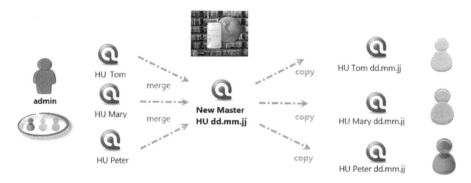

Figure 3.23 Continuous project work on a server

up a project. The standard setup in ATLAS.ti 7 is to add documents to the library. This means the documents are copied and thus use up additional space on your hard drive. If the hard drive is small, one solution is to move the library to an external drive (for instructions on how to change the library location, see 'Scenario 3 – server-based setup').

However, if you add documents to the library, no matter where the library is located, the project can only be transferred using the copy bundle function. If you work with large-sized projects (i.e. 1 gigabyte or more), creating copy bundle files and transferring projects can become cumbersome. One option is to create partial bundles to keep the file size down. Another option is to set up the project using externally linked files rather than importing all documents to the library. In this case, it is recommended to use the 'old' HUPATH setup: that is, storing all documents plus the HU file in one folder.

The additional information you need to know regarding both options is explained below.

Skills training 3.8: creating partial bundle files

You have two options to create partial bundle files: You can create a primary document family and use it as filter in the copy bundle window, or you can simply select the documents for the partial bundle in the PD Manager. As working with PD families is first explained in Chapter 5, below I explain the second option. It is also the more convenient one.

- Open the Primary Doc Manager by clicking on the P-Docs button below the main toolbar.
- Select for instance P1 to P10. Right click and select the menu option **DATA SOURCE MANAGEMENT / BUNDLE SELECTED PDs**.
- ATLAS.ti collects the selected PDs and then the Copy Bundle window opens. Click on **CREATE BUNDLE**.

Figure 3.24 Bundle selected documents

- Return to the P-Docs Manager, select the next group of documents and create a second partial bundle, and so on.

When unpacking each bundle, make sure that the HU file is always unbundled to the same location so that you do not end up with your project file at different locations. As the content of the HU file is the same, ATLAS.ti will unpack it only when you install the first partial bundle. When installing the rest of the partial bundles, it will only unpack the documents, recognizing that the HU file is the same.

Setting up a project with externally linked files

Project setup

- Create a special folder where you will store all documents that you want to add to your ATLAS.ti project. Let's call it 'project folder'. This folder can also be on an external drive. If you have lots of documents, you can organize them in subfolders. Remember to give your documents a good analytic name. This is even more important for this particular setup. You cannot later rename the original source files without having to make lots of adjustments to your ATLAS.ti project file.
- Open ATLAS.ti.
- Select the main menu option **PROJECT / ADD DOCUMENT(S) / ASSIGN EXTERNAL DOCUMENTS.**
- A file loader window will open. Navigate to your project folder and select the documents that you want to assign.
- Click on **OPEN** (it will appear in the language of your Windows system). If you store your documents in subfolders, you have to repeat the process for each folder.

You will see the File Quality Check window and can follow the process of how documents are checked and added to your project. If there is a problem with one or more documents, you will be notified. If everything works smoothly, you will be informed that all files were successfully added to your project.

- To save your newly created project, click on **PROJECT / SAVE**. The important step now is to save your project file, the HU, to your project folder! If you have organized your documents in subfolders, store the HU file in the main folder. If you are familiar with ATLAS.ti 6, this is called the HUPATH setup, where the documents and HU file are stored together in one folder (Figure 3.25).

Figure 3.25 Store all your documents + the HU file in one folder

Project backup and transfer

As you selected this project setup because your database is sizable, using the copy bundle function to back up and to transfer your project is likely not working very well. A better option is simply to back up your entire project folder and copy it if you want to move it to a different location. If your project folder is stored on an external hard drive, you only need to take the hard drive along and connect it somewhere else. It is important that your HU file is stored in the same folder as your documents.

Note also that externally linked text files cannot be edited within ATLAS. ti. Neither can or should they be modified outside of ATLAS.ti, for instance in Word. If you do so, you will jeopardize the integrity of your project. Modifying files outside of ATLAS.ti results in misaligned quotations and therefore ATLAS.ti will no longer load the files. Basically all rules that were valid for a version 6 project still apply when working with externally linked documents. You are in charge and need to take care of your documents and make sure that ATLAS.ti can access the linked data source files. If you need to make changes like adjusting the path reference, you will find the menu options under DOCUMENTS / DATA SOURCE MANAGEMENT / LINKED DOCUMENT MANAGEMENT.

Summary

ATLAS.ti supports most textual, graphical and multimedia formats. In this chapter, you have learned how to prepare various types of data and files for analysis and the issues you should pay attention to. You have seen that the ATLAS.ti way of handling documents offers flexibility and economy in handling large numbers of sizable documents and allows teams to work concurrently on shared data sources. However, it has also been pointed out that it is important to be aware of how ATLAS.ti handles documents. Knowing this can help you to avoid a number of common mistakes.

Before starting a new project, give some thought to the names and location of the documents and the HU. If you work in a team, take a look at the presented team scenarios and pick the one that suits your situation best. On the companion website you will find project planning sheets for each scenario to help you set up your project. Remember the one thing that is frequently neglected: create project backups and store them at a safe location. You never know when the next hard disk failure will occur and then you will be glad of a recent copy bundle file.

REVIEW QUESTIONS

1 Which data file formats can be analyzed with the support of ATLAS.ti?
2 What do you need to pay attention to when choosing a specific format for textual files?
3 Until the native Mac version is released later in 2014, what is important for Mac users to know when they want to work with ATLAS.ti?
4 What do you need to do if you want to work with non-Western languages?
5 What do you need to pay attention to when transcribing data? What are the recommended guidelines?
6 How does ATLAS.ti handle documents?

(Continued)

(Continued)

7   Why is it important to know this?

8   Why does ATLAS.ti handle data in such a way?

9   How would you set up a single user project?

10 What are associated documents, which benefits do they offer and how do you set up a project with associated files?

11 How do you back up a project? How do you transfer a project to a different computer?

12 How would you set up a team project? What needs to be considered?

13 How do you create user accounts and why/when is this important?

14 How do you merge projects?

15 How do you deal with survey data?

16 How do you set up a project that includes large-sized documents?

GLOSSARY OF TERMS

External document references: The basic data management concept in ATLAS.ti is that the project file, the HU, does not contain the actual files that you analyze. It only stores an external reference where the source file for each primary document can be found. This potentially allows you to work with large data sets or large data source files like videos.

Internal documents: When importing transcripts or survey data, you create internal documents. This means these documents are stored within the HU file and are referenced in the Primary Document Manager as: in HU. Further, text files created via the option DOCUMENTS / NEW / NEW TEXT DOCUMENT also become internal documents and are also referenced as: in HU.

Library: ATLAS.ti offers two library locations: My Library for single user projects and the Team Library for team projects. The libraries essentially are folders on your computer that are created when you install ATLAS.ti. The default location is a hidden location that cannot immediately be seen in Windows Explorer. The idea is that the library folders are a domain managed solely by ATLAS.ti and the user does not need to be concerned about them. It is, however, possible to move the default library location to a different place using the Library Manager.

Master HU: The Master HU is a term I invented for team projects. The project administrator begins by creating the first Master HU. This Master HU is distributed to team members. Team members add their initials to the file name and work on the part that is assigned to them. When they are done with their work, they send their (now) sub-HUs to the project administrator, who merges them into a new Master HU, adds the date, then distributes the new Master HU back to the team members – and so on.

Merging: Merging means combining the contents of various HUs into one HU. You can merge two HUs at a time. The HUs can contain either the same documents or different documents. In the first case, the documents are merged; in the second, they are added. The same applies to codes. The HUs can contain the same codes or different codes. If they contain the same codes, you merge them; if they contain different codes, you add them. If you have some codes that are the same as well as some that are different, you still use the option **Merge**, otherwise all codes that have the same name will be duplicated. This option also allows you to merge only specified objects; for example, you can add only networks or memos and ignore the rest.

Primary document/P-Doc/PD: See Chapter 2.

Project administrator: When working in a team, I recommend that one person takes on the role of project administrator. The task of the project administrator is to set up the project, to distribute it to team members, to collect project files from team members and to merge projects.

User account: All newly created objects in ATLAS.ti are stamped with the user name. The default user is 'super'. If you want to see your own name instead of 'super' in the author field for each object, you need to create a user account (under the Extras menu) and log in using your personal account name. This is a nice but not essential option if working on your own, but a necessity if you work in a team. Based on the name in the author field, each team member can see who has done what.

Variables: See document families in Chapter 5.

FOUR

Technical aspects of coding

Coding in a technical sense simply means assigning a label to a data segment. The data segment can be as small as one character in a text document, a few pixels in an image file, or less than a second in an audio or video file. Knowing about the mouse clicks does not yet tell you anything about how meaningful the attached label or the length of the selected segment might be. But before we can discuss these issues in Chapter 5, you first need to learn about the technical skills involved in coding. In this chapter, you will learn the different ways of applying codes to text and multimedia data, modifying the length of a coded segment, renaming, deleting and merging codes, and writing definitions for codes. I will use the 'Children & Happiness Stage I' project to explain the various options. You can use your own data set for these exercises as long as it is not yet coded.

Questions like what a code actually is, apart from a label in a computer program, or how to build an efficient coding system, or how to code in such a way that you can best utilize the options that software offers apart from simple retrieval, are all discussed in Chapter 5.

Skills trainings

Skills training 4.1: coding with a new code

Skills training 4.2: coding via drag and drop

Skills training 4.3: modifying the length of a quotation

Skills training 4.4: writing code definitions

Skills training 4.5: coding with in-vivo codes

Skills training 4.6: further coding-related options

Skills training 4.7: coding a PDF document

Skills training 4.8: coding an image

Skills training 4.9: working with audio and video files

Skills training 4.10: working with Google Earth documents

Variants of coding

In ATLAS.ti you can often use a number of different routes to achieve the same result. Once you see that you can use any one of three options – the main menu, the context menu or the buttons on the toolbar – you can use whichever suits you best.

For the exercises we will work with four test codes that we will simply label test 1, test 2, test 3 and test 4. Content does not matter at this point. The only exception is when I explain the use of in-vivo codes. Simply knowing how to create an in-vivo code (basically two clicks) does not help you to understand what it is used for, so I will provide a few examples.

Skills training 4.1: coding with a new code

- Open your own project that you created while working through Chapter 3. Alternatively, you can also use the 'Children & Happiness Stage I' project that you can access via **HELP / QUICK TOUR**.
- Load P3: Belkin's parenting blog discussion.
- Select a text segment with the mouse and right click on the highlighted area.
- Select the option **CODING / ENTER CODE NAME(S)** (Figure 4.1).

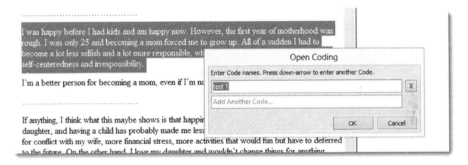

Figure 4.1 Coding with a new code via the context menu

OR: Select **CODES / CODING / ENTER CODE NAME(S)** from the main menu.

OR: Select the open coding button from the vertical toolbar on the left hand side of the screen.

- Then enter the code name 'test 1' in the field that pops up. Click on the OK button.
- Look at your screen. With one click, you have created four new entries (Figure 4.2).

You have created your first quotation and code. Each is displayed both textually (in the respective drop-down list) and graphically (in the margin area).

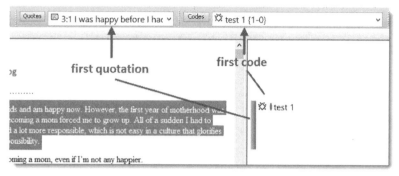

Figure 4.2   HU editor after setting a first code

The separation of quotation and code has a number of advantages. As they are independent objects, you can comment on each code and also on each quotation. Quotations cannot be linked just to codes, but also to each other and to memos. This is a prerequisite for the hyperlink function discussed in Chapter 7. It allows you to work directly at the data level without necessarily using codes.

Let's code three more segments using this method:

- Highlight a different text segment, right click, select the coding option from the context menu and enter 'test 2' as code name.
- Code two more segments using 'test 3' and 'test 4' as codes. Overlap some of your codings and observe what happens in the margin area. Also note that ATLAS.ti automatically completes the code name. If your code list gets longer, then this serves as a reminder of which codes already exist.

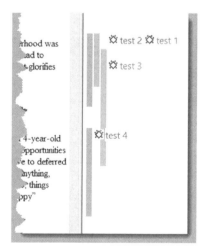

As you can see in Figure 4.3, overlapping codes are displayed in different colors in the margin area. These colors help you to distinguish which quotation bar belongs to which code word. If you were to add even more layers, the next two layers would be displayed in violet and blue. After that, silver is used again. The colors do not contain any information about the different code levels in the sense of higher or lower ranked categories. When you delete a quotation, the colors may also change. It is possible to set your own colors for codes, but not for the bars marking the length of a quotation.

Figure 4.3   Meanings of colored bars in the margin

Next, before showing you more variants of coding, I would like to explain how quotations and codes are referenced and what the entries in the drop-down lists mean.

Quotation references

The bars in the margin mark the length of the quotation graphically. The entry in the quotation field shows a textual reference for the quotation. It consists of the following elements: ID, name, start and end position.

ID: The quotation ID is composed of the number of its P-Doc and a second number indicating when the quotation was created (Figure 4.4). The ID 3:1 means that the quotation is from P-Doc 3 and is the first one that was created in this document. The reason for the chronological numbering is to do with the fact that you will not necessarily code a document from the first line to the last. You will jump between passages and modify or delete some quotations during the coding process. A linear numeration would have to be updated with every single quotation that is inserted, which would take up unnecessary computational capacity. Sorting the quotations by their start position in the Quotation Manager, for example, offers a clear linear view of your quotes. Recently an option was added to change the chronological numbering to a sequential order if need be (**Quotations / Miscellaneous / Renumber all to Docflow**). This can be useful for example when coding open-ended questions from survey data and you want to keep the cases in synch with the cases in the SPSS file.

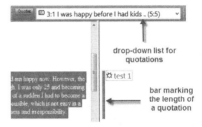

Figure 4.4   How quotations are referenced

Name: The name shows the first 30 characters of a textual quotation. This is the default setting which can be changed under Tools / Preferences / General Preferences. Quotations based on image, audio or video files show the file name. The name of a quotation can be renamed. This is a useful option for image, audio and video quotations, as we will see later.

Start and end position: The figures in brackets after the quotation name show the location (start and end position) in the document. For textual quotations, the reference given is to the paragraph numbers within which the coded segment occurs: (5:5) thus means that the quotation starts and ends in paragraph 5. Do you remember what I said in Chapter 3, when I discussed good practice rules for preparing transcripts? The suggestion was to break larger speech units into smaller paragraphs because of the way ATLAS.ti references quotations. The reason why paragraphs instead of line numbers are used as reference points is because, in digital environments, the width of a document is not set. You can move the windows splitter to the right or left, adjusting the width of the document to your computer screen. Paragraph numbers are not affected by this, whereas line numbers are.

For image files, the rectangular area marked as the quotation is referenced. Audio and video quotes use a time reference (start position and duration).

References for PDF quotations consist of page number and number of characters on the page for the start and end positions. In case the document contains columns, the column number is provided as well.

The quotation ID in combination with the start and end positions can be used when citing quotations in a report. For example:

I was happy before I had kids and am happy now. However, the first year of motherhood was rough. I was only 25 and becoming a mom forced me to grow up. (P3:1; 5:5)

The reference allows the reader of a report to trace the quote and to find it either in the original digital material or in a printed version of the coded data. There is one more issue where quotation references can serve a useful function. Remember that I suggested (in Chapter 3) naming documents according to analytic criteria whenever applicable? Assume that for an analysis of newspaper reports on a specific topic for two countries (Germany and South Africa) we had selected 600 articles and that we had thought of some meaningful data file names. The beginnings of the names are shown in Table 4.1. When assigning these files to ATLAS.ti, they appear in alphabetical order and in the order of the criteria included in the name.

This way of ordering the documents adds a bit more information to the quotation ID than it would otherwise have done. The first thing you see when retrieving quotations is the quotation ID. Let's assume that a retrieval results in quotations showing only numbers lower than 300. Then we would know – without having to enter anything further – that the quotations come

Table 4.1 Examples of analytically meaningful file names

File name prefix	PD numbering	Meaning of the prefix
G	P-Docs: 1–300	Germany
ZA	P-Docs: 301–600	South Africa
Adding further detail		
G_L	P-Docs: 1–150	Germany: local
G_N	P-Docs: 151–300	Germany: national
Adding further detail		
G_L_BS	P-Docs: 1–75	Germany: local: broadsheet
G_L_T	P-Docs: 76–150	Germany: local: tabloid
G_N_BS	P-Docs: 151–225	Germany: national: broadsheet
G_N_T	P-Docs: 226–300	Germany: national: tabloid
Adding further detail		
G_L_BS_BZ	P-Docs: 1–20	Germany: local: broadsheet: *Berliner Zeitung*
G_L_BS_FAZ	P-Docs: 21–40	Germany: local: broadsheet: *Frankfurter Allgemeine*
G_L_BS_tz M	P-Docs: 41–55	Germany: local: broadsheet: *tz München*
G_L_BS_SZ	P-Docs: 56–75	Germany: local: broadsheet: *Süddeutsche Zeitung*
	Likewise for the South African newspapers for P-Docs 301–600	

from German newspapers. Alternatively, if the IDs show numbers below 75, you know that all quotations come from German local broadsheet papers. Numbers between 21 and 40 indicate that these are all quotations from the newspaper FAZ.

Taking a less complex case, let's assume that you have interviewed 20 women and 20 men and you use their first names or pseudonyms as data file names. This could mean that P1 is Anne, P2 is Bert, P3 Chris, P4 Dana, and so on. It is much easier to label all transcripts of your female interviewees in a way that they are listed as P1 to P20 than to remember that P1, P4, P7, P12, P13, P19 and so on represent females and the rest males. This is another benefit of using good data file names in combination with the way ATLAS.ti references quotations, and it is well worth doing.

Code reference

The entered code word is written next to the quotation bar in the margin. You can recognize codes by the yellow diamond symbol. The entry in the drop-down list reads: test 1 {1–0} (Figure 4.5). I already explained the meaning of the numbers behind the code when walking you through the various features of the interface. Maybe you remember it: the first number shows the frequency (how often the code has been applied) and the second number the density (how many other codes this code is linked to). Hence the code test 1 has been used only once so far and it is not yet linked to any other code. The density remains zero for the purposes of this book until we reach Chapter 7, where the network view function is discussed.

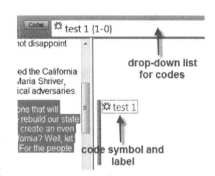

Figure 4.5 How codes are referenced

Skills training 4.2: coding via drag and drop

At the beginning of the coding process, it is normal to generate a lot of new codes. But after a while you will find similarities and repetitions in the data and want to apply codes that already exist. Your sample project should currently contain four codes. If you want to reuse them:

- Open the Code Manager and change the view to single column view (**VIEW / SINGLE COLUMN**) if not already activated.
- Deactivate the side panel as we do not need it right now: **VIEW / SHOW SIDE PANEL**.
- Highlight a text passage and select a code from the Code Manager. Hold down the left mouse button, drag the code over the windows splitter and drop it on the other side (Figure 4.6).

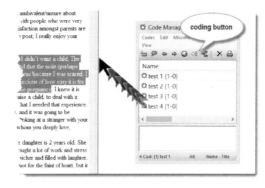
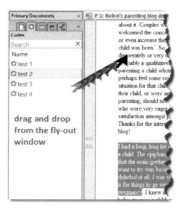

Figure 4.6 Drag and drop coding

For text documents, there is no need to drop the code in the highlighted area. It just has to be dropped somewhere on the left hand side as shown in Figure 4.6. Whatever is highlighted gets coded. Intuitively one often drags the code on top of the highlighted data segment. If you spend a long time coding, this gets very tiring on your eyes and requires more and more concentration, and the constant twisting action of your wrist in trying to hit the highlighted area may even strain the muscles. The software does not require you to do this when coding text documents. Thus, be gentle on yourself. You will also find a coding button in the toolbar of the Code Manager. This is especially useful if you want to code a highlighted data passage with multiple codes. Select the codes and then click on the coding button instead of using drag and drop.

It is quite common for more than one code to be used for coding a data segment. The segment might contain ambiguous information or different layers of meaning. You may want to code for content and also for context, use of language or aspects of time. It is difficult and also not very efficient to incorporate a variety of aspects into a single code name and it should not be done (see Chapter 5 for more information). You can later rely on the computer to find all kinds of combinations for you.

Another way to use drag and drop coding is from the fly-out window on the left hand side:

- Open the fly-out window by clicking on the three black arrows.
- Minimize the second list and click on the code tab.
- Select a code and drag it from left to right into the text area. As with drag and drop coding from the Code Manager, there is no need to hit the highlighted area when coding text. Just drop the code anywhere to the left of the fly-out window.

You will find out over time and with more practice which option you prefer – to code from right to left or from left to right, or maybe make use of both options depending on the task at hand. I prefer to code using the Code Manager because I like to use the family side panel to quickly navigate to a certain code group. I will show you how this works in Chapter 5.

You may have noticed the code-by-list option in either the context or the main menu. When you select it, a window opens showing all codes in a long list. You can select one or more codes from the list and click on **OK**. Then the list will close and you will have to reopen it again for the next data segment you want to code. Therefore the drag and drop options are much more convenient to use.

Changing a code

If you want to change a code (perhaps because you have changed your mind, found a more fitting code, used a code by accident or want to develop subcategories) then the easiest way is also to use drag and drop. This time, however, you cannot drop the code just anywhere; you have to drop it exactly on top of the one that you want to replace.

- Let's assume we want to replace the silver test 4 code in Figure 4.7 with test 2. Click on the 'test 2' code in the Code Manager, hold down the left mouse button, drag the code to the 'test 4' code in the margin area and drop it. *Voilà* – the code is exchanged.

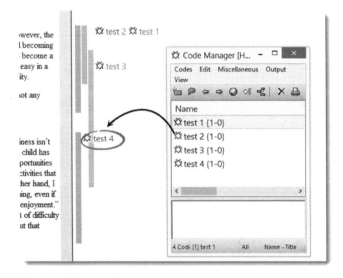

Figure 4.7 Drag and drop coding

Skills training 4.3: modifying the length of a quotation

Modifying the length of a quotation is also quite a common procedure. Maybe you discover that a chosen segment is too large or that you forgot something and need to extend the length of a quotation. Both ways of modifying are possible.

- Activate the quotation that you want to modify (e.g. with a click on the code word in the margin). The bar and the code word will be framed by a dotted line. The currently activated quotation is also displayed in the quotation drop-down list.

To enlarge a segment:

create quotation

modify quotation

- Highlight an extended area by simply overwriting the existing one. Then click on the button **Revise quotation size** in the vertical toolbar (see left).

To decrease the size of a segment

As you cannot select a segment within an already highlighted area, you first need to 'erase' the highlighting by clicking above or below it. When nothing else is highlighted you can select the smaller area that you want. Then click on the button **Revise quotation size** in the vertical toolbar.

Unlinking a code

Just as you can erase a pencil mark in the margin of a paper document, you can 'erase' a code in the margin area on-screen as well. The digital equivalent is called **unlinking**. It is mostly used when a segment is coded with more than one code.

- To unlink a code, right click on the code in the margin area and click on the option **Unlink**.

When you unlink a code from a segment that only has one code, the bar remains in the margin. If you want to 'erase' both the code and the quotation, you need to proceed as explained below. (See also Figure 4.8, which shows the difference between unlinking and removing.)

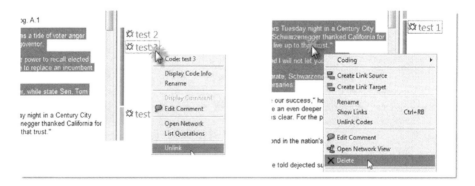

Figure 4.8   Differences between unlinking and removing a code

Removing a coded segment

- Mark the coded segment to be removed (e.g. by clicking on the code in the margin).
- Move your pointer over the highlighted quotation and select **DELETE** from the context menu.
- A message will pop up asking you to confirm that this quotation and associated links should be deleted. Click on **OK**.

Note that removing a coded segment does not delete the text or other data material that you have coded. The quotation is an object stored in the HU file. You can think of all objects stored in the HU as a layer on top of your data material. The HU only accesses the data via a reference and loads it into the HU editor. The data themselves are not touched.

Skills training 4.4: writing code definitions

If you notice something interesting while coding and you want to write it down, use the quotation comment field for it. A lot of ATLAS.ti novices attach a memo instead of using the comment field. Memos, however, are more than mere comments (see Chapters 5 and 6). As the word 'comment' indicates, it is a short note, one or two sentences long. Comments are attached directly to data segments; memos do not have to be attached to anything, or can be attached to more than one data segment. Memos can therefore be used to develop more informed ideas at a higher level of your analysis. If you use memos as comments early on you'll end up in a mess, producing an additional body of data next to the primary data that you want to analyze – and you may well get completely lost.

Thus, when you want to comment on a data segment:

- Right click on the highlighted quotation and select the option **Edit Comment** from the context menu (Figure 4.9).
- An editor will pop up. Write a comment on the selected data segment.
- Save your comment by clicking on the accept button and close the editor.

 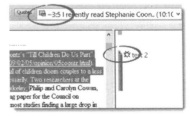

Figure 4.9   Commenting on a quotation

Quotation comments are visible in the bar in the margin area, by the tilde (~) sign in front of the quotation name and the Post-it note attached to the quotation icon in the Quotation Manager.

Skills training 4.5: coding with in-vivo codes

The term 'in-vivo code' can be traced back to grounded theory methodology. In-vivo codes according to Corbin and Strauss are 'concepts using the actual words of research participants rather than being named by the analyst' (2008: 65). Technically this means that when you highlight a text segment, the segment itself is used as a code name. In-vivo codes are especially useful at the beginning of the coding process when collecting ideas. As it is quick and easy to create them, this is what they are often used for in computer-assisted analysis. This first collection of ideas mostly takes place at the descriptive level. Description, according to Corbin and Strauss (2008), is the basis for more abstract interpretation of data and it does embody concepts, at least implicitly. Proper concept building, however, needs to happen at some point of the analysis. It does not make much sense to collect 200 in-vivo codes without developing them further. You just end up with a very long code list.

When in-vivo codes are used as a quick device for collecting things that you notice in the data, with progressive analysis they should be replaced by merging some and renaming others in more abstract terms (see below for how this works). I have seen projects gone mad – the champion being a project with over 16,000 codes. I will tell you in Chapter 5 why this is not a good idea and what has gone wrong if you end up with thousands of codes. For now, as a rule of thumb, remember that a project should only have between 120 and 300 codes. There are projects that have fewer codes and others that have more, but 16,000 is definitely too much.

Now let's turn to the technical practicalities again. The maximum length of an in-vivo code is 40 characters. If you want more, you need to modify the length of the quotation in a second step as described above.

- Mark a text passage of 40 characters maximum. Right click and select the option CODING / CODE IN VIVO from the context menu.

You can also highlight a text passage and drag it into the Code Manager. Then the limit of 40 characters does not apply. However, a code of 100 characters or so is even further away from being a proper code in an analytic sense. In addition, you will just clutter up the margin and cannot see the full name of the code anyway because it is too long.

Figure 4.10 shows an example based on the Children & Happiness project where some text segments are collected in the form of in-vivo codes. The ideas that I collected had to do with the experience of parenthood and how the various writers on the blog describe it.

After collecting some more instances and reviewing them, I could think of better and shorter names as code labels. These first ideas could, for example, be

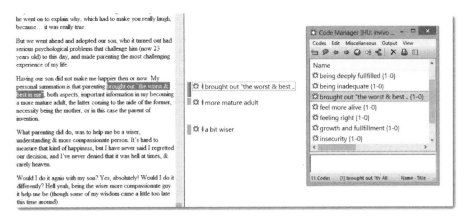

Figure 4.10 Coding in vivo

developed further into a category called 'Effects of parenting', with subcategories like all the things you can do/have less or more of. We will work with these codes in Skills training 5.3 in Chapter 5.

Skills training 4.6: further coding-related options

There are a number of other options in the Code Manager, which you can access via the menu and toolbar or the context menus. For instance, you can create new codes, and rename, delete or merge codes.

Creating a new code

You can also create a new code in the Code Manager:

- Click on the 'Create a new item' button (see right). Or select **CODES / CREATE FREE CODE(S)** from the Code Manager menu.
- Enter a code name in the first entry field, and a second and third in the fields below (Figure 4.11). Then click on **OK**. Frequency and density are both zero as the codes are not yet linked to anything.

Figure 4.11 Entering multiple codes at once

Renaming codes

The renaming option is a global option. This means that renaming a code word in the Code Manager affects all coded segments that use this code.

- Mark a code word in the Code Manager, right click and select **RENAME** from the context menu.

OR: Use the 'in-place' way of renaming entries that you may know from working with the Windows file manager.

- Select a code word with the left mouse button and then – separately – left click it again. The entry will change. You can modify the name simply by overwriting it.

Coloring codes

If you want to color your codes:

- Select a code in the Code Manager and click on the rainbow-colored circle in the toolbar.
- To make code colors visible in the margin, right click on a white space in the margin area and select **USE OBJECT COLORS**.

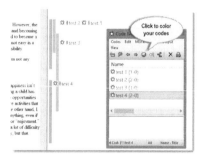

In order to still be able see which code label belongs to which quotation bar, a small bar in the same color as the quotation bar is shown in front of the code label (Figure 4.12). The code label shows the user-defined color.

Figure 4.12 Adding user-defined colors (see companion website for color image)

Deleting codes (and other objects)

The delete option also has global effects, at least within the boundaries of the HU. This means that deleting a code removes it from the entire HU and from everywhere in your primary documents, code families or network views – anywhere it was used. So use this option very carefully indeed, especially as there is no undo option in ATLAS.ti. Actually, there is one under the tools menu, but most of the time it won't help you. It can only undo simple things like the modification of a name.

There is a safeguard when using the delete option. You need to confirm a delete action before it is executed. You just have to read the message that pops up when selecting **Delete** anywhere in the program. But as I know very well, we don't always read what the computer tells us. We click on **OK** and then it is too late.

Because there is no undo option in ATLAS.ti, I can only urge you to click on the **Save** button in the main toolbar or use the hotkey **Ctrl+S** now and then, every 20 minutes or whenever you think of it. Another safeguard against data loss and undoing mistakes is to make a project backup in the form of a copy bundle file after each work session, as discussed earlier.

Having said this, of course, there are times when we want to delete codes. This is how:

- Select the code word in the Code Manager, right click and select **Delete** from the context menu. You can also click on the **Delete** button in the toolbar of the Code Manager (e.g. when you selected more than one code to delete).
- A message will pop up: 'The code you are about to delete is linked to [x] quotations. Delete code [code name] anyway?' Confirm by clicking on **Yes**.
- After you click on **Yes**, another message will pop up asking you whether the linked quotations should also be deleted (Figure 4.13).
- Don't take too much pity on the orphaned quotations. If you don't need them any longer, click on **Yes** and delete them as well.

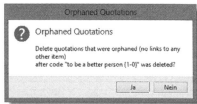

Figure 4.13   Completing the deletion process

Merging codes

The merge codes function can be used to combine two or more codes with each other. This is a common procedure when you begin to clean up your code list after initial coding, or when you work in a team and merge subprojects. You may realize that there are two codes that have different names but they essentially mean the same thing. Thus, the contents of the two codes, the coded quotations, can be combined under one code name.

- Begin with the code whose name you want to keep. Select, for example, the code 'test 1'.
- Right click and select **MERGE CODES** from the context menu.
- A small window pops up listing all other available codes. Select one or more codes (e.g. 'test 4') from this list and click the OK button. To select more than one code, the usual Windows selection procedure can be used.
- Now one more window pops up, telling you that the selected code(s) have been merged into the target code. A comment leaving an audit trail of the merge process will only be entered if the codes already had a comment before merging. All existing comments will be kept.

As you can see in Figure 4.14, before merging, both codes 'test 1' and 'test 4' coded two quotations. After merging, 'test 1' contains (2+2) four quotations. However, the numbers do not always add up like this; for instance, it wouldn't be the case if both codes had been applied somewhere to the same quotation.

If the codes have not yet been defined you won't be able to see later that the codes were merged unless you enter a comment manually. You can do this if it is important to leave an audit trail to trace your steps. Another option is to enter a comment on the codes before merging. Figure 4.15 shows an example of this. If you merge codes early on in the analytic process it will most likely

Figure 4.14 The process of merging codes

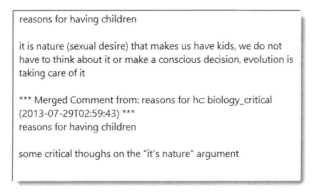

Figure 4.15 Combined comments after merging, leaving an audit trail

not be necessary to leave an audit trail, as the code labels are often still exploratory and there are not yet set definitions.

Writing code definitions

Comments can be written into the white field below the windows splitter, as we have seen in Chapter 2. When entering a comment (for codes this is in most cases a definition, a coding rule and possibly a sample quotation) the commented object is marked by a tilde (~) and a Post-it note (see Figure 4.16).

- Try it out: write a comment for one of your codes. When you are finished, click on another code: the definition is saved and you will see the tilde after the code. If you close the window immediately after writing the definition, a message will pop up asking you whether you want to save the comment.
- If you double click on a commented code in the margin area, the comment will be displayed.

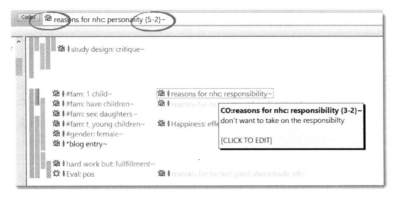

Figure 4.16   Display of commented codes

Writing code definitions is analytically speaking a very important process (see also Fielding and Lee, 1998: 94ff.). When I look at team projects, code definitions are never missing because it seems self-explanatory that in teams one has to write down what a particular code means. This is not the case when analysts work alone. They typically think that writing code definitions is not necessary, since they think they know what their codes mean. I can tell you that this is not always the case and that you cannot just take it for granted. What happens if you are ill and cannot work on your project for some time, or if you go on vacation, fly to a meeting, or have other commitments that keep you away from your analysis? Returning to your data, you sit down, click on a code and ask yourself, 'What is this code doing here? What was I thinking of when I created it?' You try to remind yourself by browsing through the quotations and perhaps you begin to remember – but if only you had written a code definition at the time, or at least some comments ….; so, you see, it does help to put some information into the code comment field.

There are other benefits as well. Coding is a process and your thoughts about the data will evolve. The meaning you attached to a code word at the beginning of an analysis may change over time. There is nothing unusual about that. If there is no definition for the code, you may not notice the subtle changes over time and in the end the code may contain quotations that in fact no longer fit under a common label. ATLAS.ti makes it easy for you to track changing meanings or associations, since you see the code definition right in front of you in the Code Manager as you use it.

Furthermore, going through all of your codes and defining them helps the analytic thought process. It forces you to draw clear-cut boundaries between codes. If you realize there are overlapping meanings, you can either merge the codes or make them more distinctive. Code definitions also add transparency to your analysis. They are necessary for a third person to understand and follow your analytic ideas. Try it out, even if it means some extra work. I promise you'll see that it is worth doing.

Handling other media types

Now I will explain the differences in handling other file formats. The differences mostly relate to selecting data segments. There are a few additional issues to pay attention to when it comes to creating output. Other than that, the different data file formats are smoothly integrated into all functions of the software. When you click on a code that codes data in different formats, all quotations are listed and you can browse through them one by one. Text quotations are displayed in context on the left hand side, audio and video quotations are played, the coded image quotation is highlighted within the image file, and Google Earth is loaded to show a geographic location that you have coded.

When you want to output coded segments, you need to be aware that the output will be in a rich text editor. Text and image segments are included. For all other data sources, only the quotation reference is provided. You can create more meaningful outputs, especially for audio and video quotations, by making extensive use of the option to rename quotations and to write comments.

We will continue to work with the Children & Happiness Stage I project for the following exercises.

Skills training 4.7: coding a PDF document

- Load P1 by selecting it from the P-Docs drop-down list. If it is displayed too small, use the zoom button in the vertical tool bar to enlarge it.
- Coding a PDF document is essentially the same as coding rtf, doc or txt files. Selecting a text segment in PDF documents, however, requires a bit of practice. If you place the cursor too far to the left of the text, you will select only a rectangular graphical image instead of the actual text segment.
- To select a string of text, place the cursor directly to the left of the first letter.
- Use any of the coding techniques described above (e.g. via the context menu or coding via drag and drop from the Code Manager).
- Try coding a few text passages in the PDF file.
- Now experiment with selecting a graphical image in the PDF file. Select for instance the title including the subtitle and the box around them.
- Modify one of your coded segments in the PDF document. This is easier than in text documents, because handles are displayed at the start and end positions (see Figure 4.17). Drag one or both handles to the desired position and click on the **Modify Quotation** button as explained in the section 'Modifying the length of a quotation'.

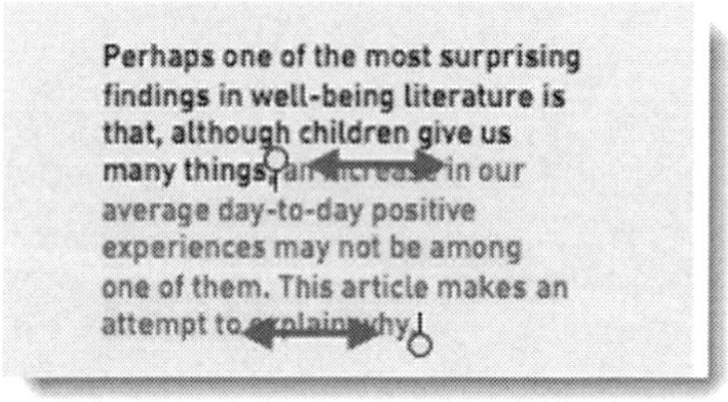

Perhaps one of the most surprising findings in well-being literature is that, although children give us many things, an increase in our average day-to-day positive experiences may not be among one of them. This article makes an attempt to explain why.

Figure 4.17   Modifying a PDF quotation

Skills training 4.8: coding an image

- Load an image document (e.g. P8), select a rectangular area and proceed to code it as described for text segments.
- You can either just see the outline of the quotation or display it filled with the color of the quotation boundary (see Figure 4.18). To change the display type, right click on the image quotation and select the option SELECTION-DISPLAY TYPE / FILLED.

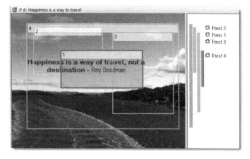

Figure 4.18   Coded image file using the filled display option for quotations

When working with image data, you may want to describe them in textual terms as well. How to make use of quotation names and comments for analytic purposes is described below (see p. 103). These options can certainly also be applied when analyzing images.

Skills training 4.9: working with audio and video files

Below I describe how to work with video files. The instructions, however, also apply to working with audio files; the difference is that instead of the video image, you see a white space.

Although it is possible to code an audio or video segment straight away in the same manner as coding a text or image segment (you highlight a section, right click and select the option CODING / ENTER CODE NAME(S)), when working with video files I prefer to set the quotation first and then think about which code I want to attach. Video files are richer in information and setting the correct start and end positions is often not as clear cut as selecting a quotation in text files. In addition, when working with audio and video files I recommend adding descriptive information in the form of segment titles and comments in the Quotation Manager (see 'First steps in analyzing video data'). Therefore the quotation itself becomes more prominent.

The video interface

- Load a video primary document (e.g. 'P6: Happiness proverbs of famous people') in the sample project (Figure 4.19).

On the right hand side, preview images are displayed. When you add a new video to a project, you do not immediately see the preview images

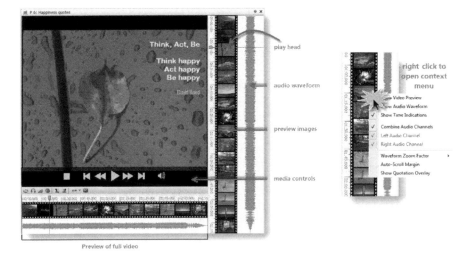

Figure 4.19   The various aspects of a loaded video document

because they first need to be created. The size of the preview images is up to 50 × 50 pixels. To create these images, one frame per second is selected. Depending on the length of the video, this may take a few seconds or up to a few minutes.

If you move the cursor inside the video pane, the media controls will appear and you can start, stop and pause the video, and skip forwards and backwards. You can also start and stop the multimedia file by pressing the space bar.

Context menu of preview pane

If you right click on the video preview, you can set a number of display options in the context menu (see Figure 4.19):

- You can hide or display the video preview and audio waveform.
- If you mark a segment by moving your mouse over the video previews, time indicators are displayed: that is, the start and end positions and total length of the segment.
- By default the left and right audio channels are displayed as one audio waveform. If needed, you can separate the left and right channels and display two audio waveforms.
- Select 'Waveform Zoom Factor' to adjust the size of the audio wave.
- Use 'Auto-Scroll' if only part of the video is displayed in the margin area and you want the margin area to automatically scroll if you play the video.
- Show 'Quotation Overlay' to see the quotation boundaries displayed on top of the video preview.

Zooming the timeline

You can zoom the timeline to select just the section of the audio or video that you want to see in the margin area:

- When you move the mouse pointer over the full preview, two orange sliders appear on the right and left hand sides.
- Move the right and left sliders to the desired position. Time indicators display the start and end positions and length of the selection (see Figure 4.20).
- Left click in the zoomed area and move it forwards and backwards. Note that the preview images in the margin area move accordingly and a different part of the video is displayed.

Figure 4.20   Zooming the timeline

Creating an audio or video quotation

Move your mouse pointer over the audio waveform/preview images. Left click roughly where you want the quotation to start and drag the mouse pointer to the approximate end position. *Or:* Move the playhead pointer to the desired start position. Select < or , (comma) to set the starting point. Move the playhead pointer to the desired end position. Select > or . (period/full stop) to set the end point of a segment. Depending on your keyboard, one of the two options (<> or ,.) is more convenient to use.

- Click on the **Create Quotation** button (see Figure 4.21).

Figure 4.21   Creating a video quotation

- Click on the Play button to review the quotation, or double click on the quotation bar in the margin area to play it.

If you are not quite happy with the start and end positions, an easy way of adjusting them is as follows:

- Move the playhead pointer to either the beginning or the end of the quotation and use the right and left arrow keys for fine-tuning the segment. Each click moves the playhead pointer in 1/1000th increments of the length of the video that is currently displayed in the margin area. This allows you to set the length of audio and video quotations quite precisely.

- Once you have located the correct position, drag the orange slider onto the red line of the playhead pointer. As soon as the orange line is over the red line, the two lines 'snap'. Repeat this for the second position as well if necessary.
- Click on the **Modify Quotation** button in the vertical tool bar (see Figure 4.22).

Smile is the key that fits the lock of everybody's heart
Anthony J D'Angelo

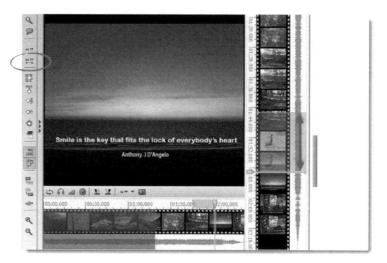

Figure 4.22 Adjusting the length of a video quotation

Display of video quotations

The default name for audio and video quotations is the document name. Each quotation can, however, be renamed. To do so, right click on the quotation name in the Quotation Manager (Figure 4.23) and select the **Rename** option (see also 'Describing multimedia quotations' below).

In addition the start position and length of the segment (i.e. the number in brackets) in the form h:min:sec:millisec is provided.

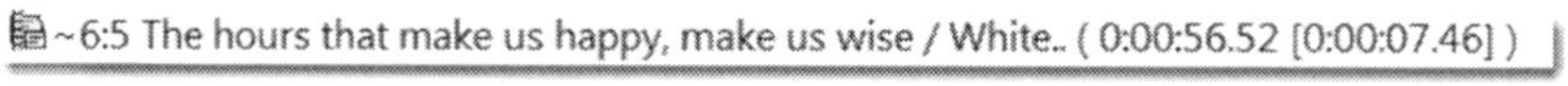

~6:5 The hours that make us happy, make us wise / White.. (0:00:56.52 [0:00:07.46])

Figure 4.23 Renamed and commented video quotation in the Quotation Manager

Adding codes

To code the video quotation, proceed in the same way as explained for text or image quotations:

- Right click on the highlighted quotation segment (or the quotation bar) and select CODING / ENTER CODE NAME(S), or drag and drop an existing code from the Code Manger onto the quotation.

First steps in analyzing video data

I recommend beginning your analytic work directly on the video file. I would not spend months transcribing a video file as some people do. All the information is self-contained and I do not see the point of repeating some of it in transcript form unless a very detailed transcript is required (e.g. for sequential analysis). But then one would probably not be working with ATLAS.ti.

Therefore, my suggestion is to add your video files to ATLAS.ti and begin your analytic work. Below I describe a few options that ATLAS.ti provides to support your analysis: making use of quotation names and comments and adding an associated text document to partly transcribe important passages, or to transcribe the words spoken in the video, or to write analytic notes that go beyond a comment for a quotation.

Making use of quotation names

As mentioned above, the name of a video quote is its data file name. In most cases this is not very useful, at least not for analytic purposes. I suggest two options: renaming the quotations and adding comments.

- In the process of creating video quotations, rename them so they can serve as titles for your video segments. To do so, right click on the quotation bar in the margin area and select **RENAME**. Alternatively, if your screen is large enough, open the Quotation Manager alongside and rename the quotations there.

The default length for quotation names is 30 characters. If you feel this is not sufficient for the titles that you want to enter, you can extend the number of characters that can be used.

- From the main menu, select **TOOL / PREFERENCES / GENERAL PREFERENCES / TAB: GENERAL**. At the bottom left, you will find the option **LIST NAME SIZE FOR QUOTES**. Increase it to the desired number of characters; 75 characters are probably enough for short titles.

On page 104 is an output of the quotes set in P6 of the stage II project, coded with codes of the code family 'Sources of happiness'. To create the output, I selected the code family 'Sources of happiness' in the query tool and set the scope to P6. As the output option I selected **LIST**, as there is no textual content apart from the quotation names and comments.

You can see the titles I have entered for each video quotation by renaming the default name. The brackets at the beginning of each line (<>) indicate that the quotations are linked to other quotations via hyperlinks (see Chapter 7). The numbers after the title show the position in the document. The first number indicates the start position; the second number in square brackets provides information on the quotation length.

Document filter:

'P 6: Happiness proverbs of famous people'

13 Quotations found for query:

'Sources of happiness'

6:1 Be happy (0:00:07.47 [0:00:08.50])

~>6:2 Think, Act, Be / Autumn leave on a green backgroun.. (0:00:17.33 [0:00:04.61])

~>6:3 Smile, it enhances your face value / Violett daisi.. (0:00:24.75 [0:00:07.91])

~6:4 Happiness is a way of travel, not a destination. /.. (0:00:36.92 [0:00:07.01])

~6:5 The hours that make us happy, make us wise / White.. (0:00:56.52 [0:00:07.46])

~6:6 Happiness is when what you think, what you say, an.. (0:01:06.91 [0:00:06.95])

~>6:7 Think of all the beauty still left around your and.. (0:01:16.10 [0:00:08.29])

~6:8 From there to here, and here to there, funny thing.. (0:01:26.75 [0:00:06.89])

~6:9 It is only possible to live "happy ever after" on .. (0:01:37.78 [0:00:04.38])

~6:10 If you never did, you should. These things are fu.. (0:01:47.43 [0:00:07.40])

~6:11 Smile, it is the key that fits the lock of everybo.. (0:01:57.07 [0:00:06.50])

~<>6:12 Don't worry, be happy / shop window (0:02:04.93 [0:00:09.97])

~>6:13 People are as happy as the make up their minds to .. (0:00:44.79 [0:00:06.83])

Making use of quotation comments

In addition to using quotation names for titles, you can add a description for each video quotation in the comment field.

- Right click on a video quotation bar in the margin area or within the highlighted area on the preview images and select Edit comment. If you have opened the

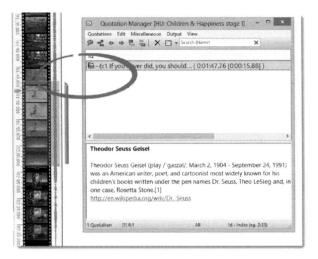

Figure 4.24 Display of commented quotations

Quotation Manager alongside, you can also write the comment into the comment field (see Figure 4.24).

The quotation bar shows a triangle on top, the quotation icon has a Post-it note and you will see a tilde (~) in front of the quotation name. If you want to output quotation lists including comments, you will find an option **List+Comments**, for example, in the query tool. If you output quotations via a selected code in the Code Manager or from the Quotation Manager, ATLAS.ti will recognize if at least one of the quotations has a comment. If so, you will be asked whether comments should be included in the output.

A quick way to access all commented quotations is by setting a filter in the Quotation Manager. Open the Quotation Manager and select QUOTATIONS / FILTER / COMMENTED (this is the last option). To output the filtered quotations, select OUTPUT / ALL QUOTATIONS (LIST). Next, confirm the message to include comments in the output as well. Below is an excerpt of the above-presented output based on the code family 'Sources of happiness', this time including quotation comments.

Document filter:

'P 6: Happiness proverbs of famous people'

13 Quotations found for query:

'Sources of happiness'

6:1 Be happy (0:00:07.47 [0:00:08.50])

~>6:2 Think, Act, Be / Autumn leave on a green backgroun.. (0:00:17.33 [0:00:04.61])

Comment:

David Baird

David Baird is a composer and theatre director who has published books on a wide range of subjects including film, art, Shakespeare, and spirituality.

~>6:3 Smile, it enhances your face value / Violett daisi.. (0:00:24.75 [0:00:07.91])

Comment:

Dolly Rebecca Parton

Dolly Rebecca Parton (* 19. January 1946 in Sevierville, Sevier County, Tennessee) ist eine US-amerikanische Country-Sängerin, Songschreiberin und Schauspielerin. Parton ist seit mehr als 40 Jahren eine der erfolgreichsten Sängerinnen und Songautorinnen im Bereich Country- und Popmusik, hatte als einzige Sängerin 25 Nummer-eins-, 55 Top-10- und 88 Top-40-Hits in den Country-Charts, verkaufte mehr als 100 Millionen Schallplatten und erhielt acht Grammys.

~6:4 Happiness is a way of travel, not a destination. /.. (0:00:36.92 [0:00:07.01])

Comment:

Roy M. Goodman

Senator Roy M. Goodman was born on March 5th, 1930 in New York City. Goodman graduated from Harvard College in 1951 and Harvard Graduate School of Business Administration in 1953, then served in the U.S. Navy as an officer.

Senator Roy M. Goodman has been widely quoted as saying, "Remember that happiness is a way of travel - not a destination."

Associating a text document with a video

In Chapter 3, I explained how to set up a project importing transcripts prepared outside of ATLAS.ti using the A-Docs function. Below I will show you how to use the A-Docs function to associate an empty text file with the video file and how to enter content.

- Select **DOCUMENTS / NEW / NEW TEXT DOCUMENT**.
- Enter a name for the new document like 'Analytical notes for Happiness proverbs'. Click on **OK**.

The document is loaded in edit mode. You can immediately begin to type. However, before we do this, we want to associate it with the video file.

- Leave edit mode by clicking on the edit button in the main toolbar.
- Load the video document into the second region. Select it from the drop-down list or the fly-out window and drag it onto the plus sign on the left hand side of the ATLAS.ti window (see Chapter 2).
- Click on the PD bar of the newly created text document to activate it. We need to associate the text with the video and not vice versa. The PD bar is yellow when the document is selected.
- Select the main menu option DOCUMENTS / A-DOCS / ASSOCIATE WITH PD FROM REGION >. The two files will be associated and the Association Editor will open.

As we do not want to code at the moment, there is no need to use space on the screen for the margin area. To hide the margin area, deactivate it by clicking on the margin button in the vertical toolbar. This hides it for the active document, the empty text file. To hide the margin for the video document, make the video document the active one by clicking on the PD bar. Then click on the margin button in the vertical toolbar (Figure 4.25).

If you come across something in your video file that you feel is important to fully transcribe or you want to write analytic notes, use the built-in transcription function and type the text into the associated text file:

Click if you do not want to see the margin area.

Figure 4.25 Hiding the margin area

- Enter edit mode by clicking on the edit button in the main toolbar.
- If you do not start at the beginning of the video, position the playhead where you want the association to start. Press F8 or click on the **Create a new anchor** button in the toolbar of the Association Editor (see Figure 4.26).

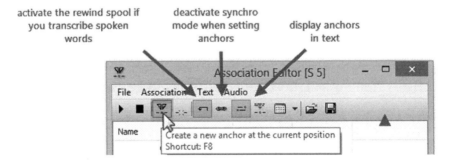

Figure 4.26 The Association Editor

- Play the video and position the playhead where you want the association to end and press the F8 key again or click on the **Create a new anchor** button in the toolbar.

By default the associations are unnamed. An easy way to enter names that helps you to find your way around the associations is the **Grab Text as Name** option (F9):

- Click on the **Text** menu and check the highlight setting. If not already selected, choose **Highlight Line.**
- Click on the first association in the list and then on the F9 key. The placeholder for the name is replaced with the text of the highlighted line.
- Proceed likewise with all other associations. The list of associations then shows the first 30 characters of the associated text for each start and end position (see Figure 4.27).
- If you click on an association it will highlight the first line of the associated text and the playhead will move to the linked position in the video.
- To play the associated video segment at full length, activate synchro mode (F3).
- Next, highlight a section between two anchors with your mouse and press **Ctrl+P**, or select **Documents / A-Docs / Play Selected Text** from the main menu (see Figure 4.27).

For further information on using ATLAS.ti for transcription see the ATLAS.ti manual.

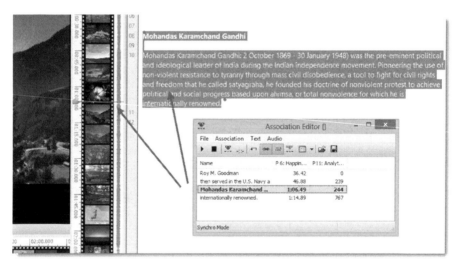

Figure 4.27   Association Editor with renamed anchors and activated anchor showing associated text and video

Skills training 4.10: working with Google Earth documents

Before you can load a Google Earth (GE) document in ATLAS.ti, you need to install Google Earth on your computer. The current sample project does not contain a GE document. Thus, in order to follow this exercise, you need to create a new GE document first.

Adding a Google Earth PD

- After installing Google Earth, select **Documents / New / New Google Earth PD**. Loading the document may take a while, depending on the speed of your Internet connection.
- Open the Quotation Manager alongside the HU editor on the left hand side. This will allow us to easily rename the quotations, delete them if necessary and to comment them. The fly-out window currently does not have the same functionality. Therefore it is better to use the Quotation Manager.
- Let's fly to New York City. In the 'Fly To' field, type the following location: 'New York City'.

Creating a GE quotation

- To set a quotation, zoom into the map and look for an interesting place. Position it in the middle of the screen and left click. Then click on the **Create Quotation** button in the vertical toolbar (see left), or select **Quotations / New from Selection** from the Quotation Manager menu.

create quotation

modify quotation

A new entry will appear immediately in the Quotation Manager. Just as with audio and video quotations, the file name becomes the quotation's name. In addition, the geographic reference is shown. Note the Google Earth symbol that is attached to the quotation icon (Figure 4.28).

11:1   Google Earth   40°46'32,83"N 73°55'33,...

Figure 4.28   Display of Google Earth quotation in the Quotation Manager

Figure 4.29   Renamed and commented GE quotations

Change the name of this quotation to something more meaningful, like the place you have marked. Write something in the comment field to describe the location (e.g. excerpts from your field notes, information you have about the location or you find online).

- Create a few more quotations and rename them.
- In order to view the ATLAS.ti tag in the GE editor, the document must be reloaded. Hold down the Shift key and click on the **P-Docs** button. You will now see the ATLAS.ti tag in Google Earth (Figure 4.29).

The ATLAS.ti tag can be displayed at various heights. In Figure 4.30 it floats 10 meters above the ground. You can set this under TOOLS / GENERAL PREFERENCES / GOOGLE EARTH PREFERENCES.

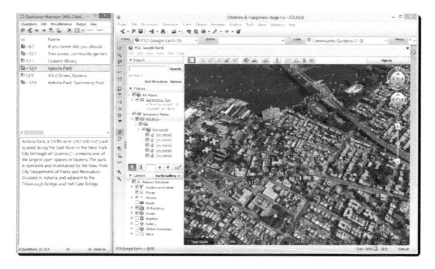

Figure 4.30   ATLAS.ti tags in GE map

Coding GE quotations

- To code GE quotations, right click on a quotation in the Quotation Manager and select CODING / ENTER CODE NAME(S). Or open the Code Manager or fly-out window and drag and drop an existing code from there onto the quotation (Figure 4.31).

You can also create a quotation and code it directly:

- Select a point on the map by double clicking on it. Then select CODES / CODING / ENTER CODE NAME(S) or SELECT CODES FROM LIST, depending on whether you would like to enter a new code or assign an existing code. Alternatively, you can use the vertical toolbar buttons for coding.

Summary

If you have worked through this chapter thoroughly you should now know the procedures of coding with ATLAS.ti. That is:

Figure 4.31   Coding GE quotations

- The various options which ATLAS.ti offers for coding.
- How coded segments of various media types can be modified.
- How codes can be renamed, merged or deleted.
- How to write definitions for code words and what this is good for.
- How to handle PDF, image, audio, video and Google Earth documents.
- How to prepare a transcript for an audio or video file.
- How to utilize quotation names and comments.

Below you will find a list of review questions to test your knowledge of the technical aspects of coding. You can practice a bit more when you go through the suggested coding exercises in the next chapter. Then you should feel quite secure in handling the technical aspects of coding. What comes next, the methodological aspects, probably needs more practice and time to learn. In Chapter 5, I want to share with you what I have learned in nearly 20 years of working with CAQDAS so that you can take a few shortcuts and speed up the learning process.

REVIEW QUESTIONS

1 Which coding options does ATLAS.ti offer?
2 What are in-vivo codes and what can they be used for?
3 Explain the quotation references in the Quotation Manager when it is set to single column view. What do the numbers before and after the quotations mean?
4 Regarding the way quotations are referenced, how does this relate to good data file names and what is the advantage of it?
5 Explain the code references in the Code Manager when it is set to single column view. What do the numbers after the codes mean?
6 Why is it important to write code definitions?
7 What in particular do you need to know when coding PDF files and non-textual data files like image, audio and video files?
8 How can you go about analyzing image, audio and video files? Which options are you likely to use more or in a different way as compared to working with text data?

GLOSSARY OF TERMS

Code: Keywords that are generally linked to quotations, but do not have to be. You can also create free codes. When you link free codes to a number of different codes, then they are called abstract codes.

Code comment: While coding you can add some notes to this field, and thoughts and questions that occur during the process of first-stage coding. If it becomes clear over time and with further analysis that something should be coded, a code definition should be entered, maybe a coding rule and a sample quote.

Code reference: This consists of the so-called groundedness and density of a code. The groundedness provides the frequency of how often a code has been applied; the density shows the number of links to other codes.

In-vivo coding: For the computer this means that the highlighted characters are used as the code name. In a computer-assisted analysis, in most cases, it does not make a lot of sense to have code words that are the same as the text they code. Generally a bit of context is needed and this requires extending the quotation beyond the characters used as in-vivo code.

Quotations: Marked data segments that have a clearly defined start and end point. Often quotations are coded, but they do not have to be. You can also create so-called free quotations. Free or coded quotations can be used as a source or target to link data segments to each other. Linked quotations are called hyperlinks (see Chapter 7).

Quotation comment: Technically, the quotation comment field acts as an editor for written text. Potentially, a comment can be added to each quotation. To avoid drowning in too much data, your comments (i.e. short notes) should be written in the comment fields rather than using an ATLAS.ti memo for them. Memos are the place to write down more extensive thoughts and ideas that you elaborate on over an extended period of time (see Chapters 5 and 6).

Quotation reference: This is made up of an ID, a name and the position of the quotation in the document. The ID consists of the primary document number that it belongs to and a number that indicates the sequence of when it was created. The quotation name is based on either the first 30 characters of a text quotation or the name of the primary document. This automatically generated name can be modified. If the default number of characters is not sufficient, they can be increased under **Tools / Preferences / General Preferences**. The location where a quotation can be found within a primary document is indicated after the name. Depending on the document type, different references are used:

- **References for rtf or doc(x) quotations:** paragraph numbers for start and end positions.

- **Reference for a PDF document:** page number and number of characters on the page for start and end positions. In case the document contains columns, the column number is provided as well.

- **References for audio and video quotations:** hours, minutes, seconds and milliseconds.

- **References for Google Earth (GE) quotations:** the geographical coordinates for latitude and longitude (e.g. 51°30'49.21"N, 0°4'41.38"W) as provided by GE.

FIVE

Embarking on a journey – getting ready and coding the data material

In Chapter 4, you learned how to handle codes on the technical level. To the software, a code is simply a code, and what you do with it, how you name it and whether you have codes on different levels are not its concern. A code might be a basic description, an indicator, a main category or a subcategory, or a placeholder modifying a link in a network view. In addition to regular codes, the software offers code families and supercodes. Technically speaking, a code family is a group of codes and a supercode is a saved query. There are no actual rules about how to use these objects; they are all at your disposal, and the software does not tell you how to use them, just like a toolbox. The toolbox contains everything you might need to build a table from a pile of wood. If you have no knowledge or experience, you might – eventually – build something that looks like a table, but you won't feel so clever if it falls over when you use

Figure 5.1 Looking at data like a landscape to be explored

it. It is much better to let someone give you instructions. In this chapter I am that someone, standing next to you with suggestions and rules of thumb on how to work with codes and all related issues. I have been through the process of trial and error myself and, 15 years ago, I was coding and approaching analysis very differently from how I do today. In the following, I would like to share with you what I have learned over the years. Therefore, before I actually send you on the journey, I would like to present a few more preparatory issues like how to organize your data and how to best prepare your project for analysis. As with most other things, the journey of qualitative data analysis also becomes easier, the better prepared you are.

Remember the data landscape that I showed you in the Introduction? I have pasted the image of it here again to prepare you for the journey that now lies ahead (Figure 5.1). Before the journey begins, I would like to call one last preparatory meeting. I would like to play a virtual jigsaw puzzle with you (see also Seidel and Kelle, 1995).

Skills trainings

Skills training 5.1: organizing documents

Skills training 5.2: commenting your data and keeping track of analytic thoughts

Skills training 5.3: creating a new memo

Skills training 5.4: developing subcategories

Skills training 5.5: building categories from the bottom up

Skills training 5.6: rules for hierarchical coding schemas

The puzzle analogy

Imagine that you and your fellow traveling companions are sitting with me, your guide, at a table in a rest house. I open a box filled with 1000 jigsaw pieces; I dump them on the table and spread them out, making sure that all the pieces are picture side up. It's your turn now. You have to solve the puzzle (Figure 5.2). How do you go about it?

Most people would answer that either they begin with the corners and the edges, or they sort by colors or shapes. Let's begin with the corners and edges. Why do you think that most people begin like that?

These pieces are easy to recognize since they have at least one straight edge. When it comes to analyzing a project in ATLAS.ti, I likewise recommend you begin with what is easiest.

Below, you will learn to make use of already known characteristics, incorporating them into the file names for easy sorting and ordering of the documents within the HU. If applicable, document groups like male, female, location, age, etc., can also be created fairly early on in the analysis process (see below: 'First

Figure 5.2 Playing a puzzle

Figure 5.3 Starting to lay the frame

steps in data organization'). By starting to work on a project in this way, literally speaking, we will frame it (Figure 5.3).

Once the frame is ready, we need to take a closer look at what is inside. Following the second suggestion, this means sorting the pieces of the puzzle by colors and shapes (Figure 5.4). The sample puzzle here depicts a castle with a forest around it and a lake in the upper right hand corner (I know this as I have seen the lid of the box!). In terms of your research projects, what is equivalent to the lid of the box?

That's right – your research questions. However, they only guide your research; they do not show a predetermined result as the picture on a puzzle box does. Some puzzles are more similar to what we do as qualitative researchers, the so-called WASGIJ puzzles (that's 'jigsaw' backwards). The finished puzzle does

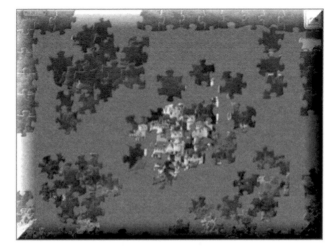

Figure 5.4   Sorting pieces by colors and shapes

not correspond to the picture on the box. The solver needs to assume the role of one of the people on the cover and the solution is the motive as seen from the perspective of this person. However, the solver does not know which of the perspectives must be taken. Only the puzzle itself provides the answer. And this is more like what we are after as qualitative researchers. We don't want prefabricated answers. The answers to our questions are somewhere in our data and our task is to discover, unravel or reconstruct them.

There are inevitably some puzzles with no picture on the box. They are comparable to a project where it is difficult to find existing literature or previous research on the subject matter. Thus, you may have a hard time developing detailed research questions based on previous knowledge and the only option you have is to go into the field and start collecting data. Like a puzzle with no premade solution, such a project is proportionately more difficult than one which is guided by research questions, so I would leave it to more experienced researchers. For smaller classroom projects or for a short-term thesis, select a research question that can be clearly outlined so it can serve as a point of orientation. When you conduct an interview study and develop an interview guideline, the questions can be used to look for themes in the data. This is similar to collecting all the pieces in the sample puzzle that look like parts of a castle, a lake or a forest.

To remind you of the three basic steps of the NCT model, collecting during the phase of qualitative data analysis means coding. Thus, our initial ideas for coding can be derived from our research questions, from theories, from the literature or from the interview guideline. Ideas for coding in the grounded theory sense can also emerge from the data, but this is not so easy for a beginning researcher, as Kelle and Kluge note: 'novices in the field of social research have a particularly tough time following recommendations like "let theoretical concepts emerge from your data material". For them, such attempts will likely result in drowning in data material for months' (2010: 19).

Staying with the puzzle analogy, a few additions need to be made. The puzzle is already broken up into pieces. In computer-assisted analysis, we actually need to

Figure 5.5 Creating subcategories of the main category castle

create the pieces first. In ATLAS.ti these are quotations. When looking for data with similar content like all the pieces of the puzzle that look like pieces of the castle, then we are 'coding' them. In ATLAS.ti there is no visual differentiation between different levels of codes, whether they are already codes in a methodological sense or just a description of a data segment. One could indicate this in the code definition, but often at the beginning of the coding process the development is still very open. Most codes are preliminary. Thus, I would not spend too much time initially contemplating whether a code is already a code or just a piece of the puzzle. It is more important to collect ideas and to develop them into proper concepts and categories over time. You will find a glossary at the end of this chapter where the various terms like codes, concepts or categories are defined.

The puzzle analogy assumes that we begin with abstract codes. It is a model, and models tend to simplify this world so we can better understand it. Keep this in mind when we continue to discuss the next steps in solving the puzzle.

So far we have put together the frame and we have collected those pieces that look as if they are related, like castle or lake pieces, into separate piles. The next step is to take a closer look at one of the piles, let's say the castle. Naturally, one now looks again for related pieces like parts of the roof, the towers, the windows or the battlements. Now we are creating subcategories; these are the properties of the castle (Figure 5.5).

By the way, you are already very skilled at constructing subcategories. You do it every day and you learned the technique a long time ago when discovering the world as a child. You may have first realized that a certain animal is a dog and then probably used the word 'dog' for all the different kinds of dogs. Later you learned that they are beagles, boxers, golden retrievers, poodles or mongrels. Developing subcategories for your data is not much different.

Let's assume you have collected lots of quotations under a common label; the next step is to look through them, as I did with the castle pieces. After reading or looking at a few quotations, you will quickly notice where the commonalities are. This is easier now than it used to be when coding a document from start to finish. The software allows you to take a focused look at only a selection of the data.

After your first day on the trail, after you have already collected a few things that we can use as examples, I have planned a feedback session and some more skills training. Then I will show you how the development of subcategories works technically. Further, I will explain what to do with descriptive codes and how to move them to a more abstract level.

To finish solving the puzzle, we need to put together the other main themes in the same way as we did with the castle pieces. The last step is to see how it all fits together. I will explain how this works in Chapters 6 and 7.

Getting ready for the journey

For the first few exercises in this chapter, I would like to ask you to open your own Children & Happiness project that you created in Chapter 3. For Skills trainings 5.4 and 5.5, I will provide specially prepared projects that you can download from the companion website.

Skills training 5.1: organizing documents

Getting started is a whole task in itself, so adding some structure is a good way to add analytic content to an as yet 'empty' project. Document groups, also called P-Doc families in ATLAS.ti, contribute to the clear organization of the data material. During later stages, they are used as filters and in queries; although exactly when to create primary document families is a question of the personal preference of the analyst and also depends on the nature of the project.

Examples of document groups are the classic socio-demographic variables such as gender, age groups, material status, profession, location, etc. In our newspaper analysis, possible groups are country, circulation, type of newspaper or media.

Documents in ATLAS.ti are grouped via the so-called document families. The term 'family' has been derived from the concept of code families used in grounded theory. A code family is basically a group of codes. This was adopted in ATLAS.ti for primary documents and memos as well. We first came across 'families' in Chapter 2 when taking a look at the object managers in the ATLAS.ti interface. In version 7, families are no longer hidden in the family managers. They are directly visible and accessible in the side panels of the managers.

- To create a document family, open the P-Docs Manager.
- Select the documents that you want to group into a family, for example P2 to P5 as these are all blog data (see Figure 5.6).

For selecting documents, common Windows procedures can be used, like holding down the Shift key to select a list of consecutive documents, or the CTRL key to select them one by one.

- Left click on the highlighted documents and drag them into the side panel. If you let go of the left mouse key, you will be prompted to enter a name for the family. If you work with the sample data, enter the name 'blog data'.
- Let's create a second family. The data set contains two documents that inform about scientific findings on the relationship between happiness and children, P1 and P10. Let's group these into a family called 'research findings'. Group the remaining documents, P6 to P9, into a family called 'about happiness'.

Figure 5.6 Adding documents to a family

It is possible to add each document to more than one family. It is not an exclusive either/or allocation. In a classical interview study, you may want to group a document into a family called *gender::female, marital status::single* and *profession::high school teacher*. Note the special syntax I am using here. The two colons are not a typo. It is possible to export a table in Excel format that contains the family allocation. This is a useful option for larger projects. See 'Exporting and importing information on document groups' below for further information.

During the course of the analysis, families can be combined in a number of ways. For instance, you can compare all blog respondents to statements made in the scientific reports. Or, in a different data set, you may want to compare all comments made on a topic by all female elementary school teachers to all comments on the same topic made by female high school teachers. The document families in ATLAS.ti are a prerequisite for such questions being asked.

A primary document can only be assigned reasonably to one or more families if the mentioned characteristics refer to the whole of the document. For example, if you interview two people, a man and a woman, or conduct a group interview with 10 people, you can assign the interview neither to the family male nor to the family female. In this case, the variables male and female have to be assigned directly to the statements of each person via codes. This is easiest done by using the automatic coding function in combination with the transcription guidelines provided in Chapter 3.

Exporting and importing information on document groups

Outputting your document groups in the form of an Excel table is an interesting option if you are working with a large number of families or your database consists of mixed quantitative and qualitative data. I insert a brief description of this option here as users often do not realize that it exists, discovering only later that it would have been useful for their projects.

The Excel table can appear in two ways, depending on the naming convention used for the families. In the Children & Happiness project, I used simple descriptive names like 'blog data', 'scientific reports' and 'about happiness'. In a quantitative sense, the appropriate variable label would be 'Type of data' with the three values 'blog data', 'scientific report' and 'about happiness'. When using a descriptive label, each family is turned into a dichotomous variable with the values 0 and 1. When adding the variable label to the name using the following naming convention, **Type::blog data / Type::scientific reports / Type::about happiness**, the Excel table will show **Type** as the variable label and the entries after the double colon (::) as nominal labels in the cells. The other example family names I used above would be translated into the variables gender, marital status and profession.

To create such a table:

- From the main menu select **Documents / Export / Export PD-Family Table**.
- Confirm that you use as separator the two colons (::). Next, you need to select whether to create an Excel-compatible csv or an xls file.
- As output destination, select **File & Run**. Accept the suggested name or enter a new name.
- Save the file. The default location is TextBank. A better location, however, is a subfolder within the folder where you store your project data anyway. You may want to call it 'Output' and store there all the output files that you create during the course of the analysis. The file is directly opened in Excel, executed by the command Run.

Figure 5.7 shows the two possible appearances based on the naming convention used.

#	documents	Name	#type of data		about happiness	blog data	scientific reports
1							
2	P 1	Powdthavee's article published in "The Psychologist"	scientific reports		0	0	1
3	P 2	Belkin's parenting blog: coments on Powdthavee	blog data		0	1	0
4	P 3	Belkin's parenting blog discussion	blog data		0	1	0
5	P 4	Rubin's happiness project: comment on Powdthavee	blog data		0	1	0
6	P 5	NY magazin blog: Discussion of "All Joy and No fun" article	blog data		0	1	0
7	P 6	Happiness proverbs of famous people	about happiness		1	0	0
8	P 7	Transcript of video	about happiness		1	0	0
9	P 8	Happiness is a way to travel	about happiness		1	0	0
10	P 9	Don't worry, be happy	about happiness		1	0	0
11	P 10	Sources of happiness: Summary of research findings	scientific reports		0	0	1

Figure 5.7   PD-Family Table showing dichotomous and nominal labels

PD-Family Tables can also be imported. This is a useful option when information is already available in spreadsheet format. The easiest way to prepare such a table is to first export a table with no families entered. This way, you don't have to create the document and name columns yourself. For further instructions on how to export and import tables, I refer you to the manual. Here I just want to point out that this option exists.

Skills training 5.2: commenting your data and keeping track of analytic thoughts

It is possible to enter a comment for each document. This may not be necessary for all types of projects, but users often do not think of adding information to the HU that they already have. My advice is to include all information in the HU that is relevant for the analysis. When analyzing interview transcripts, researchers frequently write an interview protocol. But instead of adding it to their ATLAS.ti project, they store the protocols as Word files in some other folder. The better option is to copy and paste the protocols into the comment field of the respective primary document. The likelihood that you will look at the protocols again is much greater when they become part of your ATLAS.ti project. When working with newspaper articles or reports, you could add information about the source, such as a description of the newspaper, its circulation, readership, and from where you retrieved the document.

This is how it works:

- Select a primary document in the P-Docs Manager. The white field (as you may remember from Chapter 2) is a text editor and thus the place to enter a comment.
- Type a few words into the comment area or copy and paste a text from Word.
- When you are finished, click on another document in the P-Docs Manager. This action automatically saves your entry. In addition you will see a tilde (~) after the document name. If you do not see it, you may have to extend the name column (Figure 5.8).

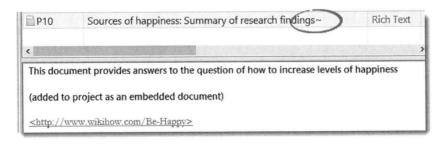

Figure 5.8 Commented primary document

Comments and memos in ATLAS.ti

Memos technically speaking provide a writing space like the comment field. In ATLAS.ti, I highly recommend that you make a distinction between comments and memos. Memos are an object class of their own. Comments are always attached to the object they describe – a document, a quotation, a code, a link or a network view. Memos have a title, you can select a type for each memo, and ATLAS.ti keeps track of the creation and modification dates. This should already hint that memos are different from comments (see also Konopásek, 2007). Users often treat them like a comment function and discover after a while that this is not very successful, or else they do not use memos at all. This is not to say that many analysts do not write memos; they probably do – but using a word processor rather than writing directly in ATLAS.ti. The disadvantage if you do this is that you are away from the data and you cannot link a Word document to a segment in your data. Within ATLAS.ti, you can link your analytic thoughts to the data segments that support them (see Chapter 6 for more).

In Table 5.1, you will find some ideas, as points of orientation, of where to write down what type of information.

Table 5.1 When to write comments and when to write memos

Content	Comment or memo?
Meta information about a document: source, where and how you found or generated it Interview protocols Note that information about the person, like gender, age, profession or company, industry, etc., is handled via document families; you do not need to write them into the comment field	Primary document comment
Comments about particular data segments: if you have a thought on a particular segment you are reading, coding or reviewing, open the comment field for the quotation (*do not* add a memo to single segments that you simply want to comment on)	Quotation comment
First ideas about what you mean with a particular code, with time a proper code definition Team work: coding rules Team work: example quotes	Code comment
Research diary	Memo (type: method)
Ideas/open questions regarding the coding system	Code memo (type: memo)
Things you want to discuss at the next team meeting	Team memo (type: memo)
Project description Research questions you already have	Project memo (type: memo)
Research questions you generate throughout the analysis process	Idea memo (type: memo)
Ideas for possible relationships	Idea memo (type: memo)
Written up analysis, one or more memos per research question	Research question memos (type: analysis)
Important definitions, theories or models from the literature that you need to refer to from time to time	Theory memos (type: theory)

Memos in the early stages of analysis

Below I describe the kinds of memos that you can start writing fairly early in the analysis process. In Chapter 6, you will find more information about how to make use of the ATLAS.ti memo function for writing up your analysis.

Research diary: If you are writing a thesis or dissertation, or working on a student or scientific research project, it is a good idea to write a research diary that you can later refer to when writing up your method section and to document the analytic process. You could do this in a Word document, but using an ATLAS.ti memo has some advantages. After an analysis session in ATLAS.ti, you can immediately write down what you have done and timestamp it without having to open another program. It becomes part of your evolving project and can later be submitted together with your project data and your analytic work in ATLAS.ti. Supervisors can follow your analytic steps and for teachers it is useful when grading a project. But there is more to it than just adding transparency: research diaries are useful reminders for the analyst too. It is difficult to keep everything in mind when a project continues over months or even years. The research diary can be reviewed, for example, when it comes to writing the method chapter for a thesis or a paper publication.

Project memo: To stay focused, adding a memo with your research questions can be done at an early stage of analysis. You probably already have a list of research questions, or at least some ideas. You can add further questions and ideas to this list with progressing analysis.

Idea memo: If you have a great idea but no time to follow it up right away, write it down before it gets lost. However, do not write a memo for every single idea you have! Collect all the good ideas in one memo that you might entitle 'Great ideas to follow up'.

To-do memo: Similar to the idea memo, you can have a memo that contains a to-do list for the next work session or a plan for the next week or analysis period.

Code memo: While your coding scheme is evolving, you may come across a code that needs further attention or a definition that you are not yet happy with. This can be written down in a code memo and, when you have the time, you can deal with all such issues. The code memo therefore collects all ideas and things to do that relate to your coding system. You can of course also add coding-related issues to your general to-do memo.

Team memos: When you work in a team, all the members can add a team memo to their subprojects. In the team memo you can write down things that you want to discuss at the next team meeting. Put all the team memos together and you already have your agenda for the next meeting. I would advise against merging team memos, as this will only work once. If you merge a second time, the previous entries will be merged again and you will end up with duplications. This also applies to all other memos that use the same title. Therefore, during a merge process, it is best to add rather than to merge memos, or to ignore them (read more about merging in Chapter 3).

Skills training 5.3: creating a new memo

Let's create a research diary. This is a 'free' memo, which means it is not connected to any other object in your project. In Chapter 6, we will see that memos can also be linked to codes, quotations and other memos.

- From the main menu, select **MEMOS / CREATE FREE MEMO**. You are prompted to enter a title. Enter 'research diary'.
- The memo editor opens (Figure 5.9). Check the Type field. ATLAS.ti offers three standard types: commentary, memo and theory. These types, however, can be changed (see Chapter 6). For this exercise change the type to 'memo' by clicking on the down arrow and selecting it from the list of available types.
- When writing a research diary, it is a good idea to keep track of when you wrote what. This can be done easily by selecting the **INSERT DATE/TIME** option from the insert menu, or simply press **CTRL+D**. Then type your entry for the day. Before you add you next entry (e.g. after the next work session), first press **CTRL+D** again, then type.
 - When you are done, either select **MEMO / SAVE** from the menu or click the check-mark button (see right). Memos are saved internally with the HU, therefore the check-mark and not the usual disk symbol is used. Then close the memo editor.

You will see that the text you have written into the memo editor also shows up in the lower part of the Memo Manager, the text editor pane. You can also continue to write the memo there, but it is less comfortable and you have fewer editing options.

- To open the memo editor again, click on the edit button in the toolbar.
 - If you continue to write the diary after your next work session, remember to press **CTRL+D** to insert the date and time in front of the new entry.

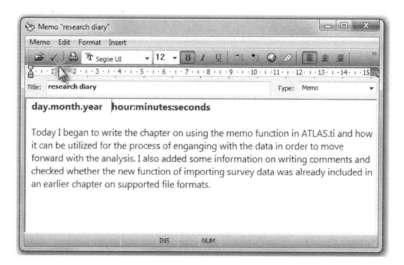

Figure 5.9   Creating a free memo

Let's add one more 'free' memo. This time via the Memo Manager:

- Open the Memo Manager by clicking on the **Memo** button. You will see your newly created memo inside. Click on the 'Create a new item' button in the toolbar (see right) and enter as the memo title: '**research questions**'. Change the type to 'memo'.
- If you work with the sample data, add the following research questions. In Chapter 6, we are going to explore these questions, plus a few additional ones. At the end of this chapter, you will find a complete list of all questions.

Is happiness defined differently by those who have children and those who do not have children?

What is the difference between parents and non-parents in terms of their attitude towards the relationship between happiness and children?

Which sources for happiness are mentioned?

What kinds of explanations regarding the statistically significant negative correlations between happiness and children are offered by the blog respondents? Do the respondents from the New York Times blog provide different answers than those writing on Belkin's blog?

Is there a difference with regard to the question 'What makes us happy?' between the answers provided by blog respondents (P3 and P5) and scientific evidence (P10)?

- Save the memo, close the memo editor and the Memo Manager.

The journey begins: noticing things and collecting them

Finally, the first day of the expedition has arrived. I hope that you are now ready and eager to embark on the journey. Remember the NCT model: if you get lost, it will remind you of the tasks that need to be done. The first day will be easy going – just keep an open mind, notice as many things as you can and collect them via coding. We will meet up again after this first day for a feedback session. Thus, there is nothing to worry about; we'll take it step by step. Here are some final instructions:

- Read the article by Powdthavee (P1 in your project if you did not change the order), which provides the backdrop.
- Next, start to read Belkin's parenting blog discussion (P3). When you start *noticing* things (Figure 5.10), begin to *collect* them by assigning them a code. Don't think too much about a perfect code label; just write whatever comes to mind and continue. You can always rename the codes later.

If you feel that it is important to read through all of the data first and to write down notes on a piece of paper before you create codes in ATLAS.ti, then this is a suitable way to proceed. If, however, after reading a few of the

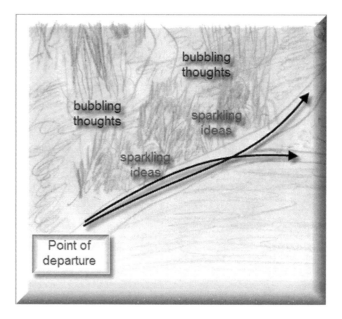

Figure 5.10   First day out – noticing things and collecting things

blog comments, you already have some ideas for codes, then go straight ahead and start coding in ATLAS.ti. This is fine as well. Do whatever feels most natural to you.

In the free memo 'research questions' that we created above, I already listed a few questions that can be examined once the data are coded. The main **research question** that you can keep in mind when reading through the blog data is: 'How do blog discussants perceive the reported relationship between children and happiness? Are there differences between parents and non-parents or between males and females? What other aspects come up in discussing the scientific findings?'

- Continue with this exercise for at least 45–60 minutes. You may create up to 20–30 codes within this time or only 6 or 7, depending on your style of coding.
- If you have questions on how to structure your list of codes and how to organize them, don't worry about it now. We will discuss it in our next feedback session. I want you to keep your mind open and notice as many things as possible without putting them into little boxes too soon. Remember, this is only your first day of coding.

Feedback session: what did you find?

How did it go? Was it fun? How did you cope with the technical aspects of coding in ATLAS.ti: creating codes, modifying quotations, renaming codes, etc.? Do write down any thoughts and questions that arose during your first day of the journey in your research diary memo before you read on.

I cannot ask you to show me your list of codes, but I have some lists created by four other coders who have already done this exercise in a face-to-face workshop (Table 5.2).

You can see from Table 5.2 that coder 1 came up with six codes, coders 2 and 3 both with nine codes, and coder 4 created nineteen initial codes. If you take a closer look at these codes, you may already get an idea of why the number of codes ranges between 6 and 19. Coder 1 has coded similarly to the way I explained in the puzzle analogy. Coder 1 collected data segments under a common term, like all reasons for having a baby. Bazeley and Richards (2000: 54) refer to this form of coding as 'broad-brush coding'. Coder 4 has more or less named the single pieces of the puzzle (labeled 'concept coding' by Bazeley and Richards). Whether you start with only a few broader codes or with a larger list of codes that are close to the data does not matter.

Table 5.2　Ideas collected by four coders

Coder 1	Coder 2	Coder 3	Coder 4
Reasons for a baby	Consequences of early parenthood	No regrets	Financial difficulties
Experience of unhappiness	Reasons for having children	More than I was before	Negative impact on career
Definition of happiness	Reasons for not having children	Richer life	Marital satisfaction goes down
Study critique	Hard work but joy	Types of happiness	More joy
Effects of parenting	Responsibility	Drop in marital quality	Becoming a bit wiser
Impact on relationships	Biological imperative	Children are more about meaning of life than happiness	Logical consequence of having a family
	Third-person perspective	Associated experience	Less burdened before
	Motivation	Biology	Love my partner more
	Critique of the concept of happiness	Questioning the sampling	More stress
			Life is richer
			Scared
			Desire of a change
			Changed feelings about own parents
			Improving the world
			Fulfillment
			Planned/unplanned children
			Less time
			Happiness is unrelated to having children
			New aspects of love

What matters is that you know how to proceed and what to do with your initial ideas. Neither coder 1 nor coder 4 should continue to code all of their data in this way; coder 1 needs to develop subcategories and coder 4 codes on a more aggregated level. Coders 2 and 3 are likely to do both. Since the codes are not hard printed in the data, you can approach coding in a flexible manner, and as it bests suits your methodology and personal style. Below, and more specifically in Skills training 5.4 and 5.5, you will learn how to proceed with coding and with developing your coding schema depending on your starting point.

Before I move on, I would like to draw your attention once again to Table 5.2. There is a considerable overlap in terms of what was coded, even though the four coders coded the data independently and at different locations. I have not counted the number of people who have coded these data, probably a few hundred by now. The results always look very similar. Therefore I allow myself to conclude (even though not scientifically proven) that qualitative research is not as subjective as it is often accused of being. See also the section on intercoder-reliability.

How to add more structure to your exploration

In order to generate sufficient ideas for developing a coding system, an hour or less is not enough. You need to plan more time for it. There are no set rules, but I can offer a few guidelines. If you conduct an interview study, select three to five interviews depending on their length. If you analyze newspaper data, you will probably need 20 to 30 articles. Begin by coding the data as we did on the first day of our journey: keep it very open, just collecting some ideas. At first you will generate lots of new codes; in time you will reuse more and more of the codes that you already have and you won't need to create new ones. You will have reached your first saturation point. In technical terms, you will drag and drop existing codes from the Code Manager onto the data segments.

As soon as you reach this point – when no new codes are being added and you only use drag and drop coding – it is time to review your coding system. If you do it at a much later stage it will require more work, because then you will have to go through all documents again to apply newly developed subcategories and recheck all other codings.

Let's assume you have taken your first round of coding up to this point. Those coders who naturally develop a mix of descriptive and abstract codes will probably end up with approximately 100 codes, depending on the project. Smaller student projects may contain around 50 to 70 codes. Generally, the cleaning up and restructuring of a first code list is done within the software. When you do it on paper, you need to apply the changes inside ATLAS.ti in a second step.

Figure 5.11 provides the visual equivalent of the various elements that were noticed in our data landscape on the first day of the excursion.

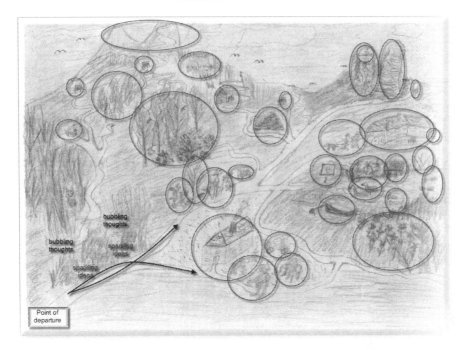

Figure 5.11   After the first day of collecting

If you have noticed a lot of things – let's say you already have 200 or 300 codes – your codes are probably very descriptive. Coders of this type often find it very difficult to let go of their codes by merging and sorting them, for fear of losing something. I can assure you that this is not going to happen. Instead of labeling almost every quotation and making a code out of it, after restructuring you will end up with a single code containing perhaps 10 quotations in their original form. This is much better than 10 codes that basically just paraphrase the original data.

The need to push codes from a descriptive to a conceptual, more abstract level is just as relevant to manual ways of coding. Corbin and Strauss wrote:

> One of the mistakes beginning analysts make is to fail to differentiate between levels of concepts. They don't start early in the analytic process differentiating lower-level explanatory concepts from the larger ideas or higher-level concepts that seem to unite them. … If an analyst does not begin to differentiate at this early stage of analysis, he or she is likely to end up with pages and pages of concepts and no idea how they fit together. (2008: 165)

This still applies to a computer-assisted analysis, even if the computer can handle 5000 or more codes. But this won't help you with your analysis. You'll just end up in what I call the code swamp. If you are a person that likes to work close to the text, at least at first, then it might be easier for you to print out the list of codes so you are forced to think on a more abstract level away from the data on a piece of paper. And this is how you do it:

- Open the Code Manager and select **Output / Code List**. Send the output to an editor. In ATLAS.ti all of these will be rich text editors. You can make changes to the text: delete it, save it, print it or copy and paste it into a Word document.

Based on the codes shown in Table 5.2 I would like to demonstrate how an initial list of codes can be sorted and structured. As the codes were generated by four coders in four different HUs, this also serves as an example of how you can develop a code list when working in teams.

I merged all four HUs (see Chapter 3 for more details on how to merge projects) to create one HU that contains the codes of all four coders. The code list then contained 43 codes. Next, I went through the list and merged all codes that have a different label but appear to have the same meaning, like 'reasons for a baby' and 'reasons for having children'. Having cleaned up the list in this way, I moved on, adding more conceptual structure to the list. Codes like 'scared' or 'biology' do not tell us much apart from the fact that the name or word is likely to be mentioned in the coded data segment. These codes have to be either renamed or subsumed under other codes. When looking at the context, 'scared' is mentioned as a reason for not having children, and 'biology/ biological imperative' on the other hand as reasons for having children. 'Becoming a bit wiser', 'fulfillment', 'more joy', 'being more than I was before' are all mentioned as positive effects of having children. As it appears, developing a category for reasons for having children/reasons for not having children and positive as well as negative effects of having children seems to be a good idea. This way, I can sort all these aspects into different subcategories.

How can this be achieved in ATLAS.ti? The code list in ATLAS.ti is linear and by default sorted in alphabetical order; therefore we need to play with the code labels in order to add some structure to the list. I usually add prefixes to the name followed by an underscore or a colon. What is important is that you clearly separate the prefix indicating the main category from the subcategory name. This way, all subcategories are automatically sorted under the main category name.

For the main category name, I use capital letters. This is a habit I developed when using version 5, when code names could not be colored. In version 6 this became possible, but I still like the capital letters for the main category name, to indicate the start of a new category. Sometimes you will need to play around with the prefixes so that the codes are in fact in the order that you want them to be, with the main category name on top. In the example provided below, I use an abbreviation, two spaces and then a clear name: RHC REASONS FOR HAVING CHILDREN. Then all subcodes are sorted in alphabetical order underneath the main category name.

RHC REASONS FOR HAVING CHILDREN
RHC: Associated experience
RHC: Desire of a change
RHC: Biological imperative
RHC: Improving the world

The categories as proposed here have provisional character as they are based on very little initial coding. With additional coding, they are likely to be developed further. I like Saldaña's idea of first-cycle and second-cycle coding. The idea of the cycle fits the nature of the NCT model where we have seen that qualitative analysis is cyclical rather than linear. First-cycle coding, according to Saldaña (2009: 45), refers to those processes that happen during the initial coding. In NCT analysis these are the ideas we noticed and collected on our first day of the journey as shown in Table 5.2. Second-cycle coding is the next step. Its main goal is 'to develop a sense of categorical, thematic, conceptual, and/or theoretical organization from your array of first cycle codes' (Saldaña, 2009: 149). The process of second-cycle coding entails the following activities: classifying, prioritizing, integrating, synthesizing, abstracting and conceptualizing. In other words, this means adding more structure to the code list. And from experience, I would add that there is at least a third and fourth cycle of coding as well. The aim of this process is to develop a structured code list, which at first is based on a subsample of your data. Once an initial structure has been developed, you can apply the codes to the remaining data material. Further refinement of your codes is probably still necessary.

Describing coding as a process that consists of at least two stages is common to a number of authors (see e.g. Bazeley, 2007; Bazeley and Richards; 2000; Charmaz, 2006; Fielding and Lee, 1998, Kuckartz, 1995; Kuckartz, 2005;

Figure 5.12   Sorted and structured code list

Lewins and Silver, 2007; Richards, 2009; Saillard et al., 2011). From my experience, telling software users that it is a good idea to develop codes into categories and subcategories makes sense to them as they will already have read about it in the literature. Richards (2009) for example refers to it as a catalogue of codes. As advantages of a well-sorted catalogue she mentions speed, reliability and efficiency. She further provides some tips for building a good code system. The problem as I observe time and time again in my everyday work is the translation of this process into mouse clicks and the technicalities of it in a software environment. Even if users know the technical aspects of coding on the one hand and read the useful tips on the other hand, they often find it difficult to apply these skills. It is actually not difficult, but neither is it self-explanatory. If you find yourself struggling, I invite you below to another skills training day offering three training sessions.

Figure 5.12 shows how the initial codes from the four coders were sorted and reordered. There are a few codes that could not be classified into a category, since it was too early to make a decision. The code 'study critique', for instance, may turn into a category of its own at some point. If there is a third-person perspective, there is likely to be a first-person perspective as well if you read on. If you look at the subcategories of 'effects pos' and 'effects neg', you may notice that they are still very close to the data. Reviewing more data material is likely to allow for formulating more conceptual labels.

What you can also see in Figure 5.12 is that I make use of the code family function. As families are much easier to access in version 7 as compared to previous versions, I changed my way of working with them. You still should not confuse them as being the equivalent of categories, though. They can represent a category in the form of a filter, but should not replace it. When I began to sort the codes and realized for instance that some codes indicated positive effects, I created the code family 'effects positive' and dragged all codes that fitted into this family. With a click on this family the list of codes is filtered. This makes it much easier to add prefixes. When you click on the 'Show all Codes' button again, the list is better sorted and structured with every group of codes you work on. You can practice this yourself in Skills training 5.5.

All codes that cannot yet be sorted into a group remain black, and if they are not already at the top of the list I add an asterisk (*) in front of the code name as a little trick to force them to be listed on top due to the alphabetical ordering. This way, it is easier to spot where you still have codes that do not belong anywhere.

Another way of sorting a code list is with the help of numbers and special characters. The sort order is as follows: special characters, numbers and letters. Sorting by numbers has the advantage that you can determine the sequence of your categories. The code list in Figure 5.13 describes a merger and acquisition process and questions regarding organizational fit come before the final results. As the label 'final results' begins with an f, it would come before the category 'organizational fit'. In addition to the number, letters were inserted indicating the major theme, like J for Justice and C for Controllability. The characters

```
1_EXOGENOUS VARIABLES
11_OP_Organizational Fit
.
2_INEGRATION PROCESS
21_J_Organizational Justice
211_J_distributive
212_J_procedural
212a_J_process evaluation
212b_J_time span
212c_J_working conditions
213_J_interpersonal
.
22_C_Perceived Controllability
212_C_explicability
222_C_transparency
.
3_EMOTIONALS RESULTS
.
.
4_FINAL RESULTS
.
```

Figure 5.13 Sorting a code list by numbers and letters

a, b, c were used when it became necessary to develop more subcategories for an already existing subcode. Continuing the number scheme would have otherwise ended up in a long chain of numbers. Inserting letters also avoids changing the sequence of numbers all the time when inserting new categories or subcategories.

Version 8 of ATLAS.ti will offer the possibility to arrange codes in higher and lower order codes. As the release of version 8 will not be before 2015 I cannot tell you at this stage what this is going to look like. Thus, until then we have to use prefixes as a way to visualize the various levels and meanings of a code.

Thoughts on inter-coder reliability

As you can see from the list of codes in Table 5.2, the four different coders dealing with the same research question did not come up with four completely different coding ideas. There are some differences but considerable overlap as well. As the saying goes, four eyes see more than two. Thus, the combined coding scheme of all four is probably better than one developed by just one person, but they will not be completely different. As Strauss and Corbin point out: 'The data themselves do not lie' (1998: 45). If we try to apply our personal view to the reality of data, we are likely to find out that it does not work and that we have a hard time relating in a meaningful way. Different coders may detect different aspects, but if they stay true to the data, it will be difficult to draw merely subjective conclusions originating from the persona of the researcher who conducted the study.

When it comes to the issue of inter-coder reliability, I am not an advocate for calculating a value that determines the degree of agreement between two or more coders. It can easily be done with the help of computers. When working with ATLAS.ti, you can upload data coded by different coders to the free Web-based software CAT (the Coding Analysis Toolkit).[1] The result is a figure between 0 and 1 and it will tell you how good the level of agreement is between two or more coders. This is suitable for studies with a large database where only few codes are used, when for instance analyzing public comments on issues like climate change, the Gulf coast oil spill, etc. CAT itself, or its sibling PCAT, is probably the best tool for such an analysis anyway.

When using ATLAS.ti, I am not greatly interested in the actual figure indicating the degree of agreement. Rather, I prefer to take a closer look at the content of those segments where the two coders do not agree and have them talk about it. It may be simply that they mean the same thing but used a different code, in which case the code definition is not yet clear enough. If they disagree on the actual content, then they have to find a compromise on how to handle such segments in the future: they might agree to apply one of their two codes or one that is more suitable, on a higher level or with a different label. In the end, there should be no differences in their coding and 'convergent validity' will have been achieved (in case you are looking for some terms for your methodology section).

If you have the opportunity to ask a second person to code one or two of your documents after you have developed a coding system and added code definitions, it could be very valuable. For me, however, this has more to do with increasing the validity of a coding scheme than being an issue of reliability. See also Charmaz, 2006; Denzin and Lincoln, 2000; or Seale, 1999 for a discussion of validity in qualitative research.

Comparing codes of two or more coders in ATLAS.ti – the mouse clicks

I suggest that you prepare a special HU file for this that contains only two or three documents. Make sure that all coders have created a user account and log in with their personal user names before they begin to code.

- Coder 1 codes the documents and sets the quotations. It would be very difficult to compare the codings if you allow every coder to set their own segments.
- All codes need to be defined well using the code comment field.
- After coder 1 has finished coding the two or three selected documents, he or she saves the HU file, plus saves a copy of it for coder 2. Rename the copy by for instance adding the name of coder 2 to the file name.

---

1 The Coding Analysis Toolkit (CAT) is available at http://cat.ucsur.pitt.edu/ or in ATLAS.ti: select HELP / MORE RESOURCES / THE CODING ANALYSIS TOOLKIT.

- Next, all codes need to be unlinked from their quotations in the HU for coder 2: CODES / MISCELLANEOUS / UNLINK QUOTATIONS FROM ALL CODES.
- Save the HU for coder 2 and create a copy bundle file. I suggest that you schedule a meeting with coder 2 to explain all the codes and their definitions. You may decide that coder 2 can add further codes if he or she sees new aspects in the data that coder 1 was not aware of.
- Coder 2 unpacks the copy bundle file and codes the data by applying the codes that are listed in the Code Manager (or new codes) to the existing quotations. After the work is completed, he or she saves the HU file and sends it back to coder 1.
- Coder 1 merges the two HU files using the following merge strategy: Same PDs and Codes. On the right-hand side of the window (see Figure 3.12), set the merge strategy for quotations to 'add' rather than unify. After merging the two files, save the resulting HU under a new name.
- Schedule a meeting with coder 2 to discuss the coding. Prepare the HU file in the following way: Open the Quotation Manager and sort all quotations by name by clicking on the column header 'Name'. Move the column 'Author' next to the Name column followed by the 'Codes' column. Now go through each quotation and compare the codes you have applied. If you applied different codes, discuss why and decide which code is the better choice or whether you need to modify the code definition.

More on code word labels, quotations and numbers

We have seen above that you can create a classification system to distinguish between different kinds of codes in the code list. A code word label should not be too long, however, even though ATLAS.ti does not dictate a maximum number of characters. The margin offers only limited space and the Code Manager, which is usually used for coding, should be no wider than necessary. Because of this, you should accustom yourself to using significant abbreviations and to writing a longer and more detailed definition in the comment field of the Code Manager instead of creating long code word labels.

Do I need to code everything?

This is a typical student question. After asking whether they need to transcribe everything, students' next question is, 'Do we need to code everything?' My answer usually is: *Yes* – with a few exceptions.

Some authors propose procedures like focused coding, where you only focus on a specific aspect of the data and leave out everything else. This might be fine when coding already existing documents or data that were not written or produced for the purpose of your own research. But when you collect your own data, why go through all that effort of conducting interviews or focus groups, only to analyze half of it? Seemingly unimportant parts of an interview may turn out to be very relevant when you look at them more closely. At first, it may seem no more than a polite gesture when an interviewee asks whether you want some more coffee. Examining the text more closely, it may turn out that the interviewee was trying to avoid answering your question and looking for an opportunity to digress from the topic or gain time to think of an answer. You cannot know this initially and therefore I don't think it is wise to transcribe an interview only partly or code it only selectively. If you don't know from the outset whether a passage is important or not, you can invent a code name that reflects this – such as 'not sure yet' or 'maybe important' or 'review later'. These codes mean that you will not completely forget about these passages. Anything not coded has no chance of being reviewed later on, and if these seemingly unimportant passages turn out to be helpful in understanding what is going on in your data, then this outweighs the little extra work required.

In contrast, some methodological approaches require researchers to look only at certain aspects of the data, for example in phenomenological research. Phenomenologists are only interested in how something is experienced and not in any of the interpretations the research participant may provide. They therefore may code only those parts that are relevant for a phenomenological assessment. Coding the entire data corpus, however, will allow the same or other researchers to look at other aspects of the data to complement the findings.

The 'right' length for quotations

As with other aspects of qualitative research, there are no set regulations, only rules of thumb. Consider the likelihood that you will not always work in the context of your data. You will create paper output from time to time, some more than others. This is user specific. The paper output only contains the quotation, not the surrounding context. A quotation should be long enough for you to understand its meaning without the context. If you know the data very well, quotations can probably be shorter. Three words might be enough to remind you of everything else that is going on in the data. When you work in a team and the labor of coding is divided, you are less familiar with all of the data and so quotations need to be longer. There could, for example, be a rule that quotations should be at least the length of a full sentence.

Quotation length also relates to the chosen analytic approach. Conversation analysts tend to code very short data fragments of only a few words. Therefore, the answer needs to be: It depends …

In order for you to test whether the quotations are the correct length for your first coding experience, I will explain two ways of creating an output of quotations for a specific code. The first way is:

- Open the Code Manager and select a code.
- From the Code Manager's menu select **OUTPUT / QUOTATIONS FOR SELECTED CODE(S)**.
- Select **EDITOR** as the output destination.
- Read through the quotations and decide whether you have chosen the right length.

The other way is provided via the query tool. The output only contains the text of the quotations and their references and needs fewer pages:

- Open the query tool via **ANALYSIS / QUERY TOOL**.
- Select a code from the list at the bottom left of the window. Double click on it.

- The results are shown in the pane at bottom right (Figure 2.13). Above this pane, you will see an output button in the form of a printer symbol. Click on the output button and select the option **Full Content – No Meta**. A window will open: accept the default settings.
- Next, select **Editor** as the output destination.

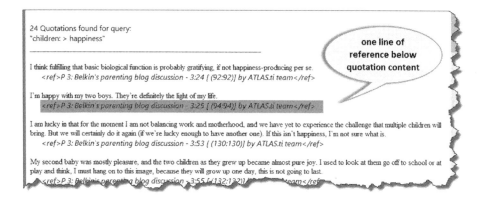

Figure 5.14   Creating output without meta information

What to do with repeated occurrences

Another question that is frequently asked is what to do when the same thing is mentioned several times in a longer paragraph. Can quotations be 'interrupted' or should the entire paragraph be coded, or every segment separately?

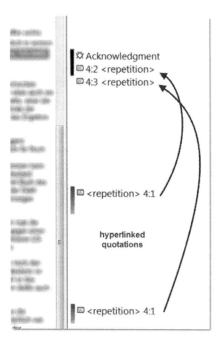

Figure 5.15   What to do with repeated occurrences

As there is no option for collecting different data segments to form one quotation, I recommend coding each instance separately. If you code the entire paragraph you cannot focus on the issue of interest, because there will be too much other information around it when retrieving the quotations later. Coding only the first occurrence and ignoring the rest is not a solution either, because this will not reflect the data adequately. If the duplications include different nuances, and thus are not mere repetitions, this is a good reason to code them. When there is no new information, you can simply code the first instance, create quotations from the repeated instances and link them to the first one via hyperlinks. This way, you do not lose anything. Everything that you do not code or mark is forgotten after a while. You are not likely to look at it ever again. An example is shown in Figure 5.15. For more information about hyperlinks and how to create them, see Chapter 7.

The 'right' number of codes

Initially, codes might be nothing more than individual named pieces of the complete puzzle. A project containing 2000 codes or more only presents the first stage of the analysis: that of breaking up the data into pieces by noticing interesting things in them. Collecting has so far only occurred very rarely. This can easily be seen by looking at the code frequencies in the Code Manager. When a project contains a large number of codes, the code frequency is usually low for most of them.

You don't need to worry if this is so in a few cases. Perhaps it is because there aren't yet enough data, or it is just one aspect of an otherwise larger elaborated category. But if most of your codes show a very low frequency then there is still some work to be done, and the development of the coding system is not yet finished. A general rule is that a developed project should show a healthy balance between the total number of codes and the frequency of each one.

After the first coding exercise you can try to evaluate yourself. Are you a person who uses more abstract terms as code labels, and thus likely to generate fewer codes containing a lot of quotations, or are you the type who works very closely at the data level creating a large number of descriptive codes, each containing only a few quotations? Or are you somewhere in between?

I have not conducted a randomized quantitative survey on coders and coding styles, but from experience and knowing that most things in this world are evenly distributed, most coders will be somewhere in the middle, using a mix of abstract and descriptive codes, while a few will be at the extremes, creating either just a few abstract codes or a lot of descriptive codes.

Let's assume you have collected lots of quotations under a common label; the next step is to look through them, as I did with the castle pieces. After reading or looking at a few quotations, you will quickly notice where the commonalities are. This is easier now as the software allows you to take a focused look at only a selection of the data. In Skills training 5.5, you will learn what to do with descriptive codes and how to move them to a more abstract level.

Developing a code list in teams

Above I have shown how I developed a preliminary code list based on the ideas of the four coders (see Table 5.2 and Figure 5.11). If you are working in a team, you can proceed likewise. The process as described below is very open. Its purpose is to develop ideas for a code list in a brainstorming fashion. The project that is set up for this purpose initially serves to generate a code list. Thus, it is small and contains only a few documents. Once the code list is established, the remaining documents are added and the 'real' coding work can begin.

In terms of project setup, proceed as follows (see Chapter 3 for details on data and project management):

- Create a Master HU file and add one or two selected documents to the Team Library. If the documents are short, select a few more.
- *Optional:* If you already have a preliminary list of codes, these can be added to the HU. See 'Importing a list of existing codes' on p. 143.
- Save the HU and then a copy bundle file that is distributed to all team members.
- Before the team members unpack the copy bundle file, ask them to create a user account and to log in under their name.
- In the process of unpacking the copy bundle file, all team members should rename the HU file by adding their name or initials.

Generating ideas for a common code list:

- All team members code the selected documents openly. If some codes have already been added to the Master HU, they can be used if fitting, and new codes can be created as necessary.
- After everyone has coded the material, they should send the HU file to the project administrator. As no documents have been added, sending a copy bundle file is not necessary.

Merging coded HUs:

- The project administrator merges the HU files. Use the merge strategy **Same PDs / Same Codes**. If none of the codes in the HUs match, then all codes will be added. Thus, the **Same PDs / Same Codes** strategy also works when everyone adds new codes.

Sorting and structuring the code list:

- Open the Code Manager and select the 'Details' view (**View / Details**). In the author column, you can see who has created which code.
- Look for all codes that refer to the same issue but have a different name. Merge these codes.
- Look for codes that are similar and might fit together under a more abstract category name. These codes also can be merged. This is how to proceed: merge the codes that have a similar meaning and then rename the merged code, giving it a more conceptual name (see Skills training 5.5).

- Try to identify very broad codes that may already be at the category level. They can be recognized by a high frequency. These need to be broken down into smaller subcodes (see Skills training 5.4).

It is best to do this while sitting together with all team members and discussing what they meant with a particular code. As all codes have an author stamp, it can easily be seen who created which code. It is possible that two coders may have chosen the same or similar labels, but they mean different things. In that case it is necessary to discuss this and to look at the data. While going through the list of codes and discussing them, it is a good idea to write down a definition for each code. Once you have agreed on a list of codes, it is very likely that you will have to recode the documents that you used for this brainstorming exercise. Due to renaming and merging codes, the coded documents probably look a mess. You can go through and adjust the quotations, but it may altogether be easier to remove the documents from the Master HU. Then add all documents that should be coded in the next step, save the HU, create a copy bundle file and distribute it to all team members.

One possible next step is to distribute the copy bundle file and to ask each coder to code different documents. Another option is to have each document coded by two persons. In the latter case, the coding needs to be cleaned up after each merge process. It is thus much more time intensive (see the section on intercoder-reliability above). There are no general recommendations when to do what, as it depends on the type of data you are analyzing, your overall methodological approach, the experience of coders, the requirements of journals you intend to publish in, and last but not least your budget.

Building an efficient code system

In Figure 5.16 we can see how the charting of the landscape is taking shape. Flowers of the same kind are identified along with different types of animals, different aspects of the forest, the benches, and various elements of the houses, the people and the various destinations. This is basically the same as I did with the codes of the four coders. I identified the various positive and negative effects of having a child, different reasons for having or not having children, and a number of issues related to parenting. As the codes were only based on a short exercise and saturation of themes was not reached, a number of issues remained unsorted. As mentioned above, when working on your own projects, you need to continue coding until you have the feeling that no new themes emerge. If you start out with a list of predefined codes, just adding to it issues that arise from the data, the point of first saturation might be reached earlier.

You already know the ATLAS.ti tools and functions that you can use to structure your coding system – but as a novice it may not be obvious how to use them. Therefore, I have organized this skills training day where I will show you:

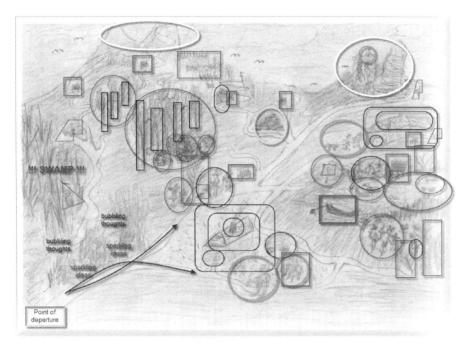

Figure 5.16 Structured landscape

- how to create subcategories from a larger group of quotations that you have collected;
- how to build a main category from small pieces of data that are still coded on a descriptive level.

I have prepared two special projects in the form of a copy bundle file that you can download from the companion website as practice material. The project 'Coding exercise I: building subcategories' contains some codes that code a lot of quotations and need more finely grained development. The project 'Coding exercise II: building categories' contains lots of descriptive codes that are still very close to the data. They demand more conceptualization.

Skills training 5.4: developing subcategories

The goal in developing subcategories is to achieve a good description of heterogeneity and variance in the data material. In principle, two approaches are possible: subcategories can be developed based on previous knowledge (i.e. known aspects from the theoretical literature), or founded empirically on the basis of the data material. In the following I will explain the empirically based approach. For those who are familiar with the writing of Bazeley and Richards (2007), this is what they refer to as 'code-on to finer categories':

- Unbundle the file for Coding Exercise I (see Chapter 3 for more details on how to handle copy bundle files).
- Open the Code Manager and look at the list of codes. All of the codes collect lots of quotations and there are too many things lumped into one code. Thus, we need to subdivide them. I will explain the procedure based on the code 'children are hard work but…'. If you want to practice more, you can repeat the exercise by selecting any of the other codes in the list.

The codes in this project are equivalent to the castle pieces of the jigsaw puzzle. They contain a loose collection of data segments relating to the 'but factor' of having children, the effects of parenting, the variety of definitions for happiness, and so on. No attempt has yet been made to separate these various aspects. When you begin to code, you may not know which aspects are salient and provide good reasons for forming a group of their own, so it is easier to collect the various aspects under a main theme first instead of wondering where a data segment might belong and how to name it. You will see when doing the exercise that it is much easier to develop suitable subcodes when reading through 20 or 30 examples of similar quotations.

- Double click on the code 'children are hard work but…' and read through the quotations. If you prefer reading the quotations in an editor, select the code and then the option OUTPUT / QUOTATIONS FOR SELECTED CODE(S). Your task is to develop subcategories based on the major theme.

The NCT model comes into play here again:

- After reading through a few quotations, you are likely to notice quotations that refer to the same aspect and others that describe another facet of the main theme. When you are at this point, start collecting these aspects. One option is to write them down on a piece of paper and run a tally. Figure 5.17 shows my notes on the category 'hard work but…'. Given sufficient screen space, another option is to type your ideas into a memo and use this memo later on to create the list of subcodes. How this works is explained below in the section 'Importing a list of existing codes'.

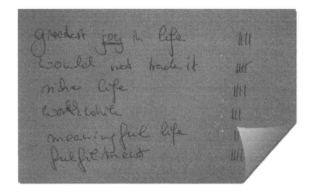

Figure 5.17   Noticing and collecting in the process of developing subcategories

Looking at the extracted terms helps to conceptualize them further. 'Greatest joy in life' might be subsumed under 'richer life'. 'Would not trade it for anything', 'worthwhile and rewarding' could be summarized under 'worthwhile trade-off'; 'life is meaningful, I feel fulfilled' can be integrated into 'fulfilment', and so on. The aim is to look at the bandwidths of issues mentioned and to come up with a label that best describes the most similar ones.

After you have decided which subcategories you want to use, you need to enter them into ATLAS.ti and then recode the data. In order for the subcodes to show up under the main code, you need to use a prefix. To stop the code word getting too long, I suggest using 'hard work but':

Hard work but_fulfilment
Hard work but_richer life
Hard work but_worthwhile trade-off
Hard work but_positive emotions

You can manually create these subcodes in the Code Manager, or you can use an option in the Memo Manager to add a list of codes. I want to show you the latter option as it is also useful to know when working with an already known list of codes:

Importing a list of existing codes

- Open the Memo Manager. You know by now how to do so.
- Create a new memo by clicking on the button for creating a new item.
- You are prompted to enter a title. As the title you could enter 'code list'.
- Type the list of subcodes into this memo, one code per line. To speed up the process, you can copy the prefix and paste it a few times. Then add the subcode name.
- Save the memo by clicking on the button with the check-mark and close it.
- Highlight the newly created memo 'code list' and select from the menu MISCELLANEOUS / CREATE CODES FROM SELECTED MEMO. A window will pop up telling you that x number of codes have been imported.

You can reuse the code list memo when developing other subcategories. This memo is not meant to document your analytic steps in any way. You do this in your research diary. Consider the code list memo as a little helper that makes your life a bit easier.

- Go back to the Code Manager and see whether you can find the new codes in the list. If you followed the above example, the subcodes do not yet appear directly below the main category code. This means that we need to change the name of the main category code to HARD WORK BUT.... Then click on F5 to re-sort the list.
- Now is a good time to color the codes of this newly developed category. Highlight the main category code and all subcodes, click on the color wheel in the toolbar, select a color and click on **OK**.

All quotations are still contained in the main category code. The next step is to distribute them to the subcodes (Figure 5.18).

- Double click on the main category code HARD WORK BUT… and select the first quotation.
- Read it and decide into which subcategory you want to move it. Select the appropriate subcode in the Code Manager and drag it onto the main code in the margin area, thus replacing it.

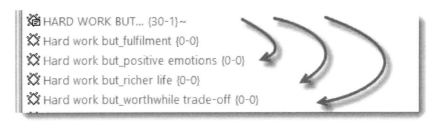

Figure 5.18   Main category code with subcodes

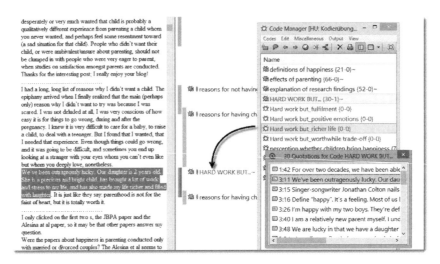

Figure 5.19   Replacing the main category code with the subcode

There is no need to leave the main category code attached to the segment – it just clutters up the margin. It is easy to collect the quotations into one main category via a code family later. For now the aim is to empty the main category code and fill the subcategories with content (Figures 5.19 and 5.20). You may need to adjust the length of some quotations or create new ones. If you come across a quotation that you find difficult to sort into any of the existing subcategories, leave it in the main category code.

The important thing is that you do not force your data into a subcategory just because it exists. Regard the developed subcategories as preliminary; they

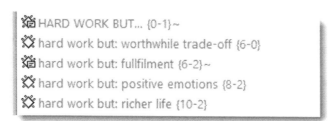

Figure 5.20 Subcategories filled with content

may change. Over time you may think of better names, or even decide that a subcategory is not suitable after all and you need to integrate it somewhere else. You have only coded very few documents up to this point and this is most likely not the final version of your code list. But you can already work with it and when coding more documents you can sort data segments right away into the developed subcategories. It is not very efficient to loosely code all of your data material now and have to go through the above process of developing subcategories later. It is best to begin quite early with this. As mentioned, a good time to do this is the first saturation point when you mainly apply existing codes via drag and drop from the Code Manager.

Skills training 5.5: building categories from the bottom up

- Unbundle the file for Coding Exercise II (see Chapter 3 for more details on how to handle copy bundle files).

This project contains 46 codes related to positive and negative effects of being a parent. These code labels are partly directly taken from the words the respondents used and thus are very close to the data. The length of the quotations was extended in order to include a bit more contextual information. For this exercise, I want you to take a closer look at the 46 codes. The aim is to learn how to move the analysis from a descriptive to a conceptual level.

Remember the puzzle analogy: most of the codes just reflect single pieces of the jigsaw. The frequency of each code word is very low. If we leave a code list like that without aggregating similar codes, there is a danger of ending up in the code swamp (Figure 5.21).

What often happens at this stage is that analysts use code families to collect their descriptive codes without further conceptualizing (i.e. summarizing and renaming) them. This is not a good idea. It leads to endlessly long code lists that are of no use in querying the data in the next phase of the analysis; it creates problems when visualizing your findings with the help of the Network View Manager; and it makes it impossible to explain your coding scheme to a third person. Below I will make use of code families as little helpers, so I can better focus on specific aspects. But remember what the F in Family stands for: not for Category ☺; it stands for Filter.

Figure 5.21   Avoiding the code swamp I

Applying the NCT process once again

The codes describing the various effects of parenting may look like real codes at first glance but they are not yet proper codes in a methodological sense. They just represent things I noticed in the data, and in order not to lose them I gave them a name. Now I can use the software to retrieve the things I noticed about the reported effects of parenting and to think some more about them. The aim is to find some commonalities within this conglomeration of terms and to add some order to it. This is what I suggest you do:

- Open the Code Manager.
- If you look through the list of codes, you will quickly notice that there are positive and negative effects of parenting. Therefore I suggest to collect first all of the positive effects into a code family that you can call 'positive effects'. Select a few code words in the list by holding down the CTRL key (e.g. codes like a bit wiser, appreciating my own parents more, become a better person, etc.). Then drag these codes onto the side panel and enter the family name. Continue to go through the list and drag and drop single or multiple selected codes into this family.
- Click on the code family 'positive effects'. According to my evaluation of what is positive and negative, the full list is now reduced to 22 codes (Figure 5.22).
- Look through this reduced list of codes. Do you notice any codes that basically refer to the same issue? I suggest that there are a number of codes that refer to personal growth. Personal growth already exists as code. Therefore, we can merge those codes that are similar into this code.

Figure 5.22   Pre-sorting the list of codes

- Right click on the code family 'positive effects' and select the option **Set Global Filter**. You will see that the icon for the code family changes to a filter, the name turns red and the main pane of the Code Manager shows up in a pale yellow color (Figure 5.23). If we now begin the merge process, we only see the reduced list of 22 codes.

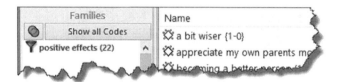

Figure 5.23   Global filter setting

- Right click on the code 'personal growth' and select **Merge Codes**. From the list that pops up select all codes that relate to personal growth. This reduces the list to 14 codes. The personal growth code now contains 8 quotations.
- Look at the remaining codes. Other codes you can merge are those related to *fulfillment*, *richer life*, *positive emotions* and *improved relationships* (parental and marital). If the more conceptual name does not yet exist, rename one of the codes with the conceptual term and then begin the merge process. This reduces the filtered list to five codes.
- As these code labels would still appear all over the place in the alphabetical code list, we need to add a prefix to all of these labels, so that they are united under a

common heading. I suggest using the prefix 'effects pos' and for the second list 'effects neg', so that the effects of parenting codes are sorted underneath each other later in the complete list of codes.

- The last thing that is missing is the main category label. As we built the category from the bottom up, developing subcodes first, it does not yet exist. Create a new code with the name EFFECTS POS. Highlight all codes and give them a color.
- Now take out the global filter: right click on the code family, select **REMOVE GLOBAL FILTER**. Click on **SHOW ALL CODES**. *Voilà*, there is your new category with subcodes (Figure 5.24).

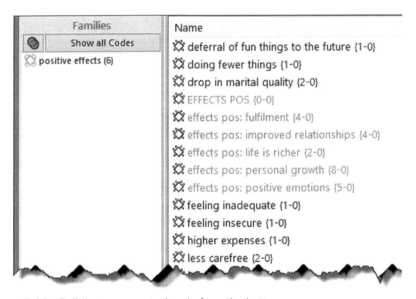

Figure 5.24   Building a conceptual code from the bottom up

When merging codes, users often express their worries that they are losing something while doing it. Yes, it is true that the original descriptive code labels disappear. However, this does not mean that you are losing something. The opposite is true: you gain more clarity and a code list that becomes more manageable. If you want to read the original data that previously were summarized by the descriptive label, simply double click on the conceptual codes and ATLAS.ti will lead you directly to the original data. Nothing is lost. If you want to hold on to the collection of individual data pieces instead, you are likely to end up in the code swamp. The symptoms are a very long code list (over 400 codes or more) and very low frequencies for most codes. If you are still worried, write down the terms of the descriptive label codes in the comment field of the merged code.

In the example used here, the original list of 46 has now been reduced to 31. Thus, there are still all the negative effects that need to be sorted and structured as well.

- Repeat the above process for negative effects of parenting starting by collecting all codes that represent negative effects in a code family. This is easy now as these are all black codes that are not yet prefixed.
- Next, look for codes that can be subsumed under a more conceptual label and merge them. A possible result could be the following list:

EFFECTS NEG
effects neg: doing fewer things
effects neg: less fun
effects neg: loss of freedom
effects neg: more worries
effects neg: on career
effects neg: on emotional issues
effects neg: on financial issues
effects neg: on relationships
effects neg: on self

When you work with the codes and the data, you will notice that some of the quotations do not yet have the proper length, or that a few quotations do not even fit at all into the category you are currently developing. It is a matter of working not only with the code labels, but also with the coded data at the same time. Through this process you will become more and more familiar with your data, learn more about their meanings and become more certain which codes apply to which data segment. The first reordering and re-sorting may not immediately result in the final version of your coding scheme. You may have to go through a second, third or even fourth cycle of re-sorting and ordering your codes. Analysis is an ongoing process and as long as it continues your code labels may change and their positions may shift.

Skills training 5.6: rules for hierarchical coding schemes

In Skills training 5.5, we learned what to do in order to avoid the code swamp. There is another dangerous track that leads us to the swamp if we are not careful. You may wander onto this track when one code is made up of two or more content layers (Figure 5.25). Looking at the Children & Happiness project, there are codes related to the various respondents commenting on Belkin's or the *New York Times* blog, like males, females, parents or non-parents. In their comments they have raised issues related to parenting, how they see happiness and how it relates to children, their views on the study design, etc. If I make the parent/childless code a category, then the code list would shape up like this:

childless_f_effects pos: fulfilment
childless_f_effects pos: improved relationships
childless_f_effects pos: life is richer
childless_f_effects pos: personal growth
childless_f_effects pos: positive emotions
childless_m_effects pos: fulfilment

childless_m_effects pos: improved relationships
childless_m_effects pos: life is richer
childless_m_effects pos: personal growth
childless_m_effects pos: positive emotions
Parent_f_effects pos: fulfilment
Parent_f_effects pos: improved relationships
Parent_f_effects pos: life is richer
Parent_f_effects pos: personal growth
Parent_f_effects pos: positive emotions
Parent_m_effects pos: fulfilment
Parent_m_effects pos: improved relationships
Parent_m_effects pos: life is richer
Parent_m_effects pos: personal growth
Parent_m_effects pos: positive emotions

… and a similar long list for negative effects and all other codes as well. Do you see what is happening? The codes of parent, childless, male and female are added to each code label they apply to, extending the code list unnecessarily.

What you need to pay attention to is that you do not lump all the different aspects under one code name. The different layers, here attribute codes and content codes, need to be kept apart and you need a category for each layer. In the sample project, I grouped the codes related to family characteristics under

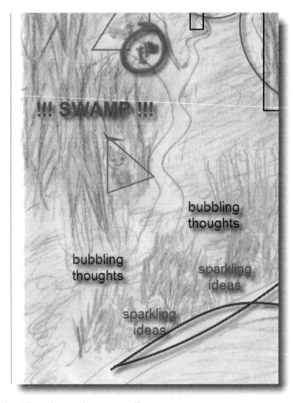

Figure 5.25   Avoiding the code swamp II

the prefix #fam, and the gender attributes under #gender. The hash sign has the effect of pushing all of these codes to the top of the list and therefore they are separated from the content codes. In addition I colored them gray to easily recognize the content codes and the attributes codes in the margin area next to the coded documents.

> #fam: have children
> #fam: don't have children
> #gender: male
> #gender: female
> Effects pos: fulfilment
> Effects pos: improved relationships
> …

Figure 5.26 shows how this looks in terms of coding in ATLAS.ti. Gender, as well as the fact of whether someone has children or not, are coded for separately. A third code indicates that this segment is a blog entry as compared to other types of data. All other aspects that occur within this blog entry are coded wherever they apply.

When you notice repetitive coding, remember the little guy you saw in Figure 5.25 standing next to the code swamp brandishing a flag. It's a warning that you're heading for the swamp. Don't continue on this route. Instead, delete the repetitions at the end of the code word labels and create a new category for the codes that indicates a different layer of content. To separate theme codes from those adding a further description like an evaluation or an attribute of some sort, I suggest marking all these kinds of codes with an asterisk (*) or a hash sign (#). This way they will appear at the top of the code list and be easy to find.

To avoid the code swamp, apply two (or more) codes to the same data segment, one code from each content layer (see also Richards, 2009; Richards and Richards, 1995; Araujo, 1995).

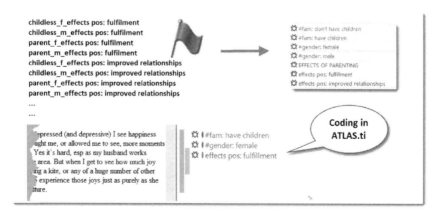

Figure 5.26 Coding for different content layers

Advantages of well-sorted and structured code lists

There are a number of advantages when you organize your code list in the way presented in the previous skills training sessions. It not only helps you to find your way around better, but also adds transparency to the research process and others can follow what you have done more easily. It also adds methodological rigor. It is when you begin to bring some order to your list that you realize what might be a good candidate for a category; it points to those codes that are in need of differentiation and it helps you to identify those codes that are not yet on the conceptual level, being too close to the data and offering no more than just a summary of a data segment (see also Fielding and Lee, 1998: 92ff.; Charmaz, 2006: Chapter 3; Saldaña, 2009).

Sorting and structuring your codes also prepares for the next level of the analysis where you begin to look for relations and patterns in the data with the ultimate aim of integrating all findings to tell a coherent story. Similar to statistical research, if you only ask questions with yes and no answers you'll end up with variables on the lowest level. This means that you cannot take the analysis much beyond the descriptive level, cross-tabulations and chi-square tests being the most sophisticated analytical procedures you can run. This is comparable to a code list that consists of a bunch of codes whose analytical level remains undetermined. An example of such a code list is shown in Figure 5.27. The total number of codes is not too bad: 168 for the entire project. Thus, the problem is not that too many codes have each been applied to only a few data segments. Rather, the list contains both: there are codes with low frequencies and codes with very high frequencies of over 150 quotations. What is missing is the development of subcategories on the one hand and the aggregation of codes under a common denominator on the other (i.e. the processes you learned about in Skills training 5.4 and 5.5).

I am allowed to criticize this code list because it is my own, developed in 1999 for my dissertation research. Learning doesn't stop even after you get your PhD! From an analytic point of view, I did develop the ideas collected in the code list further. For example, I differentiated the code 'Definition of impulse buying', which contains 157 quotations, but this is not visible in the code list. For this particular code, I used the network view function.

The study was on impulse buying and in the interview study I identified three groups of shoppers:

1. Utilitarian buyers: those who do not like to go shopping at all.
2. Compensatory buyers: those who don't mind going shopping and sometimes also shop for emotional reasons.
3. Addicted buyers: those who go shopping mostly for emotional reasons.

I asked all of them for their own personal definition of impulse buying. This is what is shown in the network views by type of consumer. On the right hand side are codes that I derived from the literature, as others before me had already studied impulse buying. In addition, the consumers' definition included

anxiety, worrying {10-0}~
appearance {50-1}~
approval (seeking), pleasing other...
assertive {19-1}~
bargain {41-1}~
beauty, order {15-1}~
being away, holiday {6-1}~
being envious, greedy {9-0}
better organized, tidy {5-1}~
boredom {39-2}~
budgeting {12-1}~
buying something for oneself {27-0}
buying something for others {41-0}
challenge {23-1}~
change of circumstances {23-1}~
change of habit {5-1}~
change of personality characteristi...
comfort {13-1}~
comorbitity {15-0}~
compensatory buyer {0-2}~
consequences {44-1}~
contributing factors {0-8}~
control, power {56-2}~
credit {70-1}~
Definition of impulse buying {157-...

Definition of planned buying {118...
dependence {7-0}~
depression /sd-statement {5-1}
depression, other mental disorder...
Diderot {1-0}~
directional {18-1}~
disillusionment {57-4}~
disregard of consequences {7-1}~
doing something for oneself {25-0...
easy going {5-1}~
education into incompetence {15-...
enjoyment, excitement, thrill {58-7...
equating love with material goods...
escape {15-1}~
experience vs having goods {127-...
extraordinary, special {13-2}~
feelings of deprivation {9-2}~
filling the empty self {31-3}~
finances {29-1}~
financial considerations {161-7}~
for the sake of buying {7-1}~
freedom, independence, getting o...
frequency {21-1}~
gambling addiction {1-0}
going shopping alone {20-3}~

going shopping with others {24-2}~
guilt {58-1}~
hiding {25-0}~
high mood {8-1}~
high point {40-1}~
hunting {8-1}~
ideal images {88-1}~
if within budget {11-1}~
impatient {4-1}~
Impulse buying {0-15}~
impulse buying episode {199-0}~
inconsist parental behavior {15-2}~
justifcation {88-0}~
kind of items typically bought on i...
learning pattern, positive feedbac...
less enjoyable, boring {13-1}~
life history {131-2}~
low feeling, bad mood {54-1}~
managing {23-0}~
media {18-1}~
mood {0-10}~
mood & choice {4-0}~
more energetic {10-1}~
more honesty {6-1}~
naughty, daring {9-1}~

need {94-1}~
newness {8-4}~
no guilt {19-0}~
no sympathy {5-0}~
not deserving of money {12-0}~
not needed, could do without, lux...
not relying on shopping {10-0}~
not within budget {5-1}~
opportunity {19-1}~
outside influence, other directed {...
over-controlling/overprotective in...
overcoming the addiction {70-0}~
parents {89-1}~
partner {8-2}~
personality {37-0}~
physical/health {15-1}~
planned buying {0-6}~
planned buying episodes {101-0}~
planned impulse buys {7-0}~
planned treats {5-0}~
plentitude {17-1}~
price/bargain not important {5-0}~
psychological aspects {0-7}~
quality {28-0}~
reason for addictive buying {61-0}~

Figure 5.27 A fully developed code list should *not* look like this one

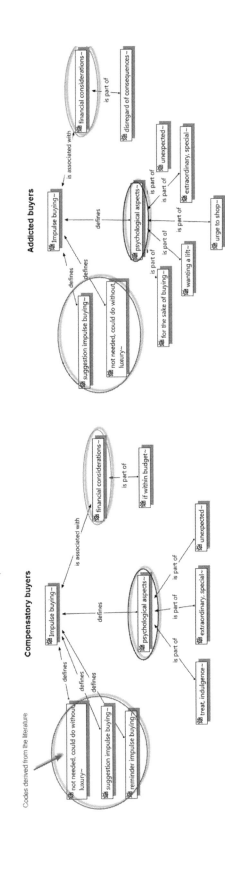

Figure 5.28 Differentiation of the code 'Definition of impulse buying' for two buyer groups

psychological aspects and financial considerations. For illustrative purposes, I show only two of the network views here. You will see that not all of the codes are relevant to each subgroup. The code 'reminder impulse buying' derived from the literature did not apply to addicted shoppers. For them the psychological aspects took up a major part of their definitions. Financial considerations were mentioned along the lines of 'well, it's on the credit card', and thus were more or less disregarded. In the network views, the analytic work that I have done becomes visible. However, for other codes it is hidden in the written-up results (Friese, 2000).

Today I would differentiate the code 'Definition of impulse buying' into three subcategories, further divided into the various facets (Figure 5.28). I would probably also work on the code labels a bit more, possibly merging codes like 'something extraordinary' and 'something unexpected'. But for this I would need to look at the data material again. Based on what I see today in the network views, I suggest the following structure:

D_DEFINITION IMPULSE BUYING
Def imp_f_disregard of consequences
Def imp_f_not within budget
Def imp_f_within budget
Def imp_psy_for the sake of buying
Def imp_psy_s.th. extraordinary
Def imp_psy_treat
Def imp_psy_unexpected
Def imp_psy_urge to shop
Def imp_psy_wanting a lift
Def imp_th_non needed_luxury
Def imp_th_reminder impulse buying
Def imp_th_suggestion impulse buying

Such a code list adds more transparency to the research and is easy to explain to another person. After more than 10 years since doing this research, it would take some time to go through the data again in order to retrace my own steps. Had I taken it a bit further and developed the codes into proper categories and subcategories at the time, it would have been much easier for me now, or you as the reader, or another third person, to see what was in the data. It would have helped me to follow my own analytic steps and remind myself about how I derived my results.

This is one advantage and, from a methodological point of view, an important one. What I have done above with the code list from my dissertation research is of course too late and should not be done just for the sake of transparency at the end of your research project. As I have advised, begin sorting and structuring quite early, after the first saturation point when coding your data. Then, during second-stage coding, apply the structured code list to the rest or to the newly incoming data. This allows you to confirm or reject the developed categories and subcategories and it suggests possible missing data and aspects to look for.

Suppose you analyze a total of 20 documents. After coding five documents, you begin to add more structure to your coding system. Then you continue to code. If you need to change it a lot, then you know that the coding system needs to be developed further. If you only need to make a few modifications, that is if you don't find many new things of interest or only a few new subcategories, then this is reassurance that your coding system fits the data well and justification for having developed a valid code system. An obvious precondition is that you need to stay alert to new, as yet unlabeled phenomena in the data and that you do not force the developed coding system onto the data.

> NOTE: After knowing how to structure and organize codes in ATLAS.ti in a hierarchical manner, I have observed that users begin to name their codes in this way quite early in the coding process. This is similar to sorting codes into trees and their branches after 5 minutes of coding in other programs that offer a hierarchical structure as built-in function of the software. The consequence often is that the category codes are not correct yet as they are decided upon too early in the process. After a while, it becomes difficult to code as nothing really seems to fit. My recommendation is to start coding a few documents or data files openly, just noticing and collecting. Don't yet think about sorting and structuring. Even if you have a deductive framework, 'listen' to your data first, and then think about where, how and whether the previously defined categories and codes fit. After coding a few documents, you will notice that you apply the codes that you already have in your list. Only few or no new codes are added and you mainly code via drag and drop from the Code Manager. You have reached a first point of saturation. Now begin to review your codes (and the coded segments) and add structure to your code list, i.e. by adding prefixes, renaming codes using more conceptual and abstract terms, merging descriptive labels and adding title codes for your categories.

Summary: moving on

We are now midway through the journey. The first days (I hope) have been very exciting for you as you discovered lots of interesting things. After the initial excitement, some duller days may follow as you continue applying your codes, plowing through the data material. When using manual methods, analysts might not have reviewed all of their material again after developing new codes, applying them consistently to all data. Now that we use software, you are more likely to do this. This allows us, for example, to pick out some numbers and see how frequently a code is applied across different data files. This is only useful if you know that all the codes have been applied to all the data, and it also means that coding at certain stages of the analysis might become a bit tedious – but there is a reward. Well-coded data are likely to reveal interesting insights when querying them. The journey is varied and there is still much to enjoy and to discover if you keep going.

Equipped with these new skills, you will be sent on your way again to continue exploring the data landscape. In Chapter 6, you will work with a fully coded project that allows you to find answers to the research questions listed below. In this context, I will show you how to prepare analytic memos that can later be used as building blocks for a written report.

List of research questions to be explored in Chapter 6

RQ1: Do blog respondents who have children define happiness differently from those without children? If so, how do they define it?

RQ2: What is the difference in attitudes toward the relationship between happiness and children between those commenting on the blogs who have children and those who do not have children?

RQ3: Compare the comments written on Belkin's blog to those written on the *New York Times* blog regarding the following issues: effects of parenting (positive and negative), definition of happiness, reasons for having children, reasons for not having children, sources of happiness.

RQ4: Compare the statements regarding sources of happiness of the two blog discussions (P3 and 5) to the article that provides summaries of research findings (P10).

RQ5: Compare the survey answers of male and female respondents with regard to the reasons they provide for having or for not having children.

RQ6: Is there a difference between male and female survey respondents WITH CHILDREN regarding their perception of parenting (positive or negative)?

RQ7: What is the attitude toward the relationship between children and happiness of those responding to the blogs and who question the study design?

RQ8: Explore the perception of various groups of blog writers with regard to how they view the relationship between happiness and children. Does it make a difference if they mention only positive or only negative or both positive and negative effects of parenting?

RQ9: Do the two groups of respondents (those who only mention negative effects of parenting and those who only mention positive effects of parenting) also differ with regard to other issues that have been raised in the blogs?

▓▓▓▓▓▓▓▓▓▓▓▓▓▓▓▓▓▓▓▓▓▓ **REVIEW QUESTIONS** ▓▓▓▓▓▓▓▓▓▓▓▓▓▓▓▓▓▓▓▓▓▓

1   Explain the puzzle analogy and how it relates to qualitative data analysis.
2   What are the last preparatory steps before you embark on the journey of coding? In other words, how do your prepare your project and how do you organize your project data?
3   What is the difference between a memo and a comment in ATLAS.ti? When would you write something into a comment field? For what purposes do you create a memo? Why is it important to know this difference?
4   How do you generate ideas for codes?
5   Which function do you need to use to import an already existing list of codes?
6   What makes a good code label?
7   Are there any rules regarding the length of a coded segment?
8   What options do you have to structure the list of codes in the ATLAS.ti Code Manager?

(Continued)

(Continued)

9   What are code families useful for?

10   How would you go about developing categories?

11   How would you go about developing subcategories?

12   How can the code swamp be avoided? What are common pitfalls?

13   After having gained some personal experience with coding, what type of coder are you? Do you start fairly broad or close to the data, or do you mix both styles?

14   How do you develop a code list for team work?

Test your understanding of computer-assisted NCT analysis

1   Explain the NCT model and how it can guide the process of developing a code system.

2   Collecting is an important aspect of the NCT model. What role does collecting play in the process of developing a code system and why is it important?

3   After reading this chapter and putting it into practice, can you describe how to apply the process of noticing, collecting and thinking when working on your own data set?

4   How is solving a jigsaw puzzle similar to qualitative data analysis?

5   How is qualitative data analysis different from solving a jigsaw puzzle?

6   What is a WASGIJ puzzle and what can be learned from it regarding qualitative data analysis?

7   What are the advantages of a well-sorted and structured code list?

GLOSSARY OF TERMS

Categories and subcategories: The aim of developing a coding system is to organize the data into main categories and subcategories. Main categories at the end of coding are likely to contain no data. They provide a common label for the subcategories united underneath. Depending on your way of coding, you may at first collect data segments within main category codes. This is likely when using a deductive framework. Then subcategories are built based on the items within this main category container by reviewing them, looking for items that are similar and uniting them under a common subcategory label until all items from the main container have found a place in one of the subcontainers.

When beginning with descriptive-level codes, main category codes are developed via the process of conceptualizing, comparing and contrasting data segments and descriptive code labels, looking for things that are similar and developing new code labels that allow for these segments to be collected under a common name. During this process it is likely that main categories and subcategories are developed at the same time.

Categories may contain more than one level of subcategories, if the main aspect can be subdivided further within the same meaning context. Subcategories should, however, not be built up from different types of aspects like reflecting content, an evaluation or a time. A category that contains three or more levels of subcategories should be closely reviewed to check whether in reality it contains different content layers that may be better coded in different categories.

Code definitions: A code definition describes the meaning of a code and how it has been or should be applied to the data. It can contain a coding rule and an example of a typical data segment coded with this code.

Writing code definitions helps to improve the methodological rigor of a study. It forces the researcher to think about the meaning of a code in comparison to other codes. It may turn out that the code system contains codes with different labels but more or less the same meaning. These can then be merged under one common label, which is then also easier to define. Writing definitions also helps to develop codes that are clearly distinct from each other so that they can be applied unambiguously.

Codes as methodological device: You turn codes into methodological devices by adding an appropriate label. Here the process of collecting becomes very important. You need to compare and contrast data segments and think of suitable names for data segments that are similar. Thinking of a common name under which similar data segments can be collected is likely to enable the researcher to move away from the descriptive to a conceptual – and over time to a theoretical – level. During this process the researcher begins to develop categories and subcategories.

Codes as technical device: Technically speaking, a code is a device that can be attached to a data segment as a label. At the beginning of an analysis, this is a useful first step in gaining an understanding of the data. With progressive analysis, however, codes need to be turned into a methodological device. For this, a human interpreter is needed. Software cannot distinguish between different meanings and levels of codes. It can handle 50 as well as 5000 codes without telling you whether they make sense or not. There is no computer function that can bring order and logic to your collection of codes.

Coding system: A well-developed coding system describes the data material in all its facets. It shows the main aspects in the data in the form of categories and the variations within a main category in the form of subcategories. The coding system can reflect different types of main aspects depending on the research questions and the aim of the study. These can be the pure content of the data, the layout, the language used, aspects of time, different speakers or actors, evaluations, level of importance, degree of expression, etc.

As a rough guide, computer-assisted coding systems contain on average about 100–250 codes and 12–25 main categories.

Collecting: The first codes that are created may just be descriptive labels. These need to be conceptualized with further coding. The aim is to collect similar data segments under a common code label and not to give each data segment a name.

Conceptualizing: This refers to the process of (1) moving from descriptive-level codes to conceptual-level codes, and (2) developing subcategory codes based on data segments collected within a too broad abstract code. Conceptual-level codes unite data segments with similar content; they fulfill the criteria of being a properly sized container where all those things are collected that have something in common and that are in some ways different from others.

Document families: Document families in ATLAS.ti can be thought of as variables. Technically they are a group of documents. You can for instance group all female and male respondents, all teachers, all postmen, all engineers, all moms, all dads, all singles and all married, unmarried or divorced respondents. You can group all documents by a

(Continued)

(Continued)

certain month, year, author or source; all documents from company X into a family called Company X; all documents from companies in industry sector X to a family called Sector X; and so on. Families can be created at any time during the analytic process, then modified, renamed or deleted. Their purpose is to serve as a filter. Thus, you can restrict a search to a particular group of documents. This applies to text searches as well as code retrievals. Using the query tool, you can restrict searches by clicking on the scope button and selecting a primary document family as filter. Document families can also be filtered via the main menu option DOCUMENTS/FILTER → FAMILIES, and you can access them via the side panel in the Primary Document Manager.

Method of computer-assisted NCT analysis: The recurrent components of the methods are noticing things, collecting things and thinking about things. They occur during the process of initial first-stage coding, are repeated when structuring the code list into higher and lower order categories, and play a role again in second-stage coding and also during the further analytic process. Then noticing, collecting and thinking shifts to collecting ideas, interpretations and gaining insights. The NCT process of analysis applies generally when analyzing data with CAQDAS and can be embedded within other methodological approaches. For a detailed description of the method, see Chapter 1.

Noticing: Noticing refers to the process of reading or looking through your data (like an explorer walking through an unknown landscape) with the aim of describing the territory in as much detail as possible. The explorer takes out his or her notebook and starts writing down notes or drawing sketches. The qualitative researcher as explorer begins to mark and label segments, creates quotations, adds first codes, writes comments and memos.

Primary document comment: You can write a comment for each primary document. The recommendation is to write meta information about a document into the comment field. For interview transcripts these might be the interview protocols or interview post-scripts. Information like age, gender, etc., is managed in primary document families, not the comment field. For other document types, you can use the comment field to specify the source of the document, the context of obtaining the information, a description of who published it, the target audience, and so on.

Variables: ATLAS.ti does not offer a spreadsheet where you enter variables like age, gender, profession, location, etc. However, you can use primary document families to represent dichotomous values like male, female, single, married, being a parent or non-parent. By adding a special syntax (::), these can be turned into nominal variables like gender::male and gender::female.

Further reading

Auerback, Carl and Silverstein, Louise B. (2003). *Qualitative Data: An introduction to coding and analysis.* New York: New York University Press.

Araujo, Luis (1995). Designing and refining hierarchical coding frames, in Udo Kelle (ed.), *Computer-Aided Qualitative Data Analysis.* London: Sage. Chapter 7.

Breuer, Franz (2009). *Reflexive Grounded Theory: Ein Einführung in die Forschungspraxis.* Wiesbaden: VS Verlag.

Charmaz, Kathy (2006). *Constructing Grounded Theory: A Practical Guide Through Qualitative Analysis*. London: Sage.

Dey, Ian (1993). *Qualitative Data Analysis: A User-friendly Guide for Social Scientists*. London: Routledge.

Evers, Jeanine C. (2011). From the past into the future. how technological developments change our ways of data collection, transcription and analysis. *Forum Qualitative Sozialforschung/Forum: Qualitative Social Research*, 12(1), Art. 38, http://nbn-resolving.de/urn:nbn:de:0114-fqs1101381.

Gibbs, Graham (2007). *Analysing Qualitative Data (Qualitative Research Kit)*. London: Sage.

Hansen, Brett (2014). Grounding ethnographic content analysis, etic as well as emic strategies; a study of context for instructional designers, in Friese, Susanne and Ringmayr, Thomas (eds.), *ATLAS.ti User Conference 2013: Fostering Dialog on Qualitative Methods*. University Press, Technical University Berlin. http://nbn-resolving.de/urn:nbn:de:kobv:83-opus4-44183.

Kelle, Udo (2004). Computer-assisted qualitative data analysis, in C. Seale et al. (eds), *Qualitative Research Practice*. London: Sage. pp. 473–89.

Kelle, Udo and Kluge, Susann (2010). Vom Einzelfall zum Typus: Fallvergleich und Fallkontrastierung in der qualitativen Sozialforschung. Wiesbaden: VS Verlag.

Kluge, Susann (2000, January). Empirically grounded construction of types and typologies in qualitative social research [20 paragraphs]. *Forum Qualitative Sozialforschung/Forum: Qualitative Social Research*, 1(1), www.qualitative-research.net/fqs-texte/1-00/1-00kluge-e.htm.

Kolocek, Michael (2014). The Human Right to Housing: Using ATLAS.ti to combine qualitative and quantitative to analyse global discourses, in Friese, Susanne and Ringmayr, Thomas (eds.), *ATLAS.ti User Conference 2013: Fostering Dialog on Qualitative Methods*. University Press, Technical University Berlin. http://nbn-resolving.de/urn:nbn:de:kobv:83-opus4-44166.

Komalsingh Rambaree (2014). Three Methods of Qualitative Data Analysis Using ATLAS.ti: 'A posse ad esse', in Friese, Susanne and Ringmayr, Thomas (eds.), *ATLAS.ti User Conference 2013: Fostering Dialog on Qualitative Methods*. University Press, Technical University Berlin. http://nbn-resolving. de/urn:nbn:de:kobv:83-opus4-44270.

Lewins, Ann and Silver, Christine (2007). *Using Software in Qualitative Research: A Step-by-step Guide*. London: Sage. Chapter 7.

Miles, Matthew B. and Huberman, Michael (1994). *Qualitative Data Analysis*, 2nd edn. Thousand Oaks, CA: Sage.

Morse, Janice M. (1994). Emerging from the data: the cognitive process of analysis in qualitative inquiry, in Janice M. Morse (ed.), *Critical Issues in Qualitative Research Methods*. Thousand Oaks, CA: Sage. pp. 22–43.

Richards, Lyn (2009). *Handling Qualitative Data: A practical guide*, 2nd edn. London: Sage.

Richards, Tom and Richards, Lyn (1995). Using hierarchical categories in qualitative data analysis, in Udo Kelle (ed.), *Computer-Aided Qualitative Data Analysis*. London: Sage.

Saldaña, Jonny (2009). *The Coding Manual for Qualitative Researchers*. London: Sage.

Seidel, John V., (1998) Qualitative Data Analysis, http://www.qualisresearch. com/qda_paper.htm (originally published as Qualitative Data Analysis, in *The Ethnograph v5.0: A User's Guide*, Appendix E, 1998, Colorado Springs, Colorado: Qualis Research).

Seidel, John and Kelle, Udo (1995). Different functions of coding in the analysis of textual data, in Udo Kelle (ed.), *Computer-Aided Qualitative Data Analysis*. London: Sage. Chapter 4.

Woolf, Nick (2014). Analytic strategies and analytic tactics, in Friese, Susanne and Ringmayr, Thomas (eds.), *ATLAS.ti User Conference 2013: Fostering Dialog on Qualitative Methods*. University Press, Technical University Berlin. http://nbn-resolving.de/urn:nbn:de:kobv:83-opus4-44159.

SIX

Further steps in the data analysis process

In this chapter you will learn how to query your data and how to write up the analysis, in order to find answers to your research questions. I have decided to put both aspects in this chapter because, when doing qualitative data analysis, they belong together. You are not just writing notes or simply querying your data. The two need to go together so you can move forward with the analysis. A lot of the analysis happens as you write, not by clicking on some buttons and outputting some results. You need to look at what the software retrieves, read through it and write it up in your own words in order to gain an understanding of what is happening in the data. Most of the time insights need to be worked at and are not revealed to you immediately by looking at the results. Simply seeing that there are, say, 10 quotations is not enough; numbers are sometimes useful, they hint that there might be something interesting there, but the important step is to take a closer look and to see what's behind them.

As you can see in Figure 6.1, I included lots of benches in the data landscape that we are exploring. The benches signal points of reflection on our journey as

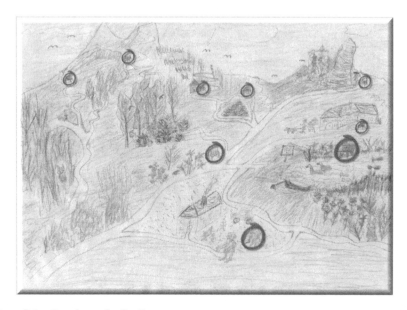

Figure 6.1 Benches of reflection

an important part of data analysis. Reflection is important throughout the entire research process. Before even beginning a project, researchers should reflect on their personal position on the issue that they plan to examine.

Skills trainings

Skills training 6.1: creating research question memos

Skills training 6.2: getting to know the query tool

Skills training 6.3: getting to know the Codes Co-Occurrence Table

Skills training 6.4: getting to know the Codes-Primary Documents Table

Skills training 6.5: code queries in combination with document attributes (working with PD families and super families)

Skills training 6.6: saving a query for later reference (or working with supercodes)

Skills training 6.7: climbing the hills and clicking on more complex queries

---

Writing up analysis

ATLAS.ti's 'benches for reflection' in the data landscape are its comment fields and the memos. We have already looked at three of the comment fields: those for primary documents (see Chapter 5) and those for quotations and for codes (see Chapter 4). As a reminder, it was explained that the P-Docs comment field is useful for adding meta information to a document like an interview protocol, which contains reflective notes on the interview situation and its circumstances. Quotation comments are useful for writing notes on a particular data segment. And code comments were described as being very useful in clarifying what is meant by a particular code. The code comment field is a place for writing down a code definition or a coding rule, forcing you to reflect more closely on its meaning. In addition to this, ATLAS.ti offers memos as a place for writing.

In 1998, Fielding and Lee reported that CAQDAS users having difficulties with the idea of writing memos within the software and after coding abandoned the package they were using and completed the analysis manually. Now, 15 years later, this still appears to be an issue. Because writing memos is an essential step in qualitative data analysis, as pointed out by the authors quoted below, I would like to make some suggestions on how to utilize memos within ATLAS.ti and the kind of advantages they offer, as compared to writing notes on a piece of paper or in a word processor. The following quotes allude to the fact that memos are different from comments or short scribbled notes in the margin:

> Memos and diagrams are more than just repositories of thoughts. They are working and living documents. When an analyst sits down to write a memo or do a diagram, a certain degree of analysis occurs. The very act of writing memos and doing diagrams forces the analyst to think about the data. And it is in thinking that analysis occurs. (Corbin and Strauss, 2008: 118)

Writing is thinking. It is natural to believe that you need to be clear in your mind what you are trying to express first before you can write it down. However, most of the time, the opposite is true. You may think you have a clear idea, but it is only when you write it down that you can be certain that you do (or sadly, sometimes, that you do not). (Gibbs, 2005)

Memos thus represent analytic work in progress and you can use some of the writing later as building blocks for your research report. I am certain that most ATLAS.ti users I have met over the years do write 'memos' somewhere, but seldom have I seen it done directly in ATLAS.ti. I don't think that this is a fault of the software design. It is more a matter of the software not 'telling' the user how the function works. It also involves some methodological awareness: knowing what memo writing is all about and that it is indeed an important part of the analysis. It is probably not by accident that Juliet Corbin includes a lot about memo writing in the third edition of *Basics of Qualitative Research*; she wants to show readers how it can be done. In a talk at the CAQD 2008 Conference about the book, she linked the poor quality of many of today's qualitative research projects to a failure to use memos. Along the same lines, Birks (2008) devotes an entire journal article to memo writing, criticizing the limited exploration of its value in most qualitative methodologies.

As this is a book on software usage, I am not going to give a definitive class on how to actually write memos. If you need some input see, for example, the third edition of *Basics of Qualitative Research* by Corbin and Strauss (2008), Wolcott (2009) or Charmaz (2006). I will teach you about possible types of memos and how to set up analytic memos in ATLAS.ti in a way that makes your research transparent and helps you engage with your data, and to enter into an internal dialog, advancing your analytic thoughts and ways of thinking. Thus, the focus of the chapter is on the thinking aspect of the NCT model of computer-assisted qualitative data analysis. Engaging with your data also means querying them and therefore you will also learn about different methods of data retrieval. At some point in your analysis, you will also want to diagram your thoughts; this will be discussed at greater length in Chapter 7, where you will learn how to do so using the ATLAS.ti network view function.

Learning how to write good memos is experiential. Reading about it and seeing examples of how it can be done is one part, but you need to do it yourself and practice it. In the previous chapter I provided you with some ideas for stand-alone memos to accompany the research process, such as the research diary, to-do memos or idea memos. Then there are the connected memos linked to your data. These might contain important bits and pieces from the theoretical framework you are using or your analytic thoughts.

Linked memos

Memos can be linked to quotations like codes, but also to codes and other memos. In the Memo Manager, you will also find a column for groundedness and density. Groundedness counts the number of links to quotations; density counts the links to other codes and memos. When linking memos to quotations, the idea is to connect a memo to the data segments that illustrate what you write in it. The direction is from the memo to the quotation and not the other way around. Thus, the memo should exist first, having a proper title and a type. Then you link it to one or more quotations. When you do it the other way around, you are using memos as comments. As I explained earlier, the quotation comment field is a better place for writing down ideas that are directly concerned with a particular data segment.

Below, I introduce two kinds of linked memos. Feel free to come up with further ideas that suit your project. What is important to remember is that memos are more than comments, in terms of both length and content. A memo could be linked to just one quotation, but more likely you will find several data segments that reflect your analytic writing in the memo. There are some parallels to building up an efficient coding scheme. We have seen that creating 1000 codes that only code a few quotations each is not a good idea. This is an indication that the codes have not yet reached a conceptual level. If you create lots of memos containing only one or two sentences and linked to one quotation each, then these are only comments and not conceptual ideas. Memos, like codes, are containers (Figure 6.2): code containers collect quotations, memo containers collect ideas. Below I present some ideas on what kinds of content you can write in linked memos.

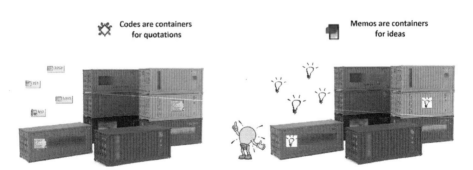

Figure 6.2 Codes and memos are like containers

Theory or literature memos

This type can be used to add information from secondary sources to the project, such as excerpts from the relevant literature, main theoretical concepts, etc. These memos partly serve as reminders; instead of having to switch programs or look through a stack of papers to remind you of important theoretical concepts and their definitions, they are right there within your ATLAS.ti project. Additionally, these memos can be used to collect empirical evidence for theories proposed in the literature. When you come across a data segment that ties in with ideas proposed in the literature by other authors, you can connect the respective memo to this data segment.

Technically, you attach a memo to a quotation just like you attach a code: by dragging and dropping a memo from the Memo Manager to the quotation. This process is described in more detail below.

Research question memos

At first I called these 'analytic memos', but I changed the name since a number of other authors use that term in a different way from what I am suggesting here. Originally, the idea of the analytic memo was developed by Glaser and Strauss (1967) to assist with the development of codes and conceptual ideas during the process of coding. Previously, this was done in the form of writing notes in the margin of the transcript (see also Fielding and Lee, 1998; Lewins and Silver, 2007). Based on this tradition, Charmaz (2006) and also Saldaña (2009) described all memos as analytical. Based on the examples provided above, you have seen that memos in a software environment can facilitate the technical handling of certain procedures or for project management purposes.

Research question memos are analytic memos. I describe them as places where you develop the interpretation of your data step by step. You can set them up early in the process of analysis, but systematic writing and development of these memos occur after coding. Thus, I suggest that you concentrate on coding the data first. Then a new phase and different process of analysis begins.

If you are familiar with quantitative research procedures, it may help to compare the two levels of analysis to descriptive and inductive statistics. The equivalent of descriptive statistics in computer-assisted analysis is the development of the coding system. When set up as explained in the previous chapter, the coding system provides an overview of what is in the data. The codes on the category level can be regarded as equivalent to the variables in a survey; the subcategories indicate the variations within the code, similar to the characteristic values of a variable.

Once we are finished with coding, we can describe the data. Perhaps we can already see a few patterns there. We then can take the analysis a step further by querying the data. After coding, it is a matter of a few mouse clicks – and knowing where to click – to dig deeper into the data material and to ask further questions. The tools employed at this stage are the **code-cooccurrence tools** and the **Codes-Primary Documents Table**, and the **query tool**. They are explained further on in this chapter. The aim of these tools is to help you find relations and patterns in the data. Thus, in qualitative research too, there are various levels of analysis. The second level is about asking questions and finding relations. This is the phase where research question memos begin to play a major role in the analytic process.

Differently from statistical analysis, the most important part of the results provided by these tools is the data behind them and not the numbers. You do need to read through, review or listen to those data and then write down your thoughts in a research question memo. These can be various things like description, interpretation or ideas for further questions and queries. You can find a more theory-oriented discussion on hypothesis examination using the various tools and operators which the software provides in Kelle (1995: part III).

Very likely you will not come up with models and highly integrated conceptual ideas from the outset. Thus, whatever you write in your research question memos does not have to be perfect and ready to be published. At some point you will get there, but to begin with your research question memos may simply contain descriptions and summaries of your data. Depending on your research approach and level of methodological knowledge, you may decide not to develop your research question memos further. A thorough description may be all that you want and need. If you take the analysis a step further, some of the descriptive memos may serve as building blocks for more abstract and theoretically rich memos (see also Bazeley and Richards, 2000: part 6; Corbin and Strauss, 2008: 119).

Hence, working with research question memos and the various tools for querying data is similar in process to inductive statistics. I call it conceptual-level work as compared to the descriptive work of developing the coding system. Before everyone jumps on me and complains that analytic steps cannot be as clear cut as I claim, I confess I am simplifying for the sake of novices who are trying to learn method and software at the same time. With more experience, you can begin to vary the sequence. However, the suggested order is not completely arbitrary: the first step is always to develop some codes and to build up a coding system. Without that, you cannot query the data. You may begin to collect ideas in research question memos as you code, but more extensive writing occurs after all the data have been coded and you start to use the analysis tools which the software provides. In order to see the benefits of this, you have to try it. If you use this book for teaching, you are likely to hear from your students that a lot of things happen when they enter this second phase of the analysis. It is now that they begin to see how the various codes relate to each other; they develop and test new questions and they may find answers that they did not expect to find. I would not exactly call it magic, rather the added value of approaching analysis in a systematic way utilizing the options available.

When you begin writing research question memos, the answers most likely will be descriptive. But in time they will become more abstract as you get ideas for further questions, add new research question memos and basically take it one step further at a time, gaining more and more understanding, exploring more and more details of your data landscape and starting to see relations between them.

Skills training 6.1: creating research question memos

Let's do some practical work now and learn the rest by actually doing it. In qualitative research, we generally do not start with hypotheses but in most cases we have some research questions. When using an inductive approach, researchers develop questions and hypotheses along the way. If you begin your project with some research questions in mind, you can create research question memos very early on in the analytic process, adjust and modify them, and add some more with progressive analysis.

At the end of Chapter 5, I listed the research questions that I had developed for the Children & Happiness project. We will now go through these questions one by one, exploring the data landscape further, and by doing so learn more about querying data and writing research question memos. A fully developed research question (RQ) memo:

- has a proper title that tells you what it is all about;
- can be identified as an analytic memo by its type;
- begins with a well-written research question, possibly followed by subquestions;
- includes the query (!);
- contains an answer to the query – when you work on a memo over a prolonged period of time, you can also insert the date and time to mark your progress;
- contains your answer and interpretation;
- is linked to quotations that illustrate the points you are making in the memo and supports your analytic thoughts (see Figure 6.3).

You do not yet know all of the mouse clicks involved and still need to learn how the analysis tools work. Let's get started with what you already know by creating a research question memo for RQ1:

- Open the Memo Manager (if it is not still open) and create a new memo.
- Enter the title 'RQ1: Definition of happiness, comparing parents and non-parents'. For the purpose of linking memos to data segments, it is a good idea to keep the title short as it will show up in the margin area. Thus, as the full question will be included in the body of the memo text, it might be sufficient to just title the memo RQ1 (compare Figure 6.5).

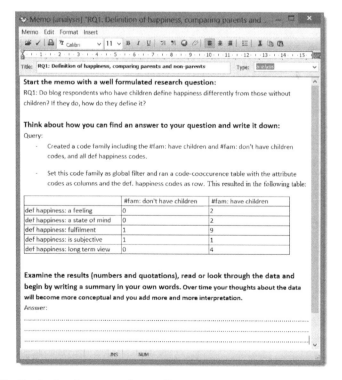

Figure 6.3   Contents of a research question memo

- Change the memo type to 'analysis'.
- Type the full research question into the editor (Figure 6.3).

Linking a memo to a quotation

I haven't yet shown you how to link a memo to a quotation. Let's pretend that you have run a query and you have come across an interesting quotation:

- Minimize or close the memo editor. Highlight one quotation in the text by clicking on the quotation bar or a code in the margin area. Then drag and drop the memo from the Memo Manager across the windows splitter to the left side of the HU editor (Figure 6.4).

Figure 6.4   Display of a linked memo in the margin area

- For this exercise, attach the memo to at least two quotations.
- Take a look at the Memo Manager. The count for groundedness has gone up.
- Double click on the memo entry. As in the Code Manager, a window will pop up showing you all quotations linked to this memo (Figure 6.5).
- When you click on the quotations, they are highlighted in context and you can see where the memo is attached.

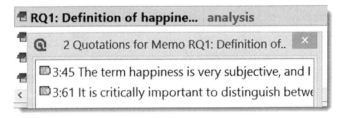

Figure 6.5   Reviewing the quotations linked to a memo

Creating output

That, however, is not the end of the story. What we want to do next is to output the memo, including the quotations. When you set up your research question memos as described, the output can be used as a building block for your research report.

- Select your RQ1 memo and then the option **Output / Selected Memo with Quotations**.
- Choose **Editor** as the output destination.

The memo output includes everything you need to write the results chapter of your research report or paper (Figure 6.6). It also adds transparency to your analysis. If someone asks how you derived your results, you can show your research question memos. If necessary, you can rerun the query. I have seen many memos that contained a lot of good interpretation, but when I asked the analysts how they came up with the ideas, they could not remember. It just takes a minute or two to spell out the query, and the return for this effort is manifold. It adds a lot to your analysis in terms of trustworthiness, credibility, transparency and dependability – in other words, the quality criteria by which good qualitative research is recognized (see e.g. Seale, 1999).

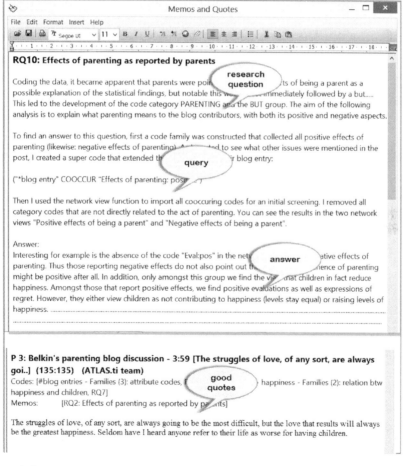

Figure 6.6   Research question memo as building block for a research report

Quoting data segments in reports

I am often asked how to reference a quote from an ATLAS.ti project. My suggestion is to use the document number that is indicated by the quotation ID plus the location in the document. The following quotation is a section from primary document 3, starting and ending in paragraph 81:

> *How about measuring a sense of purpose and fulfillment? Maybe the results would be different. Parenting is the most challenging and rewarding job there is. (P3, 81:81)*

You need to explain the references once, for example in a footnote. The coded documents where the quotation can be found in the data can be included in a paper or digital attachment to a report, thesis or dissertation. The output in PDF format is available for text, image and PDF files.

To create a PDF output of your coded documents:

* Select **Documents / Output /Print With Margin.**

As soon as you select the print with margin option, the screen view changes so you can see what the output looks like on paper or in a PDF file. Everything on the page is within the white area; everything off the page is shown in the grey area. You may need to adjust some settings to fit everything on the page and to create the output you want:

* If some codes fall off the page on the right hand side, I suggest that you set the page layout to landscape: **Project / Printer Setup.**
* You can also adjust the windows splitter (move it to the right or left) and change the font for the codes (right click in the margin, select the option Set Font) to create the view you want.
* If you want to create a PDF file, a PDF writer needs to be installed on your computer. Nowadays you can find free versions online. When creating the output, the printer dialog opens. Choose the PDF writer as your printer. Then the document will not actually be printed but saved as a PDF file. If you select a segment of text, only the selection will be included in the printout.

Recommendations for organizing research question memos

After the data material has been coded, research question memos help you approach the data analysis in a systematic way, by formulating precise queries for each individual question. The crucial point is that the memos are thematically related to contents and data segments, instead of being spread out in bits and pieces all over the place. My suggestion is to create one memo for each research question. Broader questions need to be divided into subtopics and it is probably best to create a memo for each subtopic. As we have done for codes, use letters and special characters to create abbreviations in order to structure and organize the list of memos, for example:

RQ1: title
RQ2: title
RQ3: title
:

Or:
RQ1a: title
RQ1b: title
RQ1c: title
RQ2a: title
:

Special characters like an asterisk (*) are useful when you want to place certain memos at the top of the list, like your research diary. Depending on your project design, you may know the research questions from the start. If this is the case, I suggest adding these as memos when you start setting up. This will allow you to write reflections and first ideas about a certain topic in the proper container immediately, during the process of coding. As you develop more research questions and hypotheses along the way, add more research question memos.

Querying the data

Ideally, when reading on, you have begun to explore your own data landscape and you have developed some ideas, marked those things that are interesting and collected similar items in code containers. As you now know what memos are and what to use them for, integrate them into your analysis and continue your coding work until all data are coded.

The next step is to query the data in a systematic way by going through the research questions and thinking about how to find an answer for each question in the data. ATLAS.ti offers several options to query the data. Thus, you need to attend some more skills training sessions as part of your journey. The query tool needs theoretical instruction first before we can apply and work with it. Other tools I can explain by way of example when we go through the research questions for the Children & Happiness project.

Skills training 6.2: getting to know the query tool

If you want to click along and follow the exercises, open the **Children & Happiness, stage II** project from the HELP / QUICK TOUR menu.

The query tool is used for the retrieval of coded data segments, the ATLAS.ti quotations. You have already seen and practiced the simplest form of retrieval where you double click on a code in the Code Manager. The query tool can process more complex queries by combining codes. For that, 14 different operators are at your disposal.

The results of a query formulated in the query tool are always quotations. If you are interested in the location of codes, for example which of the codes overlap, you need to use the Codes Co-Occurrence Table or explorer. That will be explained later, when examining RQ3 and 4 and RQ9. For now, I would like you to concentrate on the query tool. The schedule for the skills training session is as follows:

1. We will take a look at the query tool window and I will explain the various components of it.
2. You will get to know the three groups of operators and the retrieval language.
3. Thereafter we will run a few example queries.
4. With this knowledge, we will be ready to return to the research questions of the Children & Happiness project.

Let's begin by looking at the query tool window:

- Open the query tool by clicking on the binoculars button in the horizontal toolbar or by selecting the menu option **Analysis / Query Tool**.

On the left hand side of the query tool window (Figure 6.7) you will see the operator toolbar. You will find three sets of operators: Boolean, semantic and proximity operators.

- Move your mouse over each of the operator buttons. A comment pops up showing the name of the operator and a sample query (Figure 6.8).

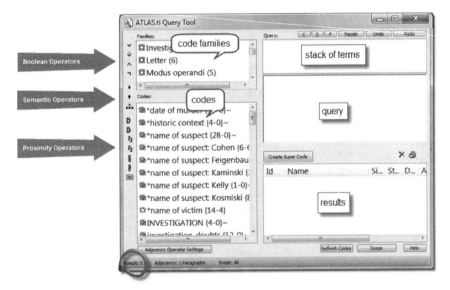

Figure 6.7   The ATLAS.ti Query Tool: searching for quotations based on code combinations

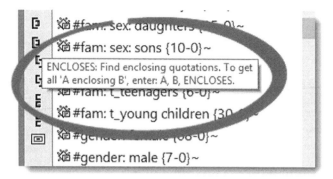

Figure 6.8 Comments explaining query buttons

In the upper left hand corner of the query tool windows you will see the code family field, listing all code families that can be used in a query. Below that you will see all of your codes. The upper right hand corner will be filled when you begin to click on a query. It lists all activated terms and is called the 'stack of terms'. This is just like other stacks that you know of from everyday life, like a stack of books (Figure 6.9) or a stack of wood. If you want to take an object from a stack, be it a book or a piece of wood, you take it from the top and don't pull out the bottom item first. This is what ATLAS.ti does with the entries in the stack of terms in the query tool. If two terms are needed for a query and there are more than two in the stack, ATLAS.ti takes the two that are on top of the stack. You will see how it works when we click on a few queries.

Figure 6.9 The stack of terms is similar to a stack of books

The middle pane on the right of the query tool windows is the place for the evolving query. It is called the feedback pane. Here you can see the arithmetical problem being addressed by the query tool. At the bottom right, you will see the results of a query in the form of a list of quotations. The resulting total number of quotations is shown circled in the bottom left hand corner of Figure 6.7.

The retrieval language

Queries are formulated following the principle of **reverse Polish notation (RPN)** developed by the Polish mathematician Jan Lukasiewicz. This sounds complicated but it is actually quite easy as it does not require you to learn syntax. Every step of the method produces a significant result and it is impossible to formulate a query wrongly. You may have found in statistics programs that you cannot run a query because you forgot the period at the end or a comma somewhere. The reverse Polish way of entering queries demands neither syntactical knowledge like commas, semi-colons, periods, etc., nor the need to enter brackets to control the order of operators.

The basic principle of RPN is that all arguments (codes or code families) are written first, followed by an operator. In RPN, this order is reversed: all arguments are written before the operators. When entering an arithmetical problem into a calculator, we are accustomed to a notation in which the operator stands between two arguments, for example in the sum 3 + 4. This form of entering terms is also called **infix notation**.

In Table 6.1 you can see some arithmetical problems in two alternative notations, the usual infix notation and RPN.

Table 6.1 Infix and reverse Polish notation

Infix notation	Reverse Polish notation
3 + 4	3 4 +
3 + (4 * 5)	4 5 * 3 + alternative: 3 5 4 * +
(3 + 4) * 5	3 4 + 5 * alternative: 5 3 4 + *

You will get the hang of it once we enter some example queries.

The three sets of operators

Boolean operators

Boolean operators combine keywords with the use of fixed operations. You probably know and have used at least two of them (OR and AND) when you do a literature search or search the Internet. For the operator OR you usually enter a vertical bar '|':

OR: A OR B
XOR: Either only A, or only B
AND: A and B both have to apply
NOT: Negation of a term

You may remember set theory from your math classes in school. Let's go back a bit in your memory to retrieve some of that knowledge. Below, the four Boolean operators found in ATLAS.ti are explained and for each a Venn diagram is shown. Your task is to mark the area that results from the query for each operator. You will find the solutions at the end of the chapter in Figure 6.43.

OR: The operator OR is the non-exclusive OR. The term 'A OR B' is true if A, B or both are true. Using this operator, the search system will return all quotations that are linked to at least one of the codes in the search term. Therefore, the query tool's mission is to find at least one of the specified arguments. When you want the quotations of a number of codes, then it is easier to create a code family rather than use the query tool. A code family basically consists of codes linked with the OR operator: (C1 | C2 | C3 | C4 | C5).

- In the following graphic, mark the area that results from the search A OR B:

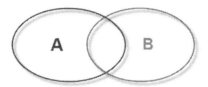

XOR: The XOR is the exclusive OR. 'A XOR B' is true if either A or B is true, but it is false if both A and B are true. XOR represents the colloquial 'either–or': 'You can have either chocolate or ice cream.' Thus, XOR means: 'You can have one of the two, but not both.' In contrast, the OR operator allows you to have both.

- Mark the area that results from the search A XOR B:

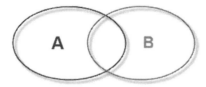

AND: The operator AND will find only those quotations that meet all conditions of the search term. It is very selective and finds only those segments that you have coded with two codes. Remember Skills training 5.4 on the rules of hierarchical coding and how to avoid the code swamp? I advised you to create different codes for different content areas like theme and dimension. Let's assume you come across a data segment that contains an opinion that children make you happier and that parenting is hard but rewarding at the same time. Instead of having one code like Children > happiness_hard work but rewarding, it is better to code the text segment with Children > happiness and hard work but: rewarding. Coded like that, you can use the AND operator in the query tool to find all data segments where someone is of the opinion that children make you happier and who perceives parenting to be rewarding.

- Mark the area that results from the search A AND B:

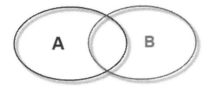

NOT: This operator is used to check if a condition is not applicable. Its formal meaning is that all results of the negated term are subtracted from all data segments in question. You only need to select one code in order to use this operator. Usually it is used to exclude the quotation of one or more codes: all A or B but not C.

- Mark the area that results from the search NOT B:

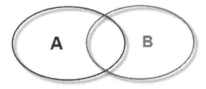

Example query

In the coded Children & Happiness sample project, happiness is defined in various ways like 'happiness is a feeling' or 'happiness is a state of mind'. The task is to retrieve the quotations of both codes. Remember that we have to enter the query in RPN: first the codes, then the operator.

- In the query tool, double click on the code 'def happiness: a feeling', then double click on the code 'def happiness: a state of mind'.

Figure 6.10   Example query with Boolean operators

The codes you select appear in the stack of terms (Figure 6.10). In the results pane you will immediately see the results of the query shown in the feedback pane; in this case, the two quotations of the code 'def happiness: a state of mind'.

- Now click on the OR operator, the top one in the row of operators.

The feedback pane displays the query: *"def happiness: a feeling"* | *"def happiness: a state of mind"*. The total number of resulting quotations is four.

- To review the results in the context of the data, click on each quotation in the results pane. To export the results, click on the printer symbol (see Figure 6.11).

Congratulations! You have clicked your first query. It was a simple process, and step by step you will get more used to it: first click on the code(s); then select an operator.

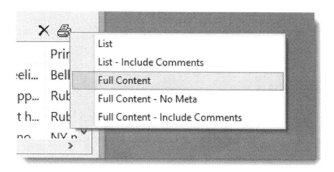

Figure 6.11   Exporting query results

Semantic operators

Semantic operators make use of the links between codes. Such links are created with the help of the **network view function**. Codes can be linked via directed or non-directed relations. When you find a causal link – for example, action A is always followed by action B, or B is a consequence of A – then you can use a directed transitive relation to link the two codes. But it is not always possible to define a directed link; at times you just want to indicate that two or more codes relate to each other, or occur at the same time or place, etc. It is neither a cause and effect relation, nor a description of situation and consequence, or anything similar. Therefore ATLAS.ti also offers non-directed relations. In a network view, this looks as shown in Figure 6.12.

Semantic operators make use of directed relations to define a hierarchy between codes. This means you can collect all quotations coded by codes that are hierarchically below, above or on the same level as another. In Figure 6.12, the codes indicating the sources of happiness are related to the two attribute codes '#fam: don't have children' and '#fam: have children'. You can collect all

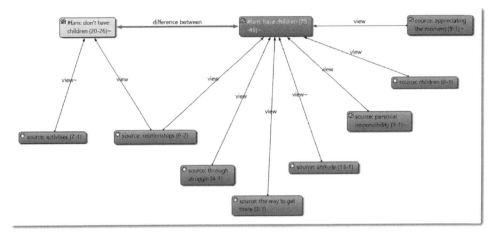

Figure 6.12   Network view showing non-directed and directed relations

'source' quotations that are related to either those who have children or those who do not have children via the SIB (sibling) operator.

SUB: all A with subgroups
UP: all A with codes of the next upper level
SIB: all quotations connected with A that are on the same sublevel

Example query   When using any of the three semantic operators, you only need to select one code and then the operator. To collect all quotations linked via a directed relation to the code '#fam: have children', this would result in lots of quotations. Try it:

- Assuming that you have loaded the Children & Happiness stage II project, double click on the code '#fam: have children'. Then click on the SUB operator. This results in 239 quotations.

In the feedback pane of the query tool, the query looks like this:

SUB "#fam: have children"

Take a look at the density of the code. It is 75 (Figure 6.12). Not all of these 75 linkages are directed links; still it is not very meaningful to query all sub-codes. We could set a filter so that only the codes of the 'source' category are queried. However, the quotations of the source category are not exclusive to blog writers who have children. Those who do not have children also write about sources of happiness. Thus, using the semantic operators for this data set does not make much sense. Only if the codes were linked in a taxonomical manner would the semantic operators be used more meaningfully. The way I explained to you about how to build up a coding system means there is no need to link all subcodes to the main category code. If you do, you 'use up' the network view function for structural purposes (i.e. sorting your codes into higher and lower order codes). At more advanced stages of your analysis, it then becomes difficult to use network linkages for conceptual-level analysis. The hierarchical linkages will always be in the way. You can read more about this in the next chapter in the section 'On the use of network views for structural purposes', after I have properly introduced you to the network view function.

Proximity operators

Proximity operators analyze the spatial relations between coded data segments like overlaps and distances. For a query with proximity operators, you have to select two codes/code families as arguments, as was also the case for Boolean operators. There is one significant difference between these operators and the ones already discussed: proximity operators are not interchangeable.

This means that you have to pay attention to the order in which you enter the codes (or code families). The query tool can only find quotations, not the lines between them.

The example in Figure 6.13 shows some lines of text where Code A is overlapped by a Code B. The query tool only returns the data segment coded by Code A or the ones coded by Code B. It cannot output just line 2, the text where the two codes actually overlap. Thus, if you want all data coded by Code A, you need to enter the query:

Code A, Code B, OVERLAPPED BY.

When you want to read the text coded by Code B, you need to enter the query the other way around starting with Code B:

Code B, Code A, OVERLAPS.

For this reason, there are always two versions of a proximity query and respectively two operators.

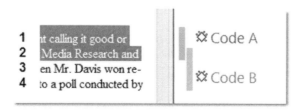

Figure 6.13   Proximity search: A is overlapped by B

Finding overlapping quotations

OVERLAPPED BY: A is overlapped by B
OVERLAPS: B overlaps A

Finding quotations of embedded codes   With the following two operators, you can find quotations that are embedded in each other:

WITHIN: B within A
ENCLOSES: A encloses B

To find the segment coded with friendship (Figure 6.14), you need to enter friendship, childhood, WITHIN. This kind of query is useful if, for example, you have coded longer segments by a time period like 'childhood'. Within this longer segment, you have coded friendship as 'first year in school', 'relations with mother', etc. It does not make much sense to enter the query the other way around ('childhood', 'friendship', ENCLOSES) as the query tool will then return the long segments on childhood. The general rule is that the first code you select should be the one you are interested in.

childhood

friendship

Figure 6.14   Querying data using the WITHIN operator

Example query   Find all quotations where blog respondents, independent of whether they have children or not, mentioned that biology is one of the main factors why human beings have children:

- Double click on the code 'reasons for hc: biology'. Double click on the code '#blog entry'. Select the WITHIN operator. This results in 15 quotations.

In the feedback pane of the query tool, the query looks like this:

("reasons for hc: biology" WITHIN "#blog entry").

Finding quotations within a set distance

The last twin-set of operators returns those quotations that do not directly overlap, but occur within a specified distance from each other. The distance can be specified based on the type of document you are working with: paragraphs for text documents, characters for text and PDF files, pixels for image files, milliseconds for audio files and frames for videos.

> FOLLOWS: B follows A
>
> PRECEDES: A precedes B

This option (Figure 6.15) is interesting when looking for coded data segments that occur near each other, for example within two consecutive paragraphs. Thus, the codes do not have to overlap directly. When the coded data segments are short, as is often the case in discourse or conversation analysis, the maximum distance between two quotations can be set to characters instead of paragraphs.

Working with proximity operators is also interesting for descriptions of plots or when analyzing filmed actions and events. Then the sequence of when what is done or happens can be very revealing.

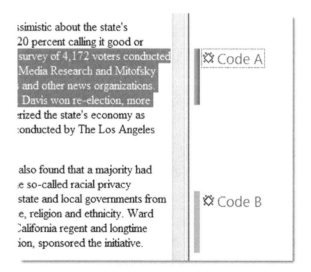

Figure 6.15   Querying data using the PRECEDE operator

When clicking on a query using the precede or follow operators (e.g. Code A, Code B, PRECEDES), a window pops up asking you to enter the maximal distance between the two codes (Figure 6.16).

You can set the default distance for all document types beforehand by clicking on **ADJACENCY OPERATOR SETTINGS**. Then the window in Figure 6.17 pops up.

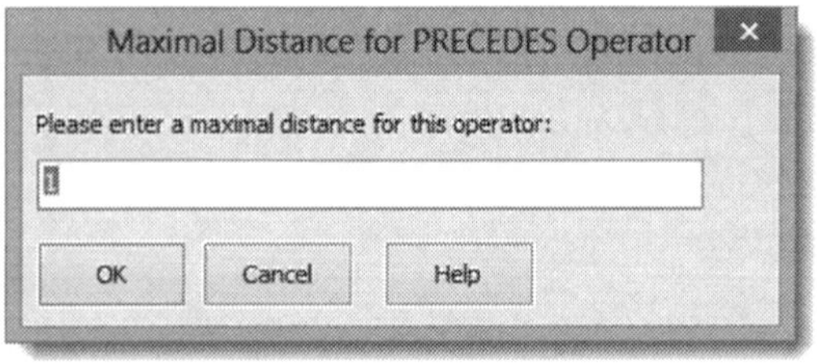

Figure 6.16   Determining the maximum distance for two codes

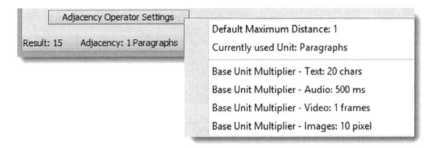

Figure 6.17   Adjacency operator settings

Example query   In the Children & Happiness project, people talk about positive and negative effects of parenting. As blog writing is sequential and people at times react to what others wrote before them, we can for instance take a look at whether writers feel obliged to write something positive after something negative was written; or the other way around, write something negative after the positive side of parenting has been pointed out.

- Double click on the code family 'effects of parenting: positive'. Double click on the code family 'effects of parenting: negative'. Select the PRECEDES operator and set a maximum distance of 2, so we are likely to catch the response of the next writer. This results in two quotations, one of them coming from the survey data. This can be seen from the quotation ID 22. Thus, this constellation does occur only once in the blog data.

The query looks like this in the query tool:

("Effects of parenting: positive" PRECEDES:2 "Effects of parenting: negative")

- To test the reversed option: Double click on the code family 'effects of parenting: negative'. Double click on the code family 'effects of parenting: positive'. Select the PRECEDES operator and set a maximum distance of 2. This results in nine quotations, mostly coming from the Belk's parenting blog (ID 3).

The query looks like this in the query tool:

("Effects of parenting: negative" PRECEDES:2 "Effects of parenting: positive")

Without looking at the resulting quotations, which should be the next step, a first conclusion is that if someone wrote something negative in the blogs (31 times), this was at times followed by a positive comment, maybe to tone down the bad part of parenting.

Finding quotations that occur together

If it does not matter in which way two codes overlap, you can use the COOCCURRENCE operator. This is a combination of ENCLOSES, WITHIN, OVERLAPPED BY, OVERLAPS and AND. The AND operator is included here as well, because it finds all quotations that are double coded with two selected codes. Thus, it describes proximity of 100%:

🖳 COOCCUR: all A together with B

When using the COOCCURRENCE operator, it is still important in which way around you enter the codes or code families. Start with the code or code family whose coded segments you want to read.

Example query   Returning to the code that we looked at when discussing the semantic operators '#fam: have children' and the 'source of happiness' code category, with the help of the COOCCUR operator we can find out what families with children have written about sources of happiness.

- As we are interested in the sources, double click on the code family 'Sources of happiness'. Double click on the code '#fam: have children'. Select the COOCCUR operator. This results in 13 quotations.

The query looks like this in the query tool:

("Sources of happiness" COOCCUR "#fam: have children")

Miscellaneous useful query tool functions

On the top right hand side of the query tool you will find some buttons facilitating the process of clicking on queries (Figure 6.18).

Clear: The **C** button clears the whole stack of terms. After you finish one query and review the results, it is best to click on the C button to clear all entries before you enter the next query.

Swap: When clicking on the **S** button, the first two elements of the stack switch places. This option is very useful if you have entered the codes or code families in the wrong order.

Put: The **P** button creates a copy of the first element and puts it on top of the stack. This can be used for reproducing a complex expression.

Recalculate: If you have created and coded new quotations while the query tool window is open, you can use the **Recalc** button to recalculate the current query results.

Undo: The **Undo** button removes the element at the top of the stack if you have, for example, selected the wrong code.

Redo: The **Redo** button puts the last removed element back on the stack.

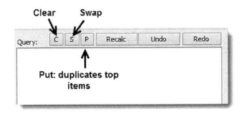

Figure 6.18   Useful buttons when clicking on a query

Reviewing results

Even though you can see (at the bottom left of the query tool) how many quotations the query is yielding, the really important result is the content of the quotations. It is essential to read, review or listen to the contents of the quotations to be able to interpret them. The number of results can serve as an initial point of orientation and thus is also meaningful, but only together with the corresponding content. You can review the results in context either by clicking on each quotation in the results pane of the query tool, or by creating a report. The various output options can be seen when you click on the printer symbol (Figure 6.11).

The List and the List – Include Comments output options are useful for outputting multimedia (audio, video, image, Google Earth) quotations when you have used the quotation name as title (see Chapter 4, p. 103).

The Full Content output is useful for text and image documents. The Full Content – No Meta option is quite handy for reducing the number of output pages. The regular output includes a reference for each quotation plus information about other codes, memos and families linked to the segment. This takes up a few lines of space. The 'no meta' option reduces the output to the minimum necessary, which is often sufficient. You can compare the two output formats in the box below.

Full Content output

P 3: Belkin's parenting blog discussion - 3:62 [As for the question of "why does have children in ..] (138:138) (ATLAS.ti team)

Codes: [reasons for hc: biology - Families (2): for Quick Tour: Cooccurrence Example, reason for having kids]

No memos

As for the question of "why does have children in the first place?", well that's easy. Beyond the choice to have them, as per the statement above, people are VERY motivated by sex, and children are very often a by-product. In humanity's distant past and for most other species, there is little to no thought about whether to have children... it just happens, and we're wired to care for them, thankfully.

Full Content – No Meta output of the same segment

As for the question of "why does have children in the first place?", well that's easy. Beyond the choice to have them, as per the statement above, people are VERY motivated by sex, and children are very often a by-product. In humanity's distant past and for most other species, there is little to no thought about whether to have children... it just happens, and we're wired to care for them, thankfully.

<ref>P 3: Belkin's parenting blog discussion – 3:62 [(138:138)] by ATLAS.ti team</ref>

If you have written quite a number of quotation comments and want them all to be included in the output, the 'no meta' option cannot be used. Then you need to use the option Full Content – Include Comments.

As usual, you can send the output to an editor or the printer, or save it directly as a file. The 'File & Run' option is useful when creating Excel tables as output. You will see how this works a little later.

Exploring the data terrain further – the journey continues

I will now take you on an excursion to explore the Children & Happiness data terrain in a bit more detail. Our program for the day is to look at nine research questions and how to find an answer to them using the analysis tools that ATLAS.ti provides. These examples prepare you to explore more of the terrain on your own and to transfer this knowledge to investigations of other data landscapes in the form of your own projects.

For the following exercises, please download a specially prepared version of the Children & Happiness project from the companion website. It is a copy bundle file with the name: '**Children & Happiness analysis exercises**'. Alternatively, you can use the Stage II project that you can access via the Help / Quick Tour menu. However, it contains more codes and code families that are needed to follow the exercises and thus is more difficult to handle.

- Unpack the copy bundle file 'Children & Happiness analysis exercises' (see Chapter 3, page 67).
- Open the Code Manager in order to get a feeling for what was coded and what kind of categories and code families are available.

Skills training 6.3: getting to know the Codes Co-Occurrency Table

Research question 1 can be explored in three different ways. You can use the query tool, the code-cooccurrence tools and the network view function. The analytical capabilities of the network view function are explained in the next chapter. So, here, I focus on the first two options.

RQ1: Do blog respondents who have children define happiness differently from those without children? If so, how do they define it?

If you look at the Code Manager, you will see that the Def Happiness category has five subcodes. The codes indicating that someone is a parent or not are: '#fam: have children' and '#fam: don't have children'. The 'def happiness' codes occur within each of the blog entries. Thus, we can use either the WITHIN operator or the COOCCUR operator. The result in this case is the same.

In order to find an answer to this question, we could run single queries in the query tool for each 'def happiness' subcode with the two attribute codes (with or without children). A quicker way of gaining an overview that includes all codes is to create a Codes Co-Occurrence Table. To remind you, for calculating code-cooccurrences, ATLAS.ti combines four of the proximity operators and the Boolean operator AND.

I prefer to create code families that include the codes I need in order to answer a particular research question. This way, I can always review it later and use them as a global filter, which makes selecting the codes much easier. Let's do it, so you can see how it works:

- Open the Code Manager.
- Create a code family including the '#fam: have children' and '#fam: don't have children' codes, and all 'def happiness' codes. If you forgot how it works, see for example Skills training 5.3 in Chapter 5.
- Set this code family as the global filter: right click on the family in the side panel and select the option SET GLOBAL FILTER.
- From the main menu select ANALYSIS / CODES CO-OCCURRENCY TABLE (Figure 6.19).

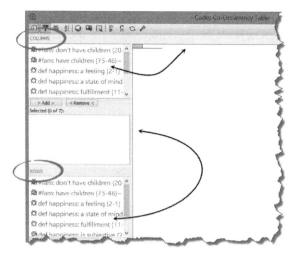

Figure 6.19 Opening window of the Codes Co-Occurrency Table

- Select the '#fam: have children' and '#fam: don't have children' codes to be displayed in the columns, the 'def happiness' codes to be displayed in the rows. You can either double click on each code, or select multiple codes and click on **ADD**.

If two codes cooccur, the cells of the table show two numbers (Figure 6.20). The first one is the frequency of cooccurrence, the second is the c-coefficient. If the two codes do not cooccur, you see the entry n/a for not applicable. The lighter the color of a cell, the higher the frequency of cooccurrence.

The c-coefficient indicates the strength of the relation between two codes, similar to a correlation coefficient in statistics. As with statistical analysis procedures, you need to make sure that your data fulfill the requirements for running a particular test. Here we analyze the data of two blogs and clearly the case numbers are too low for the c-coefficient to yield a meaningful result. If you import open-ended questions from 300 survey respondents or more, then it makes much more sense to look at this value.

	#fam: don't have children
def happiness: a feeling	n/a
def happiness: a state of mind	n/a
def happiness: fulfillment	1 - 0,03
def happiness: is subjective	1 - 0,05
def happiness: long term view	n/a

Figure 6.20 Display of results in the Codes Co-Occurrency Table

Normally, the value of the c-coefficient is somewhere between 0 and 1. But as we are not dealing with standardized quantitative data, it might be that the value is higher than 1. If this is the case, you will see on-screen a red circle next to the coefficient. When the c-coefficient is low but the data segments overlap quite considerably, then the field is marked by a yellow circle. The message is: even if the coefficient is small, it might be worthwhile to look at the data behind the cell.[1]

For anyone interested in the mathematics behind the c-coefficient

The coefficient is based on the 'Normalized Cooccurrence' measure as used for quantitative content analysis. In the case of pairwise cooccurrence, that is co-citation frequency between two and only two terms k1 and k2, the C-index is given by

Eq 1: C12 – index: n12 / (n1 + n2) – n12

where:

* c12 = 0 when n12 = 0, i.e. k1 and k2 do not cooccur (terms are mutually exclusive).

* c12 > 0 when n12 > 0, i.e. k1 and k2 cooccur (terms are non-mutually exclusive).

* c12 = 1 when n12 = n1 = n2, i.e. k1 and k2 cooccur whenever either term occurs.

- The c-coefficient is automatically displayed if you create a Codes Co-Occurrency Table. You can deactivate it by clicking on the c-coefficient button on the toolbar (see right). Do so now, because the coefficient is not applicable to the Children & Happiness data.

To make your table look like the one displayed in Figure 6.21, you need to change a few preference settings:

- Click on the wrench icon on the toolbar to change the column and row header width and if you want to use code colors as header background.
- To change the color scheme, click on the colored circle in the toolbar. The cells can be displayed in green, blue or red. Green is the default setting. Choose 'None'.

	#fam: don't have children	#fam: have children
def happiness: a feeling	n/a	2
def happiness: a state of mind	n/a	2
def happiness: fulfilment	1	9
def happiness: is subjective	1	1
def happiness: long term view	n/a	4

Figure 6.21   Result of RQ1

1 See also: www.atlasti.com/395.html.

- To look at the data behind the numbers, double click on any of the fields that show a result. A drop-down list with the list of quotations opens (Figure 6.22).
- Click on a quotation in the list and it will be highlighted in the context of the data.

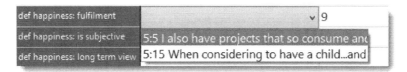

def happiness: fulfilment		⌄	9
def happiness: is subjective	5:5 I also have projects that so consume and
def happiness: long term view	5:15 When considering to have a child...and

Figure 6.22   Data behind the Codes Co-Occurrency Table

The drop-down list contains more quotations than are indicated by the frequency. Recall from Skills training 6.2 that ATLAS.ti can only find something that is a quotation and not the stuff in between. Thus, when looking for cooccurring codes, ATLAS.ti always finds two versions unless the segment is double coded by two codes (i.e. an AND occurrence). If not, then the alternatives are:

- A is overlapped by B and B overlaps A.
- A within B and B enclosed A.

Thus, per hit, a maximum of two quotations can be shown in the drop-down list.

Exporting results

If you want to continue to work with the resulting numbers, you can export the table as an Excel file. If you want to export the data, or those parts that seem to be interesting when looking at the table, you will need to use the query tool. See below.

NOTE: In the future, further output options will be provided in the Codes Co-Occurrency Table directly. You will for instance be able to display a report of all quotations of a selected cell, choosing whether you want to view or read the quotations of the row or the column code.

Clustering

If you have coded multiple segments within a larger segment with the same code, for example all parts of an interview where the interviewee talks about friendship during childhood (the larger segment), then you may not want to count these as five cooccurrences but as one. This can be achieved by clicking on the clustering button.

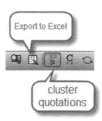

- Try out the various options so that you become familiar with the tool.
- Explore the results and write down your observations in the research question memo for RQ1 (Figure 6.3).

As you might have noticed, the Codes Co-Occurrence Table is exploratory and provides a quick overview of what parents and non-parents wrote. We have seen that parents provide a larger variety of definitions than non-parents, but we have to keep in mind that the blog comments contain answers from 75 parents as compared to 25 of non-parents. This probably explains part of it. If we look at the table, we might decide that we would like to take a closer look at the code 'def happiness: fulfilment'.

- Close or minimize the Codes Co-Occurrence Table. Open the query tool.
- Double click on the code 'def happiness: fulfilment'.
- Double click on the code '#fam: with children'.
- Select the COOCCUR or WITHIN operator. Result: nine quotations.
- Take a look at the resulting quotations and repeat the query for the code '#fam: don't have children'. Result: one quotation.

In the query tool, the query looks as follows:

("def happiness: fulfilment" COOCCUR "#fam: have children")

("def happiness: a fulfilment" COOCCUR "#fam: don't have children")

Tip: A quick way to reset one or more filters is via the main menu: TOOLS / RESET ALL FILTERS.

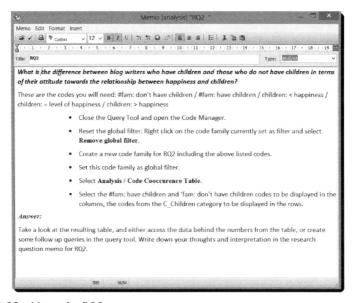

Figure 6.23   Memo for RQ2

	#fam: don't have children	#fam: have children
children: < happiness	5	6
children: = level of happiness	1	11
children: > happiness	2	19

Figure 6.24 Result of RQ2

RQ2: What is the difference in attitudes toward the relationship between happiness and children between those commenting on the blogs who have children and those who do not have children?

RQ2 can be explored in the same way as RQ1. Start by creating a code family that includes the codes that you need in order to answer this research question. Set this family as a global filter and create a Codes Co-Occurrence Table. Explore the interesting findings further by using the query tool.

Look at the memo for this research question (Figure 6.23), where I explain this in more detail.

Your Codes Co-Occurrence Table should look like that in Figure 6.24. You could for instance take a closer look at the five or six quotations where those with and without children write that children make a person less happy. Is there a qualitative difference between the two respondent groups?

Skills training 6.4: getting to know the Codes-Primary Documents Table

If you want to compare and contrast on the document or case level, you need to use the **Codes-Primary Documents Table.** It is always a good option when you want to compare the distribution of codes across documents or document families, depending on how your cases are defined. The output of an analysis in the Codes-Primary Documents Table is an Excel table or an internal report as a text file. The latter only works well if the number of codes and PDs included is small. Mostly I use the Excel output option because Excel provides further options to work with the data. Furthermore, you can decide to export frequency counts: how often a code was applied, or the number of words within the coded segments per code. The latter option is used for instance by communication researchers who code rather small data segments and are more interested in the number of words rather than the pure frequency count.

Let's create a Codes-Primary Documents Table now to find an answer to RQ3:

RQ3: Compare the comments written on Belkin's blog to those written on the *New York Times* blog regarding the following issues: effects of parenting (positive and negative), definition of happiness, reasons for having children, reasons for not having children, sources of happiness.

- Open the Codes-Primary Documents Table via the **Analysis** menu (Figure 6.25).
- Select all codes from the 'Effects neg:' and the 'Effects:pos' category in the codes pane. You can either double click on each code to move it into the 'Selected Codes/ Families' pane to the right, or you can highlight the entire group of codes and click on the button with the right arrows (see below).
- Select the two documents P3 and P5 in the documents pane and move them to the 'Selected PDs/Families' pane.
- On the right hand side of the window, make your choices on what the output should look like. Then click on the **Create Report** button.
- Excel opens (it may take a few seconds) and will ask you whether it is OK to open the document as it is only in an Excel-compatible and not a native Excel format. Click on **Yes**.

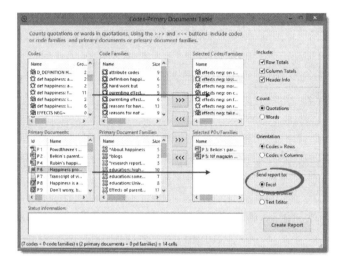

Figure 6.25   Creating a Codes-Primary Documents Table for RQ3

Tip: When sending the report to Excel, ATLAS.ti automatically stores the files in a Reports folder. This folder can be found under *My Documents / Scientific Software / ATLAS.ti / Reports*.

You can visually support your interpretations by creating charts in Excel. Thus, also a quantitative charting of the data terrain is possible. But numbers need to be interpreted with care. The chart shown in Figure 6.26 is based on a two blogs only. In addition there are 47 comments in the *New York Times* blog and 92 in Belkin's blog. So I calculated relative frequencies in order to make the two blogs comparable. What can be seen is that the importance of the various issues differs in the two blogs. The negative effects on relationships are prominent in both blogs. When looking at the positive effects, it becomes obvious that this is mainly mentioned in Belkin's parenting blog (Figure 6.27).

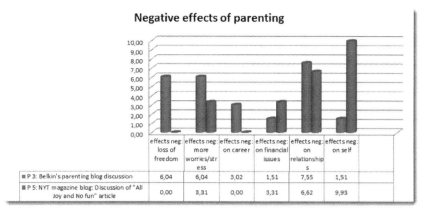

Figure 6.26   Excel chart for negative effects of parenting

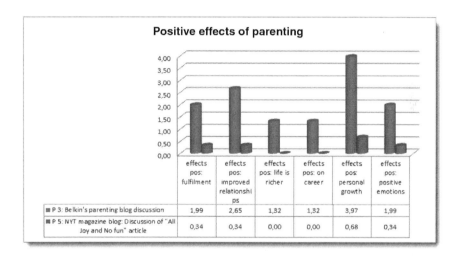

Figure 6.27   Excel chart for positive effects of parenting

As was the case with RQ1 and RQ2, in a second step you can use the query tool to look at the data behind the numbers. For instance, you may want to read why parenting affects relationships negatively and what type of relations.

- Open the query tool.
- Double click on the code 'effects neg: on relationships'. This results in 13 quotations, but across all data. If you only want to read what the writers on Belkin's blog wrote:
- Click on the **SCOPE** button. This opens the Scope of Query window. On the left hand side, you will see the primary document families and the list of all documents. These can now be applied as a filter:
- In the Primary Documents pane select P3: Belkin's parenting blog. The result will always be shown in the query tool window (five quotations), not in the Scope of Query window. Technically what happens is that ATLAS.ti calculates the intersection

between all P3 quotations – these are the ones you see in the Scope of Query window – and the quotations listed in the query tool. Read the five quotations in context or create an output to read them.

- Select P5 in the Scope of Query window to read the comments of the *New York Times* blog. Compare the answers and write down your thoughts and interpretation in the memo for RQ3.

The memo for RQ3 might look as shown in Figure 6.28.

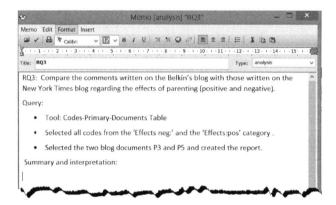

Figure 6.28   Research question memo for RQ3

Practice working with the Codes-Primary Documents Table by examining the comments of the two blogs for the remaining issues: the definition of happiness, the reasons for having and for not having children, and the sources of happiness that were mentioned. You will find the solutions to these exercises on the companion website.

For RQ4, I would like to go through this together with you:

RQ4: Compare the statements regarding sources of happiness of the two blog discussions (P3 and 5 = PD family *blogs) to the article that provides summaries of research findings (P10).

In order to answer this question, we can use the Codes-Primary Documents Table again. This time we cross-tabulate codes with both a PD and a PD family:

- Open the Codes-Primary Documents Table.
- Select the codes from the 'Source' category.
- Select the PD family *blogs (which contains the two documents P3 and P5); select the single document PD10 (Table 6.2).

As P10 is much shorter, once again one cannot base the interpretation on the absolute numbers. What can be seen is that the everyday perspective with respect to the question 'What makes us happy?' coincides only partly with

Table 6.2 Codes-Primary Documents Table for RQ4

	P10: Sources of happiness: summary of research findings	*blogs
source: relationships	4	3
source: activities	1	3
source: appreciating the moment	1	2
source: attitude	5	3
source: balance of mind and activities	0	0
source: baseline level	1	1
source: children	**0**	**5**
source: financial security	**3**	**0**
source: laughter / smile / fun	1	0
source: personal responsibility	**1**	**8**
source: the way to get there	0	1
source: through struggle	**0**	**4**
TOTALS:	17	30

what is proven scientifically. The writers on the two blogs strongly emphasize personal responsibility. Financial security as found by a number of studies was not mentioned at all by the blog writers. Both mention relationships, activities and personal attitude as sources for happiness. Based on the numbers provided by the table, you can return to the data querying specific codes individually. To compare the two groups, use the query tool in combination with the scope button.

Skills training 6.5: code queries in combination with document attributes (working with PD families and super families)

RQ5: Compare the survey answers of male and female respondents with regard to the reasons they provide for having or for not having children.

In order to answer the above question, you do not need to learn a new tool. You only need to turn a switch in your head in thinking about the data material. So far we have worked with the blog data and some associated material. As the blog comments are written by a number of different people, I needed to code for attributes like gender, whether they have children or not, etc. This is also the case when you work with focus group data, of if you have documents that contain multiple actors that you want to keep track of. As described in Chapter 3, if you prepare your transcripts accordingly, you can use the auto coding function to automatically code all speaker attributes in focus group data. When coding the blog data, the attributes of the writers only became obvious when reading the data. Therefore they needed to be coded manually.

If you look at P15 to P38 in the sample project, you will see that these are case-based data generated through the survey import option (see Chapter 3). When working with case-based data like surveys or interview transcripts, there is no need to code for attributes like gender, profession, marital status, and the like. This is handled via primary document families in ATLAS.ti and always applies if an attribute encompasses the entire document. Thus, if you catch yourself wanting to code the entire document, stop and think of an appropriate document family that you can add this document to.

When importing survey data, the document families are already created and the documents are sorted into the respective families based on the information provided in the Excel table. This was also the case for P15 to P38 in the sample project. Open the Primary Document Manager and select for instance case 6 (P20 in the quick tour project and P12 in the analysis exercise project): it is a single woman with some college education, who has no children and who answered the single choice question whether children bring happiness or not with 'Yes' (see highlighted families in Figure 6.29).

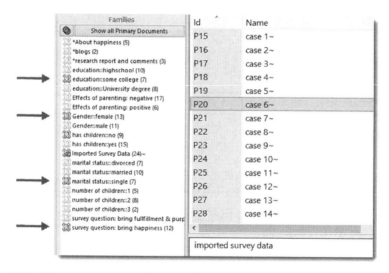

Figure 6.29 The assignment of document families for case 6

You are already familiar with the tools that you need to use in order to compare answers across different documents or document groups. These are the Codes-Primary Documents Table and the query tool in combination with the Scope button. So let's find an answer to RQ5:

- Open the Codes-Primary Documents Table via the **ANALYSIS** menu.
- From the list of codes, select all reasons for having children and all reasons for not having children codes.
- From the list of PD families, select the families gender::female and gender::male.
- On the right hand side of the window, make your choices on what the output should look like. Then click on the **CREATE REPORT** button.
- Excel opens and as before will ask you whether it is OK to open the document in an Excel-compatible format. Click on **YES**.

There are only 24 survey cases and you queried over 20 codes. So don't expect the numbers to be very meaningful. Remember that this is just a small sample project for you to practice on. Imagine a larger survey with 500 respondents or more. Then the results are more likely to be meaningful. What you can still see is that the following reasons did not come up in the survey (0 hits):

reasons for hc: focusing illusion
reasons for hc: personality
reasons for hc: richer life
reasons for nhc: adoption
reasons for nhc: don't feel the need
reasons for nhc: personality

By now you should be able to check whether these are reasons that are only mentioned by the blog writers ☺.

Tip: The easiest way to find out is to create another Codes-Primary Documents Table cross-tabulating the codes of the two categories 'reasons for hc' and 'reasons for nhc' with P3 and P5.
   The adjusted table without the 0 hits looks like Table 6.3.

Table 6.3   Codes-Primary Documents Table for RQ5

	Gender::female	Gender::male
reasons for hc: altruism	1	2
reasons for hc: always knew it	0	2
reasons for hc: biology	2	1
reasons for hc: cultural embedded beliefs	0	1
reasons for hc: feel good about trade-off	1	0
reasons for hc: for oneself / self-centered	2	1
reasons for hc: influencing course of the world	1	0
reasons for hc: shaping a human life	1	2
reasons for hc: unconditional love	3	0

(Continued)

Table 6.3 *(Continued)*

	Gender::female	Gender::male
reasons for nhc: being there for others	3	0
reasons for nhc: not worth the trade-off	1	1
reasons for nhc: responsibility	0	2
reasons for nhc: self-centered	7	6
reasons for nhc: state of the world	1	1

Let the data speak to you and follow up on something that appears interesting to you, for instance the views of males and females regarding the issue of self-centeredness. Both groups have mentioned it quite a few times. Do you have an idea about how to go about it? Think for a moment before you read on.

- Open the query tool.
- Double click on the code 'reasons for nhc: self-centered'.
- Click on the **SCOPE** button and select the PD family gender::female. Read the quotations. Remember that the results are always shown in the query tool window not the scope window.
- Change the scope to gender::male and read the quotations.
- Write down your thoughts and interpretation in the research question memo for RQ5 (Figure 6.30).

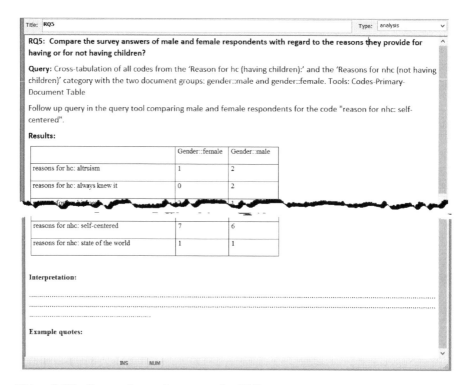

Figure 6.30 Research question memo for RQ5

Creating super PD families

Next, I want to show how you can combine various attributes. This can be done more easily in version 7 of ATLAS.ti as compared to older versions. Combining document attributes technically means creating super PD families. Let's consider the following question:

RQ6: Is there a difference between male and female survey respondents WITH CHILDREN regarding their perception of parenting (positive or negative)?

In order to answer this question, we first need to create two super PD families, one for males with children and one for females with children:

- Open the P-Docs Manager.
- Click on the Venn diagram so that only the intersection is colored in gray.
- Select the two PD families 'Gender::male' and 'has children::yes' by holding down the CTRL key. These two characteristics apply to six documents. You can see the frequency at the bottom left of the P-Docs Manager (Figure 6.31).

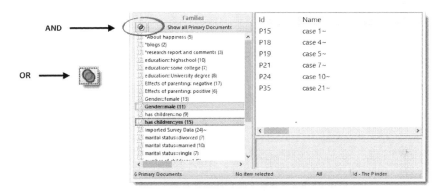

Figure 6.31   Creating a super PD family with the help of the Venn diagram

- Right-click on any of the two selected families and select the option **Create Super Family**. The new super family is immediately created and ATLAS.ti assigns a default name. You can rename the family later.

All 'super' objects in ATLAS.ti are colored red, hence also super PD families (Figure 6.32). Further, instead of the frequency value that you see behind each regular family name, an asterisk (*) is displayed behind super families. The reason is that super families are updated dynamically. If you enter more survey respondents and thus more documents are added to the 'gender::male' and 'has children: yes' families, the affected super families are automatically updated. The same happens if you remove documents from a project.

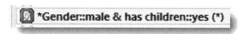

Figure 6.32   Display of super families

- Next, create a super family for all female survey respondents who have children.
- Open the Codes-Primary Documents Table. Select the two new super families in the Primary Document Families pane, and the two codes families 'effects of parenting: negative' and 'effects of parenting: positive' in the Code Families pane. The result is shown in Table 6.4.

Table 6.4   Codes-Primary Documents Table for RQ6

	female & has children:	male & has children
effects of parenting negative	3	5
effects of parenting positive	2	0

As before, the results are not really interpretable because of the small number of cases. In addition, the survey data are entirely fictional – I made them up based on statements I found on the Internet and assigned attributes in an arbitrary manner. If the numbers were higher by a factor of 10, one could deduce that males only mention negative effects of parenting, whereas females are more balanced in their views, providing evidence for both positive and negative effects. The next step would be to examine the various subcodes for positive and negative effects and to read the data behind them. This can be achieved – you should know it by now ☺ – with the help of the query tool and the scope function.

Skills training 6.6: saving a query for later reference (or working with super codes)

We have already come across super families, which are a combination of already existing families. They are created with the help of Boolean operators AND and OR. In fact, a super family is a saved query. The one we have just created in Skills training 6.5 was: 'gender::male' AND 'has children:: yes'. Every time you click on this family, ATLAS.ti retrieves all responses from the male survey respondents who have children.

There is a similar option for code queries. If you want to rerun a query in the future, you can save it as a super code. When you add, modify or delete quotations during the progress of your work, this will be detected by the super code. Every time you click on a super code, the query will be newly calculated and the results will reflect the current state of your coding. Depending on the chosen analytic approach, super codes could be regarded as 'frozen' hypotheses and thus be used to test hypotheses based on newly collected data.

Properties of super codes

- Super codes are symbolized by a red icon in the program rather than the standard yellow icon.
- You can select super codes just like other codes in the Code Manager or in network views and display their virtual connections to quotations.
- Super codes can be part of a code family or a network view. They can also be an argument in other queries. With the aid of super codes, you can therefore create highly complex queries in a few steps. Super codes can contain super codes, which contain super codes, etc.

What super codes cannot be used for

- Coding: super codes cannot be directly linked to quotations. Thus, drag and drop from the Code Manager is not possible and super codes are not shown when selecting the option 'code-by-list'.
- Super codes do not remember filters. A filter set in the Scope of Query window is ignored during the creation process of a super code. The list of results always displays the quotations from the entire project. Thus, when rerunning a super code, you need to apply filters again if you want to break down the results to a subgroup of data.

Creating super codes

The first step in creating a super code is the formulation of a query. For that matter, it is irrelevant whether the query returns any results or not. Super codes are 'intentional', meaning you can also create them based on a query without results. This saves the trouble of having to reformulate the same query later in the analytic process.

- Open the query tool and click on a query.
- Then click on **CREATE SUPER CODE**.
- Accept the default name suggested by ATLAS.ti or enter your own name and click on **OK**.

The suggested default name contains the query details and starts with an asterisk (*). This means super codes are displayed toward the top of the Code Manager when sorted alphabetically. If you change the name or if it is too long, remember to add the query as a definition to the code to indicate what the super code is based on.

If you want to use a different name, I suggest that you leave the default name at first, then go to the Code Manager, copy the default name (= query) into the comment field and enter a new name as code label.

The quotation frequency is not displayed immediately since super codes, like super families, are dynamic; instead of a number, an asterisk is shown (see Figure 6.33). Only when you activate the super code will the valid number of quotations be displayed for the duration of the current work session. If you close and reopen the project, you will see the wild card until you double click on the super code.

Let's consider a research question that can best be solved by creating a super code. The super code will be created to be used in the continuing query.

RQ7: What is the attitude toward the relationship between children and happiness of those responding to the blogs and of those who question the study design?

In order to answer this question, we need to use the following codes. If you do not want to be distracted by the other codes in the list, create a code family for RQ7 that contains the codes listed below and set it as a global filter.

> children: < happiness
> children: = level of happiness
> children: > happiness
> children: unrelated to personal happiness
> study design: asking the wrong question
> study design: critique
> #blog entry

Looking at the codes for study design, the two codes 'study design: asking the wrong question' and 'study design: critique' contain the comments of respondents who question the study design. We need to combine them using the Boolean operator OR. However, since we do not want just the quotations on the study design but the quotations for the entire blog posts where people among other issues question the study design, we need to start the query with the code '#blog entry':

- Open the query tool.
- Double click on '#blog entry' → 139 quotations.

Next, we combine the two study design codes:

- Double click on 'study design: asking the wrong questions'.
- Double click on 'study design: critique'.
- Select OR → 30 quotations.

Now we can identify those quotations that occur within the blog entries:

- Select ENCLOSES (or COOCCUR) → 23 quotations

This is how the query looks in the query tool:

("#blog entry" COOCCUR ("study design: asking the wrong question" | "study design: critique"))

- To save this query, click on the **SUPER CODE** button and enter a new name for the super code (e.g. #those who question study design).

Figure 6.33 Super codes display a wild card for the code frequency until you activate them

Having created this super code, we can explore the attitude these people have regarding the relationship between happiness and children:

- Click on the C button to clear the previous query.
- Double click on 'children:<happiness'.
- Double click on the newly created super code.
- Select COOCCUR (or WITHIN) → 0 quotations

Display of query in the query tool:

(*"children: < happiness" WITHIN "#those who question study design"*)

Repeat this for the three other codes in the C_CHILDREN category (Figure 6.34). Or, create a Codes Co-Occurrence Table. This is the quicker option. You will find two quotations for 'children: = happiness' and three for 'children: unrelated to personal happiness'. Thus, these findings are not very exciting.

| Title: | RQ7 | | Type: | analysis | ⌄ |

RQ7: What is the attitude toward the relationship between children and happiness of those responding to the blogs and of those who question the study design?

The following codes were queried:
  children: < happiness
  children: = level of happiness
  children: > happiness
  children: unrelated to personal happiness
  study design: asking the wrong question
  study design: critique
  #blog entry

("#blog entry" COOCCUR ("study design: asking the wrong question" | "study design: critique"))
---> super code #those who question study design

("children: < happiness" WITHIN "#those who question study design")
("children: = happiness" WITHIN "#those who question study design")
("children: > happiness" WITHIN "#those who question study design")

Result and interpretation:
....
....
....

Example quotes:

Figure 6.34 Research question memo for RQ7

Nonetheless, you learned three things: how to create a super code; how to use it in a continuing query; and, as a side effect, that it does not take very long to create such a query. Even if some questions lead to a dead end, it won't take you a whole day to figure it out.

Miscellaneous: editing supercode queries

If you get into the habit of clicking on queries and develop a taste for complicated queries that you want to store as super codes, you have the option to edit the query directly. Some ATLAS.ti users will definitely want to use this option, so this is how it is done:

- Right click on the super code and select **MISCELLANEOUS / EDIT QUERY**.

Figure 6.35 shows what the syntax for a supercode query looks like and provides some instructions on how to edit it. You can see the instructions when you click on the help button in the editor window.

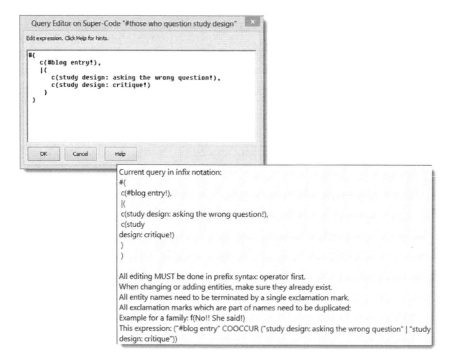

Figure 6.35 Editing a super code query

Skills training 6.7: climbing the hills and clicking on more complex queries

The next exercises are for those who like brain gymnastics.

RQ8: Explore the perception of various groups of blog writers with regard to how they view the relationship between happiness and children. Does it make a difference if they mention only positive or only negative or both positive and negative effects of parenting?

How would you go about it? You have now learned all the skills you need to figure it out on your own. If you get stuck, you will find step-by-step instructions at the end of this chapter. If you want to test your understanding of the ATLAS.ti analysis tools, especially your understanding of the query tool, try it yourself first. I will guide you by providing general instructions, but without spelling out each mouse click.

This is how you need to get started to create the three subgroups:

1. Find all blog entries where people only mention negative aspects of parenting.
2. Find all blog entries where people only mention positive aspects of parenting.
3. Find all blog entries where people mention both positive and negative aspects of parenting.

Once you have found the 14 blog posts where only negative aspects are mentioned and saved them as a super code, continue with finding the blog posts that only contain positive aspects (12 quotations). Save the result as a super code. And lastly find those where both aspects have been mentioned (8 quotations) and save the result as a super code.

Explore how these three respondent groups see the relationship between children and happiness (subcodes of C_Children).

Table 6.5 shows the final result. Even though the numbers are small, there appears to be a tendency that those who report only negative effects of parenting perceive that children do make you unhappy, or at least not happier. Those who report only positive effects either take a neutral stand or believe that children add to happiness. As the blog data are not fictional, this is an interesting finding.

Table 6.5   Result of RQ8

	#blog entries both pos. and neg. effects	#blog entries only neg. effects	#blog entries only pos. effects
children: < happiness	0	4	0
children: = level of happiness	1	3	3
children: > happiness	1	0	5
children: unrelated to personal happiness	1	0	0

Let's continue to query the data based on three subgroups we have created:

RQ9: Do the two groups of respondents (those who only mention negative effects of parenting and those who only mention positive effects of parenting) also differ with regard to other issues that have been raised in the blogs?

This question is best answered by using the Cooccurrence Explorer, which I have not yet introduced. It works on the same principles as the Codes Co-Occurrence Table, but displays the result in a different way. This is what it looks like (Figure 6.36):

- From the main menu, select **ANALYSIS / CODE COOCCURRENCE EXPLORER**.

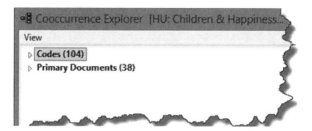

Figure 6.36   Opening window of the Cooccurrence Explorer

- Click on the arrow before **Codes** to open the tree. The number of codes may differ on your screen, depending on how many super codes you have created in the meantime.
- Expand the tree for the two super codes created to answer RQ8: '#blog entries only incl. pos effects' and '#blog entries only incl. neg effects'. The actual names may differ depending on how you have named your super codes.

   In order to create the tree shown in Figure 6.37, I have created a code family that does include all codes except the effects of parenting codes as these are

Figure 6.37   Cooccurrence Explorer expanded to code level

already included in the super codes and only the two attribute codes '#fam: have children' and '#fam: don't have children'. This helps to focus the view. If you work with the sample file prepared for this chapter, look for the code family RQ9 and set it as a global filter before you run the Cooccurrence Explorer. Otherwise, you need to create this family yourself.

What you can see is that we are only dealing with blog entries written by parents. Those exclusively mentioning positive effects of parenting offer a broader range of reasons for having children, only providing one reason for not having children: adoption. They also mention children to be a source of happiness and see the positive sides behind the hard work of having children. Those who focus on the negative sides of parenting offer fewer reasons for having children and two for not having children.

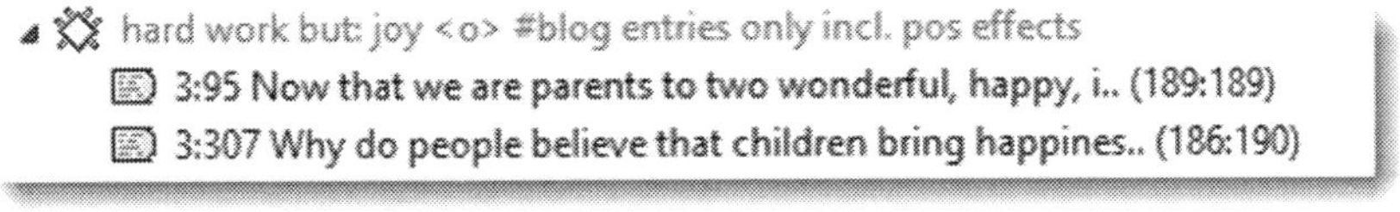

Figure 6.38 Cooccurrence Explorer expanded to quotation level

- If you want to read the quotations, click on a cooccurring code of your interest and expand the tree further.

In Figure 6.38, the **View** option in the Cooccurrence Explorer has been set to show images. You see two cooccurring quotations for 'hard work but joy' <o> '#blog entries only incl. pos effect', but it is only one cooccurring event. Recall Skills training 6.2, where I explained the proximity operators. As

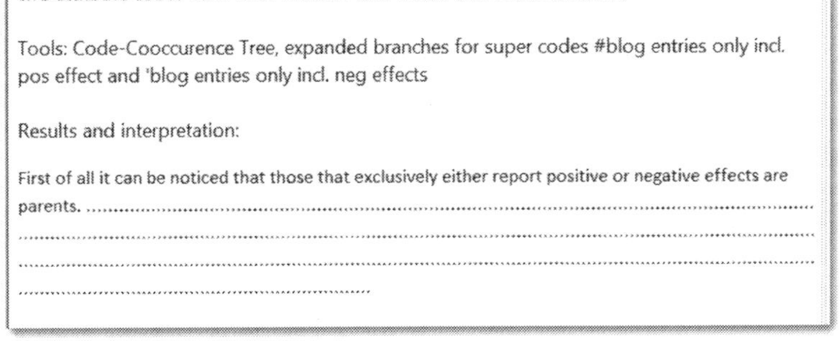

Title: RQ9 Type: Commentary

RQ9: Do the two groups of respondents (those who only mention negative effects of parenting and those who only mention positive effects of parenting) also differ with regard to other issues that have been raised in the blogs?

prepared a code family as filter that includes all codes but the effects of parenting codes + the two attribute codes 'fam: have children' and '#fam: don't have children'.

Tools: Code-Cooccurence Tree, expanded branches for super codes #blog entries only incl. pos effect and 'blog entries only incl. neg effects

Results and interpretation:

First of all it can be noticed that those that exclusively either report positive or negative effects are parents. ....

Figure 6.39 Research question memo for RQ9

ATLAS.ti cannot find lines or segments in your data that are not quotations, the actual overlap between two quotations cannot be shown – unless it is an AND occurrence. Therefore, for an overlapping occurrence you will see two quotations. The first one here is the one coded with 'hard work but joy' starting and ending in paragraph 189; the second is the quotation for the super code '#blog entries only incl. pos effects', ranging from paragraph 189 to paragraph 190. If you double click on a quotation in the Cooccurrence Explorer, you can view the data in context.

The research question memo is shown in Figure 6.39.

You are probably somewhat exhausted by now. This is normal when you're going uphill, but the view from the top is your reward (Figure 6.40). I hope that at least sometimes you felt, 'Yeah, I am getting there. This is great. I can see things in my data landscape that I did not dream of when I started to explore.'

While you take a rest, open your backpack, take out something to eat and drink, maybe a notepad to write down some notes as well, and let me point out a few last issues.

Figure 6.40   Rewarding view from the top

On the use of code families

In Chapter 5, I mentioned that it is best not to use code families as higher order category codes in a hierarchical sense. I showed you how to go about developing subcategories and how to aggregate codes from a lower level to a conceptual level, making use of code families as a filter tool. In this chapter you have seen how useful code families are in formulating queries. For this reason, I generally create code families from all main categories and their subcodes once the code scheme is developed. I advise against using code families solely for the purpose of creating categories. This results in an unstructured list of codes that is difficult for you to handle and for others to comprehend.

What also often happens when code families are used to aggregate codes is that early descriptive codes are not developed further into 'proper' codes. They are just grouped into a family without being further conceptualized. As I mentioned in Chapter 5, neither ATLAS.ti nor any CAQDAS package can recognize the different levels of codes. It is up to the software user to make this distinction. If a code remains at the descriptive level and is not conceptualized, there is no warning sound or flashing red light indicating: 'Please take a look at this code; it is not yet a proper code. You need to work on it a bit more!'

To the software, a code is just an object that can be attached to various other objects and whose content can be searched and retrieved. Everything else is up to you.

A further aspect that needs to be considered is that although code families can be included in network views, they can be linked neither to each other nor to other codes using named relations (Figure 6.41).

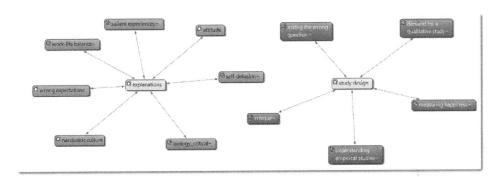

Figure 6.41   Code families displayed in a network view

Well you might say that this is not much of a disadvantage as most of the interesting linkages are not on the category but on the subcategory level. I agree. The greater danger I see when using code families as category codes is that descriptive label codes are not conceptualized properly and remain unsorted in the Code Manager. This is demonstrated in Figure 6.42 with just a small selection of 33 codes and 5 'code family categories'.

A second reason for not using code families as categories is methodological rigor. The first step should always be to develop the coding system in a proper manner. This means that codes should not be all over the place on different levels with no indication of which code belongs where and what kind of meaning it has. If you use the code family function in ATLAS.ti too early, it undermines this process and the families will get in the way of building a systematic, transparent and comprehensible coding system.

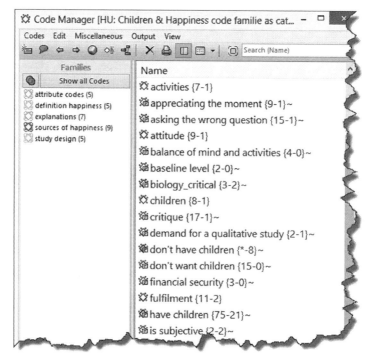

Figure 6.42   You don't want your code list to look like this

On the use of numbers and how perfect does the code system need to be?

We have seen throughout the chapter that quotation frequencies, the number of codes and subcodes, provide an initial overview but need to be interpreted with care in a qualitative context. It is always good advice to review the data behind the numbers. In addition, remember that the output is only as good as your coding. While preparing the exercises for the book, running through them, testing and reviewing the data, I came across quotations where I wondered why I had coded them the way I did. When the assignment of a code no longer appeared to be meaningful, I unlinked the code, assigned others or modified the segment length. I am sure that this will also happen when you work on your own data. Querying data means you view them from different perspectives, you begin to understand more and more, and with that also your views on how segments should be coded change. Thus, coding and recoding never really finish. If your coding system is built up well, the changes are not huge; however, subtle changes are likely. The hermeneutic circle continues. The more you work with your data, the better you understand what is going on and the closer you approach the underlying meaning.

Thus, when you stop your main coding phase to begin conceptual-level analysis, keep in mind that your coding system does not have to be perfect: 95% perfect is good enough – don't spend another three months trying to reach 99% perfection. As the coding system in most studies is something that continuously changes with progressive analysis, this tells you something about how to make use of and interpret the numbers that ATLAS.ti provides. Use them as indicators, but not as facts.

Summary

In this new chapter you have learned all you need to know about second-level conceptual analysis. We started by looking at the memo function and how to work with linked memos. I emphasized the role of memos as containers for ideas and explained in detail how to set up research question memos so that they can be used as building blocks for the research report. Then it was time for some further skills training to get to know the ATLAS.ti analysis tools. What I hope you have seen in this chapter is that only a well-built-up code system based on categories with subcodes allows you to ask the kind of queries that we have gone through in this chapter. You learned how to click on queries in the query tool; how to create cross-tabulations of codes and cross-tabulations of codes by documents and document groups; how to combine code queries with variables; how to create special filters in the form of families and super families; and how to save queries for later reuse in form of super codes. We also discussed that certain types of data require the use of different tools depending on how you need to treat data attributes. While exploring the Children & Happiness terrain in greater detail by working through nine research questions, you learned how to apply the analysis tools in conjunction with writing research question memos. Knowing which analysis tools are available to ask questions should also feed back to what you have learned in Chapter 5 on how to build an efficient coding system. Your data must be coded in the recommended way in order to be able to ask more complex questions. If for instance none of your codes overlap others, then you can at most use the OR, PRECEDES and FOLLOWS operators. In such a case, your coding system is probably quite simple and you probably won't go any further than simple code retrieval in the Code Manager. The scope button in the query tool may nevertheless be an interesting option for comparing and contrasting groups of documents. You can test your knowledge now by taking the next open book assessment.

REVIEW QUESTIONS

Can you answer the following questions on how to write up the analysis in ATLAS.ti and its analysis tools? If so, you have already gained a good understanding of the second phase of analysis. Congratulations! If you are not sure about some of the answers, fortunately this is a book and not a fleeting lecture. You can go through the chapter again at your own pace and review what you're not yet sure about. Use the provided sample data and click on the instructions to see what is happening on the screen. Or wait until you have coded your own data and can then apply the analysis tools with your

(Continued)

(Continued)

own questions in mind. I have often seen the 'Aha!' effect when users apply the analysis tools to their own data and suddenly see the light.

Here are the questions for you to work through:

1   What is a memo and what are memos used for in qualitative data analysis?
2   ATLAS.ti offers the option to create different memo types. What types will you need for your project and why? What can you use them for?
3   What kind of information should a research question memo contain in order to add transparency to your research and to be used as a building block for your research report?
4   Thinking about your own research project, what kind of memos would be useful to you and why?
5   What kinds of analysis tools are available?
6   Explain the query tool window.
7   Which operators are available to create queries? Explain them.
8   How do you click on a query in the query tool?
9   How can code searches be combined with variables?
10 How do you store a query for later reuse?
11 How do you create reports from query results?
12 What is the purpose of the Codes Co-Occurrency Table and Cooccurrence Explorer? When would you use the tree and when the table explorer?
13 What does the c-coefficient indicate? When is it useful to use it?
14 How do you create and apply filters to restrict a query to a particular part of the data set?
15 Which function do you need to create a frequency table showing code frequencies by documents or document groups?
16 Do you need to use different analysis tools depending on the type of data you have, or are the tools only related to the type of questions you are asking, or both? Why?

GLOSSARY OF TERMS

Cooccurrence tools: The cooccurrence tools can be used for a cross-tabulation of codes. Before you run the tool, it is often advisable to set a code family as filter. The quantitative results of the Codes Co-Occurrence Table can be exported in the form of an Excel table. The findings often need further exploration in the query tool.

The **Codes-Primary Documents Table** shows the frequency of codes or code families across documents or document families. It can be exported as an Excel table. It works well as an exploratory tool in combination with the query tool for further in-depth analysis.

Memos in ATLAS.ti: Regard memos in ATLAS.ti as containers for ideas. Do not create a memo for every single idea. If the idea cannot be developed or expanded over time, then consider whether your thoughts might better be entered as a comment for a quotation.

Operators: ATLAS.ti offers a total of 14 operators that you can use to formulate a code query:

Boolean: OR, XOR, AND, NOT

Semantic: DOWN, UP, SIBLING

Proximity: WITHIN, ENCLOSES, OVERLAPPED BY, OVERLAPS, FOLLOWS, PROCEEDS, COOCCUR

Within a given project, you will probably never use all operators.

Query tool: The query tool can be used to build queries based on codes or code families and a number of different operators. ATLAS.ti provides three sets of operators: Boolean, semantic and proximity operators. The result of a query formulated in the query tool is a list of quotations. Furthermore, code queries can be combined with variables via the scope button within the query tool. Variables are created via the so-called primary document families (see Chapter 5).

Research question memos: These memos form the building blocks for the results section of a research report. They begin with a well-formulated research question, a description of how the answer to this question was found (e.g. in the form of the query that was run) and how it was developed by the analyst over time, and some linked quotations that provide good examples. These linked quotations might later be used as citations in the research report. Research question memos can be added to the project at any time. Some research questions might be known already from the beginning; others may be added or existing questions may be modified throughout the analytic process.

Reverse Polish notation: A code query in the query tool is entered using reverse Polish notation (RPN). This means that you first select the codes or code families and then select one of the operators. Thus, you enter **Code A, Code B, OR** instead of **Code A OR Code B**. The logic of reverse Polish notation bypasses the need to learn syntax.

Role of families in the analytic process: Primary documents and code families are very handy when it comes to querying the data. You need them as filters to ask focused questions. In addition to the filter options in the side panel of the managers, primary document families can also be set as filters via the scope button in the query tool.

Super codes: Super codes represent a saved query. They can be created within the query tool after having clicked on a query. They appear by default in red in the Code Manager and only show frequencies once selected. Each time you activate a super code, the query that it consists of will be run. Thus, a super code is always up to date and changes when the code content that it is based on changes.

Super families: When you need a combination of two or more families (e.g. to prepare a special filter for a code query in the query tool or a Codes-Primary Documents Table, or before you run cooccurrence table or tree explorer), you can create super families. This option is available within the Family Managers.

Further reading

On memos and writing

Birks, Melanie (2008). Memoing in qualitative research: probing data and processes, *Journal of Research in Nursing*, 13, 68–75.

Charmaz, Kathy (2006). *Constructing Grounded Theory: A Practical Guide Through Qualitative Analysis*. London: Sage. Chapter 4.

Corbin, Juliet and Strauss, Anselm (2008). *Basics of Qualitative Research: Techniques and Procedures for Developing Grounded Theory*, 3rd edn. London: Sage. Chapters 6–12.

Lewins, Ann and Silver, Christine (2007). *Using Software in Qualitative Research: A Step-by-step Guide*. London: Sage. Chapter 9.

Okeley, Judith (1994). Thinking through fieldwork, in Alan Bryman and Robert G. Burgess (eds), *Analyzing Qualitative Data*. London: Routledge. pp. 111–28.

Richardson, Laural (2003). Writing: a method of inquiry, in S.N. Hesse-Biber and P. Leavy (eds), *Approaches to Qualitative Research: A Reader on Theory and Practice*. Oxford: Oxford University Press. Chapter 22.

Wolcott, Harry E. (1994). *Transforming Qualitative Data: Description, Analysis and Interpretation*. London: Sage.

Wolcott, Harry E. (2009). *Writing up Qualitative Research*, 3rd edn. London: Sage.

On querying data

Ayres, Lioness, Kavanaugh, Karen and Knafl, Kathleen (2003). Within-case and across-case approaches to qualitative data analysis, *Qualitative Health Research*, 13(6), 871–83.

Bazeley, Pat (2002). Issues in mixing qualitative and quantitative approaches to research. Presented at the 1st International Conference on Qualitative Research in Marketing and Management, University of Economics and Business Administration, Vienna. www.researchsupport.com.au/MMIssues.pdf.

Kelle, Udo (ed.) (1995). *Computer-aided Qualitative Data Analysis*. London: Sage. Part III.

Kelle, Udo (2004). Computer-assisted qualitative data analysis, in C. Seale et al. (eds), *Qualitative Research Practice*. London: Sage. pp. 473–89.

Lewins, Ann and Silver, Christine (2007). *Using Software in Qualitative Research: A Step-by-step Guide*. London: Sage. Chapter 8.

Miles, Matthew B. and Huberman, Michael (1994). *Qualitative Data Analysis*, 2nd edn. Thousand Oaks, CA: Sage. Chapters 5–10.

Solutions

A reminder of set theory for understanding Boolean operators

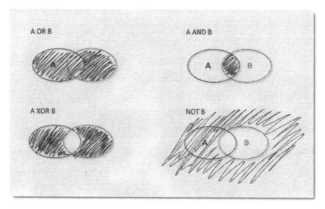

Figure 6.43   Solutions to Boolean queries

Step-by-step instruction to answer RQ8

Explore the perception of various groups of blog writers with regard to how they view the relationship between happiness and children. Does it make a difference if they mention only positive or only negative or both positive and negative effects of parenting?

At first we need to find all blog entries where writers mention positive (resp. negative) effects of parenting and store the result as super code:

- Open the query tool.
- Double click on the code '#blog entries'.
- Double click on the code family 'effects of parenting positive'.
- Select the operator ENCLOSES (alternatively COOCCUR). → **12 quotations**

Your query in the query tool:

(*"#blog entries" ENCLOSES "effects of parenting positive"*)

- Click on the SUPER CODE button to save the query. Leave the default name or enter a new one. I used '#blog entries incl. pos effects'.
- Repeat the above steps to create a super code for all blog entries that include negative effects of parenting. I called it '#blog entries: incl. neg effects' → **14 quotations**.

Based on these two new super codes, we can now create two more super codes that only include either positive or negative statements related to effects of parenting. Let's start with the exclusive positive statements.

- Double click on the supercode '#blog entries: incl. pos effects'.
- Double click on the supercode '#blog entries: incl. neg effects'.
- As we want to exclude all statements containing reports on negative effects of parenting, select the NOT operator.

The next step is to combine the two arguments currently listed in the stack of terms: the blog entries containing statements on positive effects of parenting and everything else that is not blog posts containing negative reports. If you look at Figure 6.42, we need the dark gray area that only contains statements on positive effects. And this is the intersection of the two terms currently in our stack.

- Therefore click on the AND operator. The resulting query looks like this:

(*"#blog entries incl. pos effects" & NOT "#blog entries incl. neg effects"*)

When looking at the resulting query in the feedback pane, it is easy to see what we did. You can read it as 'blog entries including pos. effects statements' *but not* 'negative effects statements'. In Figure 6.44, the query is illustrated in the form of Venn diagrams.

Generally, if you want to exclude quotations from a code or code family you must:

1. Choose the code or code family from which you want to exclude something, or create a query first.
2. Select the code/code family whose quotation should be excluded.
3. Negate it with NOT.
4. Combine the two resulting terms with AND.

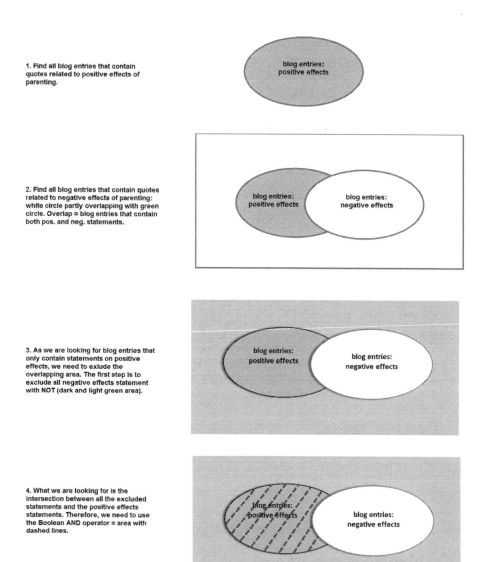

Figure 6.44   Illustration of the Boolean queries needed to solve RQ9 with Venn diagrams

SEVEN

Working with network views

The ATLAS.ti network view function is a tool that allows you to explore your data visually. We started the journey by looking at an unknown landscape (see the Introduction, 'Computer-assisted analysis is like exploring a data landscape'). Then we began to explore it by noticing interesting things. After a while we were able to label what we noticed and we gained a better understanding of the data landscape during the process of first- and second-cycle coding (see Chapter 5, 'The journey begins'). At first this was a descriptive understanding. With a prolonged stay and further exploration we were able to describe the various aspects of our data landscape and their specifications in the form of a well-developed code system (see Chapter 5, 'Skills trainings 5.4 and 5.5').

This enabled us to dig a bit deeper and to ask more specific questions utilizing a number of different tools provided by the ATLAS.ti toolkit (see Chapter 6). Our notebook (the memo function) became even more of an indispensable companion. In order to be able to explain later how we discovered something, we noted down every step of the analytic process and described each examination in detail, writing down what we found. We added some example quotes to our notes so that later we would be able to illustrate our findings to others. All this was achieved by writing research question memos. By writing these memos, step by step we gained an understanding of what the data landscape is like and how the various aspects are related and linked to each other.

Visualizing these links in the form of the ATLAS.ti network views is the natural next step. Graphic illustrations enable a different kind of exploration. Images, as compared to words, activate different parts of the brain and lead to different ways of processing (e.g. Khateb et al., 2002). The ATLAS.ti network views illustrate findings in the form of concept maps. Concept maps are known to aid creativity and to help in detailing the entire structure of an idea or a line of argument. They enhance metacognition in the form of elucidating and thinking about knowledge. On the receiver end, they support the creation of a shared understanding and help to communicate complex ideas and arguments (Novak and Cañas, 2006; Novak and Gowin, 2002).

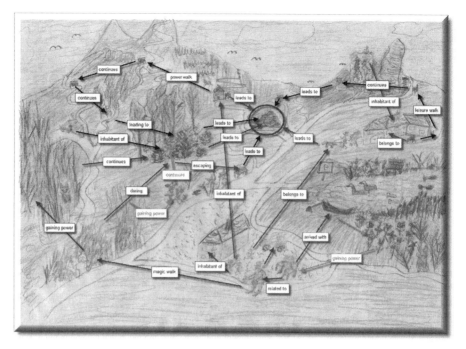

Figure 7.1 Concept map of the data landscape

Figure 7.1 shows the story that can be told about our imaginary data land-scape. You can see which people belong together, who is living where and related to whom, and furthermore the secret attraction of this valley: the cairn of wisdom. Not everybody has access to the cairn of wisdom; some can only observe from the outside while others undergo various rituals in order to gain entry – though this requires such mental strength and willpower that not all inhabitants of the valley or its visitors will succeed ... If you enjoy storytelling, look at the concept map laid over the data landscape and try to continue the story. You can embellish it with further detail, mystery and possibly a happy ending.

In this chapter, I will first provide some ideas for you about for which purposes the network view function can be used. This includes how to make use of the network view function for analytic purposes, a new feature that was added in version 7 of ATLAS.ti. You will also learn how to create a nice-looking code book illustrated by network views. After this pragmatic intro-duction, I will explain the technicalities of working with network views. Once again this will require some skills training. You will need to learn some new terminology, how the network view function is integrated within the HU, and of course how to create links and relations. In this chapter, the order in which you go through the skills training after Skills training 7.1 doesn't matter. Some may prefer to start with the technicalities (Skills training 7.4); others may like the pragmatic approach and first want to learn about the application of network views.

Skills trainings

Skills training 7.1: learning terminology

Skills training 7.2: using network views for conceptual-level analysis

Skills training 7.3: using network views to pimp up your code book

Skills training 7.4: creating network views

Skills training 7.5: working with the Relations Editor

Skills training 7.6: saving and exporting network views

Skills training 7.7: working with hyperlinks

Skills training 7.1: learning terminology

The ATLAS.ti concept maps are called **network views** because each of the views you create offers some insight into the whole network, which is your HU. Basically, everything you do in ATLAS.ti – each link you create, be it a code–quotation link, a code–memo link, a memo–quotation link, a code family linked to its code members, and so on – can be visualized. The entire HU consists of links and thus represents the total network. The process of coding has already generated a great number of links between individual codes and the data segments they encode.

Figure 7.2 shows the code 'effects pos: improved relationships', which codes six data segments and is linked to two other codes. Incidentally, each object that becomes part of a network view is called a **node**.

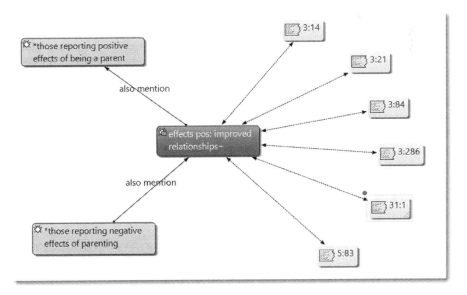

Figure 7.2   First- and second-class relations

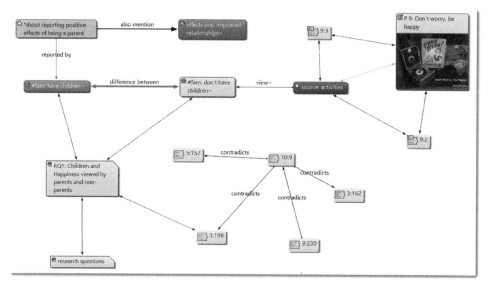

Figure 7.3   Examples of the various possible links and visualization options

As you can see from the network view here, there are different types of relations – just a line linking two objects or a line plus a name for the link. The named links are referred to as **first-class relations** and the unnamed links as **second-class relations**. First-class relations can only be created between two codes or between two quotations. All other links are second class. In Figure 7.3 you will see an overview of possible links.

First-class relations can be **directed**, that is pointing from A to B (A -> B), or **undirected** (A <--> B). In Figure 7.3 you can see an example of each one. The property of directed relations is **transitive** and those of undirected relations **symmetric**. We need to know these terms when creating new relations, as I will show in Skills training 7.5.

Second-class relations can be created between memos and quotations, codes and quotations, and memos and other memos. Further existing links between quotations and primary documents, codes and primary documents, and between families and their members can be visualized as well. These links are second class, thus cannot be named. When you open a network view on a family, the lines between the family node and the member nodes are shown automatically. The same happens if you import quotations or codes for a PD.

In Figure 7.3 you can see an image PD that has been added to the network view. You cannot manually link the image, or any other PD for that matter, to anything. But existing linkages, for example to codes that have been applied to the PD, can be visualized (see also Figure 7.10).

You can choose from a number of display options. I will not describe all of them in this chapter as most are self-explanatory, but here is a list of things you can do. Figure 7.3 only shows quotation IDs, but you can extend the display up to the full text for each quotation. Code nodes can be shown with and without their groundedness and density counts (Figures 7.6 and 7.7). If you don't like the node bitmaps, you can deactivate them, and so on. You will explore the available options in Skills training 7.4.

In addition to the various layout options, a number of actions are also available. Network views do not simply display your project items: you can also access the data behind the image. Double clicking on a memo in a network view will display the memo text. Video and audio quotations are played when you click on them in a network view. Double click on a quotation and you will see the full content. If you right click on a quotation, you will find the option 'Display in context'. When right clicking on a code, you have the option to list all quotations coded by that code and to access the data from the list (Figure 7.8).

Skills training 7.2: using network views for conceptual-level analysis

In version 7 of ATLAS.ti a little thing was changed that has a large effect on what is possible with network views. This little thing is that filters also have an effect on network views. In previous versions this meant that some functions produced pretty pictures, which, however, only cluttered up the network view and could not be interpreted in a meaningful way due to the missing filter settings. As filters have an effect now, network views can be used for conceptual-level analysis. I would like to introduce this new functionality to you in a pragmatic manner by going through a few examples without first telling you the more boring technicalities of the network view function. This way, you will learn some of the mechanical stuff just by doing it. If you are more the theoretical kind of person, you may want to go through Skills training 7.4 and 7.5 first and then return to this section.

Exploring code–cooccurrences in network views

Let's take a look at RQ1, which we have already explored in Chapter 6, and see how we can find an answer to it using the network view function.

RQ1: Do blog respondents who have children define happiness differently from those without children?

If you want to click along, you can continue to work with the 'Children & Happiness analysis exercises' project from the companion website. It is a coded project that does not yet contain links. The stage II project that you can directly access from within ATLAS.ti already includes links and network views.

- Open the 'Children & Happiness analysis exercises' project.
- Open the Code Manager and set the code family '*RQ1: Skills training 7.2' as the global filter. If you need a reminder of how this works, see Skills training 6.3. The code family contains all the codes that we need for this query. You will see a few steps further down below why it is necessary to set a global filter.

- Select the code "#fam: have children' and click on the network view button to open a network view editor for this code.
- Right click on the code (node) in the editor and select the option **Import Cooccurring** (Figure 7.4). By that cooccurring codes are meant.

Now ATLAS.ti runs the same query as it does when preparing a Codes Co-Occurrence Table or when you use the COOCCUR operator in the query tool. This means the following five combinations of cooccurrences in the data are tested: A OVERLAPS B, A is OVERLAPPED BY B, A WITHIN B, A ENCLOSES B, A AND B. If you do not set a filter, this query is run for all codes that cooccur with '#fam: have children'. However, this is not what we are interested in. We only want to see how parents define happiness (in comparison to non-parents). Therefore, it was necessary to set the global filter. The result of the import is shown in Figure 7.5.

Figure 7.4   Network view editor displaying a single code

Figure 7.5   Network view displaying imported code nodes

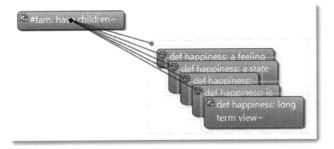

Figure 7.6 Linking codes in a network view

Cooccurring codes are not automatically linked. In order not to lose the connection between the codes, I am going to show you how to link them:

- Highlight all cooccurring codes (green on-screen) by drawing a frame around them with your mouse. As shown in Figure 7.5, all selected nodes display a dot (red) in the top left hand corner.
- Click on the **LINK NODES** button in the toolbar and move the mouse pointer on top of the '#fam: have children' code. Left click. A list of relations opens. Select for instance the relation **VIEW**.
- You could work a bit on the layout of the network view, but this is not important at this stage. You can for instance move the nodes with your mouse pointer to a different position, or select **LAYOUT / SEMANTIC LAYOUT** to spread the nodes in the network view editor (Figure 7.6). Try it out if you like and then minimize the network view.

Let's repeat the process for those without children:

- In the Code Manager select the code '#fam: don't have children' and open a network view on this code. Import the neighbors for this code and link them to the '#fam: don't have children' code in the same way as was explained above. This time there are only two cooccurring codes.
- Close the second network view. You will be asked whether you want to save this network view. Select the option **DISCARD CHANGES**. The links you have created are not deleted just because you close the view. The view, however, is no longer necessary as we only needed it to find the cooccurring codes and to link them to the '#fam: don't have children' code.
- Open up the minimized network view that we created first on the '#fam: have children code'. Now drag and drop the '#fam: don't have children' code from the Code Manager into this network view. The two codes that we have linked before to the '#fam: don't have children' code will show automatically. Thus, you see that ATLAS.ti remembers established links even if you close a view.
- Now arrange the codes in such a way that the story this network view is telling starts to make sense. For instance, position the two codes that apply to both parents and non-parents between these two codes, and the three others that only have been mentioned by parents on the right hand side of the network view (compare Figure 7.7).

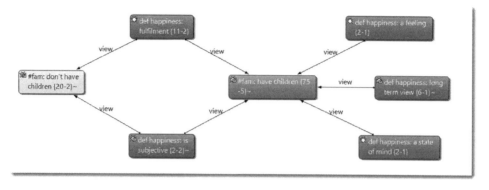

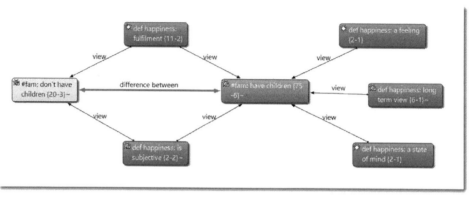

Figure 7.7 Building a network view to represent the results of a research question

Next, you can link the parent and non-parent codes to each other by expressing what you want to point out in this network view: the difference between their views.

- Select for instance the '#fam: don't have children' code and drag the red dot to the '#fam: have children' code. As relation select 'difference between'. This relation is not one of the standard relations that come with the program – I have created it for the sample project. You will learn in Skills training 7.5 how to create your own relations. Figure 7.7 shows a possible layout for visualizing the findings of RQ1.

In Figure 7.7, you can see the frequency and density counts behind the code labels. The density count shows how often a code is linked to other codes. To activate this option select DISPLAY / EXTENDED CODE LABEL. Whether the network view already tells the complete story can only be discovered after reading the data behind the code nodes. Thus, you can either follow up on what the network view shows you by using the query tool as was explained in Skills training 6.2, or directly access the data behind the code nodes:

- Right click on a code node and select the option LIST QUOTATIONS (Figure 7.8). This opens a quotation list, as you know from double clicking on a code in the Code Manager, for instance. Select each quotation with a single click to view it in the context of the data.

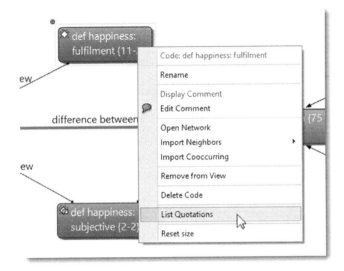

Figure 7.8 Accessing the data behind code nodes in a network view

After reading the data behind the network view, and finding that the links are correct and that the relations apply, you can save the network view. This way, you preserve the view in the way you have created it and can always review it later or continue to work on it. This also allows you to insert the network view into a report or presentation. You can also export it as a graphic file.

- To save the network view select **Network / Save As...** and enter a name for the view like 'RQ1: Different ways of defining happiness by parents and non-parents'. If you close the network view without saving it, ATLAS.ti will ask you whether you want to save it. Then you can still decide to do it.

How to export a network view as a graphic file or insert it into a report or presentation is explained in Skills trainings 7.3 and 7.7.

If you would like to practice this analytic feature of the network view function, here is one more research question for you to explore:

RQ10: Is there a difference between those with one child and those with two or more children with regards to the negative effects of parenting they report? This is how you go about finding an answer:

- Remove the global filter that you have set for RQ1 (e.g. **Tools / Reset all Filters**) and set '*RQ10: Skills Training 7.2' as the global filter.
- Proceed as described above to import cooccurring codes, first for the code '#fam: 1 child' and next for the code '#fam: 2 or more children' in two different network views. Link the attribute codes with the effects of parenting codes, for example by using the relation perceive.
- Close the network view for '#fam: 2 or more children'.
- Drag the code '#fam:2 or more children' from the Code Manager into the network view that contains the '#fam: 1 child' code. You may wonder why there is only one link that is established between the '#fam: 2 or more children' and the effects of

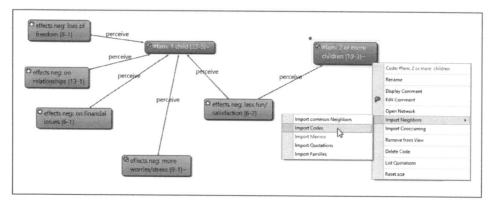

Figure 7.9 Importing linked codes

parenting codes (see Figure 7.9). Look at the density count. It tells you that this code has been linked to three codes altogether. The reason why you do not see these codes is that they are not also linked to the '#fam: 1 child' code. This was different when we examined RQ1. There, the two codes linked to '#fam: don't have children' were also linked to '#fam: have children'.

- To import the remaining two linked codes into the network view, right click on the '#fam: 2 or more children' code and select IMPORT NEIGHBORS / IMPORT CODES (Figure 7.9).
- As there appears to be a difference between first-time or one-child parents and those who have two or more children, as before with RQ1, you can also link these two codes with the relation *difference between*.

Even if this is a very small data set, I am always surprised how well the data can be interpreted. I find the network view quite telling. Those with two or more children seem to have put up with the loss of freedom; difficulties with relationships have been overcome; and they no longer seem to experience children as stressful (or have got used to it) and they worry less. Does this finding motivate you to look immediately at how the two groups compare in terms of the positive effects they mention? Go ahead and check – the data are coded and the ideas and queries that come to mind are just a few mouse clicks away. I can tell you already that the findings are also interesting.

Case-based analysis in network views

Another new option in ATLAS.ti 7 is the object sensitive import. You have already seen in Figure 7.9 that you can choose the type of objects that can be imported. Depending on which object you select (code, quotation, memo or PD), the *Import Neighbors* submenu shows different options. When combining this new import option with filters, it is possible to compare documents in terms of their coding. Let's take a new look at RQ3 and explore it in a network view:

RQ3: Compare the comments written on Belkin's blog to those written on the *New York Times* blog regarding for instance sources of happiness.

- Set the 'Sources of happiness' code family as the global filter in the Code Manger.
- Open the P-Docs Manager, hold down the CTRL key and select P3 (Belkin's blog) and P5 (*New York Times* blog). Click on the network view button in the toolbar.
- A network view editor will open displaying the two documents in *full image* view. If you do not have sufficient space on your screen, deactivate this option under the **DISPLAY** menu. If you do not see full images, you can also activate the option via the **DISPLAY** menu (see Figure 7.10).
- To see which of the 'sources' codes have been used in either P3 or P5, right click on P3 and select the option **IMPORT NEIGHBORS / IMPORT CODES**. Repeat this for P5.
- Move the code nodes around with your mouse to see which code is linked to which document. Codes that have been applied to the documents are linked with a thin gray line. Arrange the two documents so you can see whether there is a difference between them.

Let's extend the research question a bit and add P10 to the network view. P10 contains summaries of research findings regarding sources of happiness. Adding this document allows us to see the difference between what has been written on the blogs as compared to what science tells us:

- To add P10 to the network view, drag and drop it from the P-Docs Manager into the network view.
- To see whether it contains further codes, you also need to import the codes for this document. Thus, right click on and select **IMPORT NEIGHBORS / IMPORT CODES** once again.

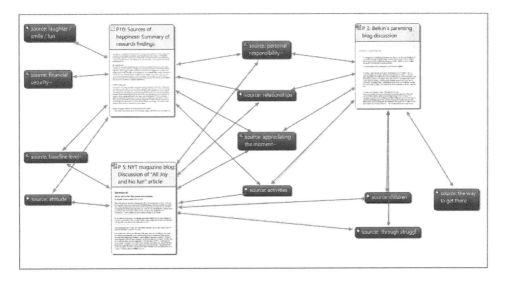

Figure 7.10 Case-based network view

- Arrange the network view in such a way that you can see which of the 'sources' codes apply to all three documents, which to only two documents and which to only one of the three (Figure 7.10).

What can be seen is that most scientifically proven sources of happiness have been mentioned by those responding to the blogs. What they did not take into account was that financial security and simply the fact that putting a smile on your face make you happier. Explicitly mentioned by the blog writers but not in scientific reports were children and that happiness is something that needs to be achieved either through struggle or as a never-ending pursuit.

Using network views to discuss findings with your adviser or colleague(s)

As already mentioned above, visual images activate different regions in our brains and stimulate us to think in different ways. You may send your adviser or colleagues an excerpt from your analysis chapter before scheduling a meeting, so they can get an idea about your work. Prepare one or two network views that visualize the main arguments that you want to discuss and bring a printout and possibly also your laptop to the next meeting (see Skills training 7.6 on how to prepare a printout). Instead of going through pages of text, you can explain your ideas while looking at and discussing the network view(s). You can clarify why you linked the nodes the way you did and why you used a particular type of relation. If there are questions related to the underlying data, you can open the network view(s) in ATLAS.ti on your laptop and access the data from within the network view (see Figure 7.8).

Talking about the findings based on the printed-out network view might, however, already be sufficient. Working with a different medium, paper in this case, can be a nice change, especially when it comes to visualizing ideas. You can extend your ideas by scribbling notes on the printout or by drawing new 'network views' on paper. After the meeting take these back to your office and transfer your ideas, notes and paper-based network views to ATLAS.ti. As the data in ATLAS.ti are only a few mouse clicks away, you can verify whether the ideas are valid and still hold when checking them against the data. If so, you can refine your current network views and the analysis you wrote in your research question memos.

Using network views to present findings

Below, I present some example network views from various studies in order to provide some ideas on how network views can be used to present findings. For smaller projects, like a Master's thesis, it might be possible to integrate all findings into just one network view, but sometimes several are needed.

These 'final' network views can be saved as graphic files and inserted into reports or presentations. You can also copy and paste network views directly. In Skills training 7.3 you will learn how to do it.

Illustrating results from the Schwarzenegger project

The network view shown in Figure 7.11 illustrates a result from analyzing the sample data set used for the first edition of this book. The data consisted of newspaper articles from Germany and the USA collected one day after Arnold Schwarzenegger was elected Governor in California in the 2003 recall election.[1] You can insert the network view as a graphic into a PowerPoint or Prezi presentation and explain what you found. Prezi has the advantage of being able to zoom to the parts of the network view you are currently talking about. The text that goes along with the network view shown here could be something like this:

> The network view shows that there are differences in topics covered by the German local and the German national press. As can be seen from the network view, the local press did not provide background information on the recall process; instead it focused on the election results, the reactions to the results and the person of Arnold Schwarzenegger. In comparison, the national press provided background information as well as reporting on the person and the election results, with a strong focus on Schwarzenegger's political program.

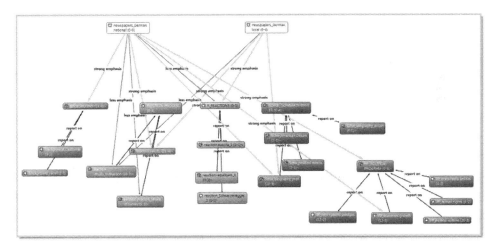

Figure 7.11 Network view of the issues covered by the German local and national press

---

1 Incidentally, the data set is still available on the companion website in case you are interested in using it as sample data.

Illustrating results from a media analysis of the financial crisis

Figure 7.12 shows the results of a study comparing media reports from 2008 and 2009 on the financial crisis and illustrates how you can make your data come alive in presentations. This requires you to run ATLAS.ti in the background, or alternatively to use ATLAS.ti to present your findings. You could for instance:

- present your project setup and sampling showing the Primary Document Manager and the families;
- explain your major categories by showing the Code Manager;
- show the major findings in the form of network views;
- bring the data to life by showing or playing quotations that illustrate the results (see Figure 7.12);
- show a few of your research question memos if anyone questions how you derived your conclusions.

The network view in Figure 7.12 shows factors that have been mentioned by experts as contributing factors to the financial crisis (green on-screen), and a number of immediate, long-term and individual consequences accompanied by their research question memos (red on-screen). The codes at the bottom (violet on-screen) indicate the source: expert opinion, political opinion, statistical figures, news agencies and personal experiences.[2]

Also shown are an activated video and a text quotation. If the quotations are not included in the network view, you can always right click on a code node and select the option **LIST QUOTATIONS** (Figure 7.8).

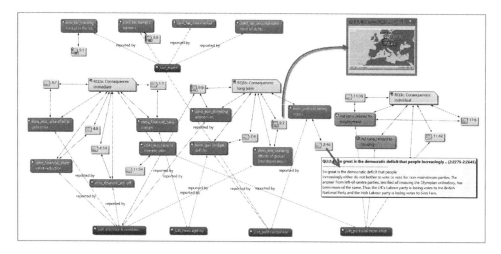

Figure 7.12   Integrating findings from a study on the financial crisis (Friese, 2011)

---

2 The study was developed as a sample study based on a small data set. Therefore the results are fictitious.

Using network views in publications

The following two network views are included in genuine publications and represent central findings. Figure 7.13 shows one result of my dissertation research illustrating the phases of an addictive buying experience. The original network view published in my dissertation (Friese, 2000) looked a bit different as a number of options were not yet available in version 4 of ATLAS.ti. And, as mentioned, I would not have coded my data in the same way as I did back then and therefore I modified the original code labels to reflect how I would probably code the data today.

For the next example I am indebted to Eddie Hartmann for allowing me to use his data material (Hartmann, 2011). He conducted 20 interviews and developed a case structure for each person. For each case he developed a network view based on four main criteria: **affirmation, negation, rejective negation and positive substitution**. As you can see in Figure 7.14, each case shows a different pattern visualized (on-screen) by the colors used for the different criteria. Quotations were added to each network view to show the sequence of arguments that comprise the story of each interviewee.

Skills training 7.3: using network views to pimp your code book

A code book usually consists of a long list of codes with definitions. To make it more comprehensive to read, you can break it up into categories and insert a network view image for each category. For this purpose we can put code families to good use again.

How to open a network view on a code family

- Open the Code Manager. Right click on a family (e.g. Effects of parenting positive) and select the option OPEN NETWORK VIEW.
- The network view displays the code family and all its members linked via a dotted line (red) (see example code book below).
- Arrange the code family and the member nodes manually by dragging them to the desired position with the mouse.

How to insert a network view into Word or any other application

- To insert the network view into your code book, select the option NETWORK / COPY TO CLIPBOARD / COPY ALL NODES. The network view is placed on the clipboard.
- Open your word processor. Pasting the network view (e.g. via CTRL+V) will insert it as text only. To insert it as an image, select the **paste special** option. In older Office versions of Word, this option can be found under the Edit menu. In Office 2007 and newer versions it is the first option under the Start tab. In the Paste Special window,

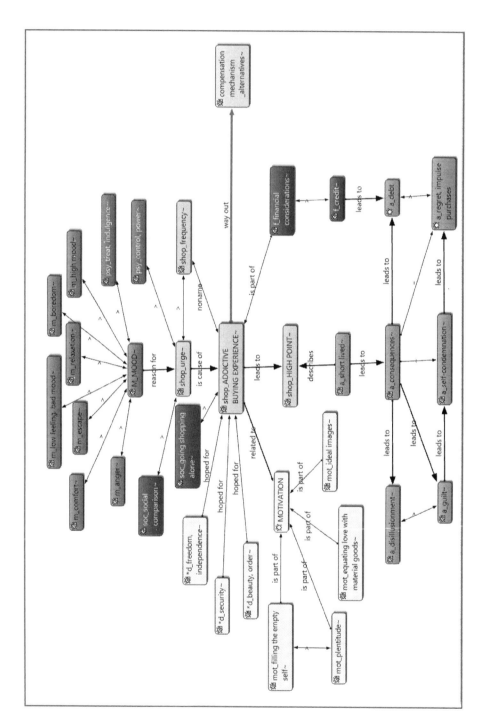

Figure 7.13 Illustrating the addictive buying experience (adapted from Friese, 2000)

Case reconstruction

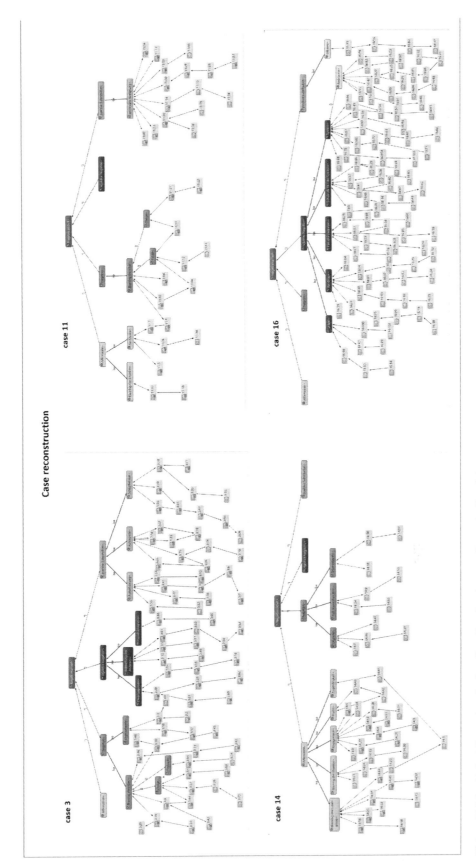

case 3

case 11

case 14

case 16

Figure 7.14 Using the network view function to show patterns in the data

as format select 'enhanced windows metafile', or 'device independent bitmap' and click on **OK**.

Now you know how to insert an image of a code category into your code book. What I have not shown you yet is how to create a code book. This works best via the XML export option.

How to create reports based on XML style sheets

In case you don't know what XML is, the short explanation is that XML, similar to HTML, is a document mark-up language. Based on an XML file in combination with style sheets, ATLAS.ti can create a variety of reports. A style sheet is a way of prescribing how the content of an XML file should be rendered. Based on the same XML source, a variety of outputs can be created, such as a list of code, PD or memo families with their members, all memos with their content and linked quotations, all codes with their quotations, or – and this is what we are interested in at the moment – all codes with their comments.

- Click on the **XML** button in the main toolbar (or click on the down arrow next to it and select the option XML Explorer).
- A window with a list of reports will open. Select the first one *Codes: Code Book*.
- When creating reports based on XML style sheets, you have three export options: to not include the primary documents, to include meta information on primary documents and quotations, and to include the quotations content as well. The option that is applicable to the selected report is framed in a light blue color. For creating a code book, this is the option *Do not include Primary Documents*.
- The code book will open in Windows Explorer in html format. You can copy it into a Word document by highlighting everything (**CTRL+A**), copying the content (**CTRL+C**) and pasting it (**CTRL+V**).

With a bit of formatting, your code book could look like this:

@ atlas.ti report

Illustrated code book

Number of Codes: 97

Effects of parenting positive

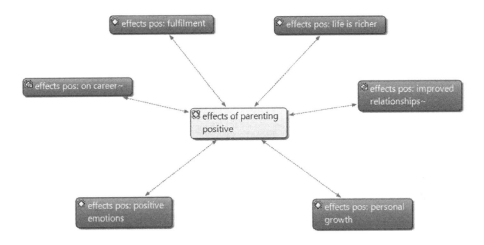

EFFECTS POS	■	statements that deal with the positive effects parenting has on one's life
effects pos: fulfilment	■	Leading a meaningful and fulfilled life. This code is used when persons talk about meaning and purpose as compared to 'richer life', which is related to life content
effects pos: improved relationships	■	Improved relationships to partners, spouses or own parents
effects pos: life is richer	■	Children add value to life
effects pos: on career	■	The fact that one has children has positive effects on professional life, because one is more efficient, uses available time better
effects pos: personal growth	■	Becoming a better and more mature person because of being a parent, learning about one's own values
effects pos: positive emotions	■	Being joyful when observing own children, being reminded of one's own childhood, being happy to see own children laugh and have fun

Effects of parenting negative

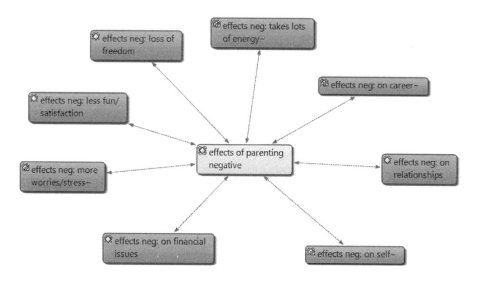

EFFECTS NEG	■	statements that deal with negative effects parenting has on one's life
effects neg: less fun/ satisfaction	■	Doing fewer fun things like going out and decreased satisfaction because of it
effects neg: loss of freedom	■	Complaints about/expectations that freedom is lost
effects neg: more worries/ stress	■	more worries, more stress/or formulated the other way around: less burdened before children, more chaos
effects neg: on career	■	negative effects on professional life due to being a parent
effects neg: on financial issues	■	Children cost money, expenses are higher
effects neg: on relationships	■	Mostly with reference to relationships with partners and spouses, decrease in marital satisfaction – references to reports and descriptions of personal experiences
effects neg: on self	■	feeling inadequate, losing identity, sacrifices
effects neg: takes lots of energy	■	you need lots of emotional and physical energy, less sleep, you have less time or no time

Skills training 7.4: creating network views

In the next few pages, you will learn about various ways of linking and handling network views. The exercises are intended to teach you the technicalities of working with network views. We will not create 'meaningful' networks in an analytic sense. You can choose any of the existing codes to practice with, similar to what we did in Chapter 4 with the four test codes when I showed you how to code.

Learning how to link

- Open the Code Manager and choose four codes by holding down the CTRL key. Then click on the network symbol in the toolbar of the manager.
- A network view editor will open. As a title, the name of the selected code(s) is chosen. The window contains the code you have selected. If you want to add more codes, move the network view window next to the Code Manager and drag and drop other codes into the network view.
- Select one of the code nodes with a left mouse click. A red dot will be displayed in the top left corner. Drag the red dot with your mouse to another code and release the mouse button. A list of relations will open. Select the **is associated with** relation.

This relation is a symmetric relation showing a double-ended arrow. It indicates that the two codes are related somehow but no direction can be specified.

Depending on the type of project you are working with, the list of relations on your computer screen might be shorter than the one shown in Figure 7.15. In addition to the default relations that ATLAS.ti provides, it includes a few others that I have created for the sample project. Basically, you can create any relation you want and need, and in any language you want (see Skills training 7.5).

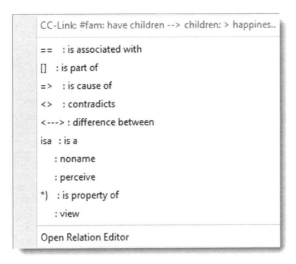

Figure 7.15   List of code–code relations

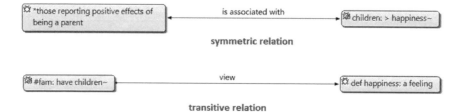

Figure 7.16   Examples of a symmetric and a transitive relation

Let's try out another way of linking. This time, let's select a transitive relation. Figure 7.16 shows an example both of a symmetric (non-directed) relation and of a transitive (directed) relation.

- Left click on another code so that you see the red dot. This time click on the **LINK NODES** button in the toolbar. Drag the black line on top of another code and left click. From the list of relations that is shown, select for instance 'is part of' or 'view'.
- Practice linking code nodes by linking the remaining codes in your network view.

Exploring the links

- The link labels are interactive. Right click on a link label and explore the options like flipping a link, changing the relation or cutting a link (Figure 7.17).
- Each link can be commented individually. Try it. All commented links are marked with a tilde (~) as you already know from other commented objects in ATLAS.ti.
- End this exercise by unlinking all codes from each other because I want to show you next how you can link multiple objects to each other at the same time. For this we need free unlinked nodes.

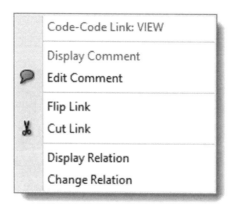

Figure 7.17   Context menu for links

Linking multiple nodes simultaneously

- Select three of your nodes by holding down the CTRL key, or by drawing a frame around the three nodes with the mouse cursor.
- Now you need to select either the main menu option **Links / Link Nodes** or the toolbar button. The number of the black rubber bands that show up corresponds to the number of selected nodes.
- Move the cursor to the target node, left click and select a relation. The chosen relation is used for all links. If the relation does not apply to all links, you can change the relation later via the link context menu as explained above.

The various ways of linking explained here apply to all objects that can be linked to each other in network views. When linking codes to codes and quotations to quotations you are offered a list of link labels to choose from.

Importing nodes

- You can import objects into a network view editor via drag and drop from all managers or the margin area. Another option is via the menu **Nodes / Import Nodes**. Select this menu option (Figure 7.18).
- Click on the down arrow to select a different node type. Then select the objects to be imported and click on the button **Import**.
- The imported nodes are placed in the upper left hand corner. To distribute them evenly in the network view, select **Layout / Semantic Layout** from the network editor menu.

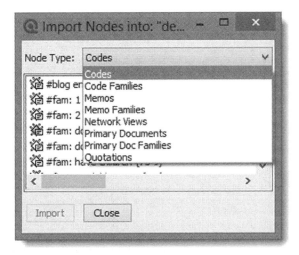

Figure 7.18   Importing nodes into a network view

Removing nodes

If you want to remove an item from a network view, you must take care to select the correct option. When right clicking on a node in a network view, you have two options: **Remove from View** and **Delete 'object name'** (see Figure 7.19).

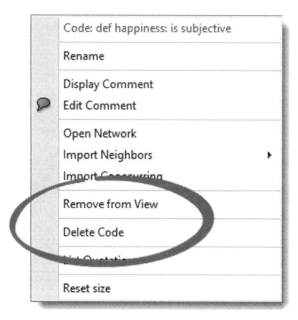

Figure 7.19   Removing vs. deleting a node

As all objects inside a network view are called nodes, users often think that the node is not the 'real' object. But it is. When you delete a node in a network view, the object is deleted from the HU itself (i.e. from your entire project). When selecting the **Delete** option, you are asked whether you really want to do this. Regardless of this warning, many users have learned the hard way by clicking on this option. So, if you no longer want an object to be visible in the network view, select the **Remove from View** option or press **Del**. The delete key on your keyboard is the equivalent of the 'remove from view' option.

You may wonder why the delete option exists at all when it is so dangerous. It can be useful, for example when creating new code nodes or memo nodes as placeholders or modifiers of relations (see p. 251, 'Dealing with case-based network views'). However, if it turns out that they do not work in your network view as you hoped and you want to get rid of them, it is quite handy just to right click and delete them in the network view instead of having to go to the Code Manager.

Moving nodes

If you want to move the whole or parts of the network view within the editor, first some nodes need to be selected:

- To select all nodes, use the key combination **Ctrl+A**. To select only a few nodes, hold down the CTRL key.
- Then point to a node with the cursor, press the CTRL key and move the selected nodes by dragging the cursor to a different location.

Layout options

Take a look at the semantic or topological layout of your network: **Layout/ Semantic Layout** or LAYOUT/TOPOLOGICAL LAYOUT.

- The semantic layout can be used to evenly distribute all nodes in a network view. This is especially useful when importing a number of objects at once.
- The topological layout arranges your codes from the upper left hand corner to the lower right hand corner, based on the relation types. This is useful when you want to visualize a sequence of events or activities.

If you don't like the result of an automatically created layout, you can use the undo function by selecting UNDO POSITIONING in the main toolbar, or use the hotkey CTRL+Z.

Display menu

Click your way through the different options and try out the display options. Here are a few exercises and explanations:

- Display the nodes with and without the bitmaps for the respective object type. Option: DISPLAY NODE BITMAPS.
- Switch between the normal view of the nodes and a three-dimensional (3D) view. Option: DISPLAY NODES 3D. Which one do you like better?
- Hide or show the 'groundedness' and 'density' for your code nodes. Option: EXTENDED CODE LABEL.
- Display code definitions. Option: CODES WITH COMMENTS.
- Add primary documents to a network view, for example via drag and drop from the P-Docs Manager, and activate/deactivate the option 'Full image for PDs'.

Display options for link labels

ATLAS.ti offers three alternatives for displaying the label of a link. These are called label 1, label 2 and menu text. You could, for example, use label 1 as an empty label in case you don't want the name to show, label 2 for labels in English, and the menu text for labels in another language. You can set the alternative displays under **DISPLAY / LINK DISPLAY**.

- Try out the three options to see what happens when you select **LABEL 1**, **LABEL 2** and **MENU TEXT**.

The default relations that come with the software show a symbol for label 1, a letter for label 2 and a text for the third label (menu text). But you can define the labels in any way you want. This is done in the Relations Editor, which you will learn about in Skills training 7.5.

Preference settings

There are various ways to utilize colors in network view displays. For instance, in the window NETWORK PREFERENCES, you have the option to set fonts and colors for nodes and the background (Figure 7.20). The modifications you make here apply to all network views and not just to individual ones.

In a network editor, select the menu option SPECIALS / PREFERENCES.

- Click on the tab GENERAL and set a new background and node color.
- Click on the tab FONTS and select a different font and size (e.g. for the links).

Code colors in network views

You probably have set colors for your codes in the Code Manager. If they do not show up automatically, you can find the color settings by clicking on the colored circle in the network view editor (Figure 7.20).

It the option 'Fill Nodes' is deactivated, then only the label is shown in the user-defined color. If the option is activated, the code label is shown in black

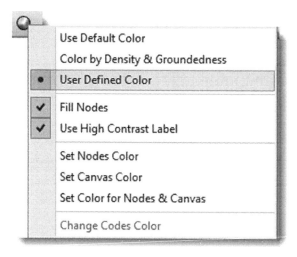

Figure 7.20   Use of code colors in a network view

Figure 7.21   Variations of displaying code colors

(or white) and the node is filled with the code color. It is advisable to activate the high-contrast option. This changes the node label to white when a dark color is used for the node itself (Figure 7.21).

Network view preview images

Version 7 allows you to see preview images in the Network View Manager and in the fly-out panel (Figure 7.22).

- Open the **Network View Manager** via the main menu Networks.
- From the menu select **View / Tiles** and **View / Preview Size / Jumbo**.

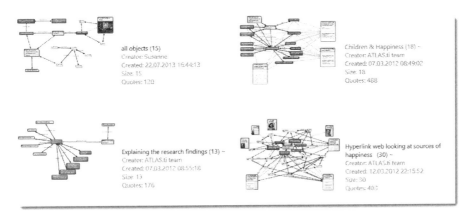

all objects (15)
Creator: Susanne
Created: 22.07.2013 16:44:13
Size: 15
Quotes: 120

Children & Happiness (18) ~
Creator: ATLAS.ti team
Created: 07.03.2012 08:49:02
Size: 18
Quotes: 488

Explaining the research findings (13) ~
Creator: ATLAS.ti team
Created: 07.03.2012 08:55:18
Size: 13
Quotes: 176

Hyperlink web looking at sources of happiness (30) ~
Creator: ATLAS.ti team
Created: 12.03.2012 22:15:52
Size: 30
Quotes: 480

Figure 7.22   Preview images in network view manager

- If you want to see preview images in the fly-out windows, click on the three arrows in the middle of the vertical toolbar to open it (see Chapter 2).
- Select the network view tab. Right click and select **Show Preview**. If you double click on a network view, it will be opened in a network view editor. Incidentally, the preview option is also available for the document tab and quite handy if you work with image data.

Skills training 7.5: working with the Relations Editor

The Relations Editor gives you an overview of the existing relations and their attributes. Additionally, you can define new relations. In the following, you will learn how to customize relations so that you can illustrate the kinds of relations that are relevant for your data material.

Above, I introduced you to the concept of first- and second-class relations. We have seen that codes can be linked to other codes and quotations to other quotations via first-class relations. For this process, ATLAS.ti offers a distinct set of link labels for each of the two object types, as the nature of the relations between codes is different from that of the relations needed for quotations. The link labels offered for quotations include 'discusses', 'justifies' or 'explains' as compared to 'is a', 'is associated with' or 'is part of' for codes. Accordingly, there are also two **Relations Editors**: one for code–code relations and one for quotation–quotation relations. The latter types of relations are called **hyperlinks**. In terms of handling, there is no difference between the code–code relations editor and the hyperlink relations editor. When you know how to create new code–code relations, you also will know how to create new hyperlink relations.

Explaining the Code-Code-Relations Editor

• In the main menu of the network editor, select LINKS / EDIT RELATIONS / CODE-CODE-RELATIONS.

The Relations Editor can also be accessed from the main menu of the HU. From the main menu, select **Networks / Edit Relations / Code-Code-Relations**. The window in Figure 7.23 will open. If you do not see the main menu, increase the size of the window by dragging it with the mouse.

Figure 7.23   Code-Code-Relations Editor

Description of the data fields

Internal ID: Each relation has an internal ID by which it is recognized. By default it uses capital letters, but this is not a requirement. When creating a new relation, you just need to make sure that this ID has not already been used. My suggestion is to continue to use capital letters and to use the first three or four letters of the new relation as ID.

Link labels: Next you can define the three link labels. You can leave label 1 and label 2 empty, but it is necessary to create an entry in the menu text field.

Line style: You can define the width, color and representation (dashed or solid) of the line. Try out different colors and widths. The width allows you to add some more graphic elements to your network view (I think this is an unintentional option; see Figure 7.24). For instance, when you use a width of 35 characters, the line can be shown as a triangle. If the display looks a bit awkward as you move nodes around, click F5 to refresh the display.

Preferred layout direction: You can influence the automatic layout algorithm by defining the layout direction of the different relation types. Most of the time, however, one drags the nodes manually to the desired position in the network view.

Formal properties: The definition of the formal properties is more important. It not only has a cosmetic effect, but also affects the representation of the codes in the **code forest** and the use of the semantic search operators in the **query tool** (see Chapter 6).

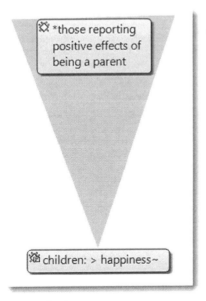

Figure 7.24   Customizing link displays

All codes can be displayed in a sideways tree called the code forest in ATLAS.ti.

Object Explorer
Code Forest
Code Tree
Code Cooccurrence Explorer

Figure 7.25 How to open the code forest from the main toolbar

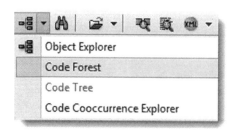

- Select **CODES** / **MISCELLANEOUS** / **CODE FOREST** from the main menu, or select the option from the main toolbar as shown in Figure 7.25.

The display is not strictly hierarchical. All codes appear at the first level. If you link two codes via a transitive (directed) relation, you begin to arrange them in a hierarchical order. However, if you link two codes using a symmetric (undirected) relation, then the codes point reciprocally to each other. This is shown in Figure 7.26.

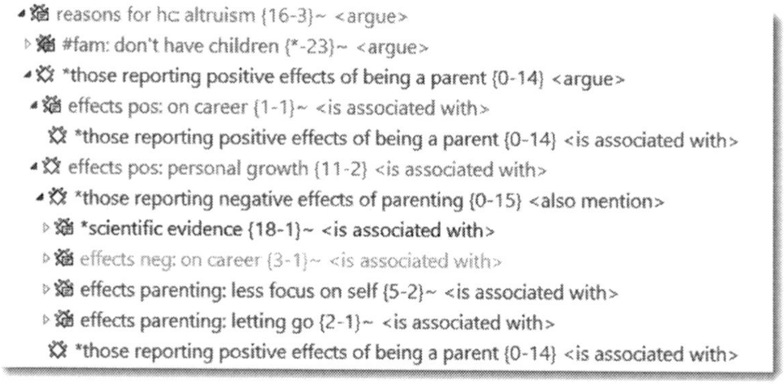

reasons for hc: altruism {16-3}~ <argue>
#fam: don't have children {*-23}~ <argue>
*those reporting positive effects of being a parent {0-14} <argue>
effects pos: on career {1-1}~ <is associated with>
*those reporting positive effects of being a parent {0-14} <is associated with>
effects pos: personal growth {11-2} <is associated with>
*those reporting negative effects of parenting {0-15} <also mention>
*scientific evidence {18-1}~ <is associated with>
effects neg: on career {3-1}~ <is associated with>
effects parenting: less focus on self {5-2}~ <is associated with>
effects parenting: letting go {2-1}~ <is associated with>
*those reporting positive effects of being a parent {0-14} <is associated with>

Figure 7.26 The ATLAS.ti code forest

Thus, the code forest is not equivalent to the code tree in other CAQDAS packages and I advise against using it in such a way unless you do not want to go beyond descriptive-level analysis. I explain this at greater length below in the section 'On the use of network views for structural purposes'.

Modifying an existing relation

- Activate one of the entries in the Relations Editor and customize the relation according to your preferences.
- For example, edit the relation *is associated with*. Think of a more meaningful name for label 2, change the width of the line and select a different color.
- Click on **APPLY** to save the changes.
- Then go to network view and link two codes using the 'is associated with' relation and see how it looks now.

Creating a new relation

Let's create the relation **is reason for:**

- In the Relations Editor, select the menu option **EDIT / NEW RELATION**. All input fields are empty and can now be filled with new information.
- Enter an internal ID (e.g. REA).
- Enter label 1, label 2 and the menu text (see Figure 7.27).
- Then, select the width and color for the line.
- Set the formal property to Transitive.
- Click on **APPLY** to accept the new entries.

In order to make this relation available to all HUs in the future, you need to save it:

- Select **FILE / SAVE RELATIONS**. Accept the default setting and save the relation to the standard relation file DEFAULT.REL by clicking on **SAVE**.
- You are asked whether it is OK to overwrite the existing file. Click on **YES**.

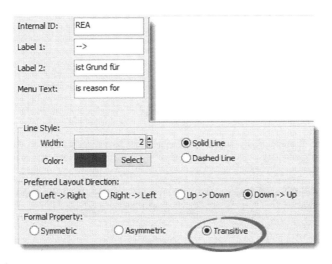

Figure 7.27   Creating a new relation

Skills training 7.6: saving and exporting network views

Saving network views

- To save a network view, click on the menu option **NETWORK / SAVE AS** and enter a name for the network view.

All saved network views (Figure 7.28) are listed in the **Network View Manager** that you can access from the main menu **NETWORKS / NETWORK VIEW MANAGER**.

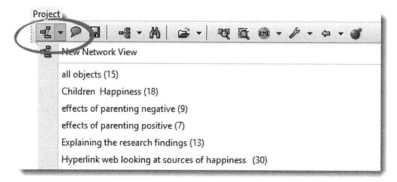

Figure 7.28   How to open existing network views

Or click on the network view button in the main toolbar. It is the first button on the left hand side under the main menu **PROJECT**.

When you link objects in a network view and you do not want to save the image itself, there is no need to save each network view. The relations that you create between two objects are saved in the HU. Thus, save only those network views that show a particular constellation that you want to preserve or those views that you want to continue to work on.

Exporting network views

You can save the network view as a graphic file or use the copy and paste option to export it to word processing or presentation software. The latter option has already be explained in Skills training 7.3.

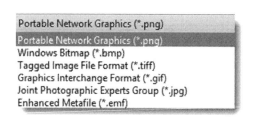

Figure 7.29   List of graphic file formats to choose from

- To save a network view as a graphic file, you need to open it in the network view editor.
- Select the option **NETWORKS / SAVE AS GRAPHIC FILE**.
- Enter a name and select a format by clicking on the down arrow in the data type field. Version 7 offers a number of graphic file formats to choose from (see Figure 7.29).

Dealing with case-based network views

When you link two codes to each other in one network view, the link is not just a private link for this one view. It is used for these two codes in the entire HU. Thus, if you pull the two codes into another network, the link between these codes immediately becomes visible.

But what if you want to link Code A with Code B using the relation 'is a consequence of' in a network view in the case of Paul, but need to use the label 'is a prerequisite of' for the network view in the case of Mary? The solution is to add more information to the network. If A is a consequence of B for Paul, there is probably a reason for this that you know from reading the data. If A is a prerequisite for B in the case of Mary, there are likely to be circumstances that explain this relation too. This information is what you need to add to the network view. Thus, it becomes even more meaningful as you add more to it.

If the reason that applies to Paul and the circumstances relevant to Mary are not yet covered by existing codes, you need to create them. These codes then will not contain data; you use them as modifiers to show the kinds of relations that exist in your data. The term for such codes in ATLAS.ti is **abstract codes**. The frequency is zero and the density is at least one or higher. Creating abstract codes occurs quite regularly when creating network views. You often need to add codes at this stage to let the network view visualize the story you want to tell. Codes as compared to memos have the advantage that you can link them via first-class (i.e. named) relations.

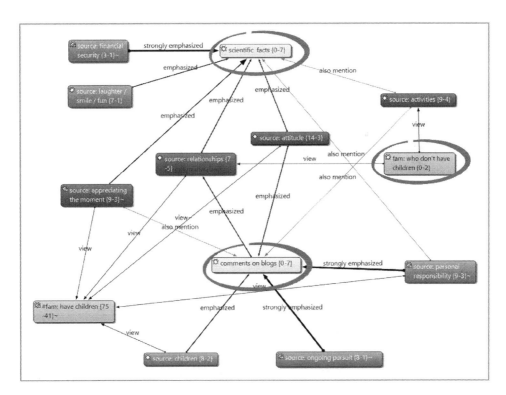

Figure 7.30 Using abstract codes to express what is going on in your data

The network view in Figure 7.30 contains three abstract codes. Two represent cases on the document level, 'scientific facts' and 'comments on blogs', and one is a double for a code: 'fam: who don't have children'. All of these codes show a 0 for frequency. If you go back and review Figure 7.10, it shows the same codes linked to the data sources P3, P5 and P10. Links between documents and codes are, however, second class and cannot be named. By creating a code node for P10 and one combined node for the two documents PD and P5 representing the blog comments, the various emphases that are put on the various sources of happiness can be expressed via the relation names and the width of the links. I also recolored those codes that have only been mentioned by one side. In a next step I added the two attribute codes for parents and non-parents. As these two are already linked with a thick red line and the relation name 'difference between', I didn't want to have this relation in this view (see Figure 7.7). Therefore I added a new abstract code for non-parents ('fam: who don't have children') and linked it to the two codes that are also linked to the 'real' code.

On the use of network views for structural purposes

After 'Skills training 5.6' on p. 149, I told you about the advantages of a sorted and structured code list and presented my own dissertation research as an example of how not to do it. Instead of utilizing the Code Manager, I used the network view function to put some order into my thoughts. The danger of this is that the code system remains messy. The brainwork is done, but one forfeits transparency. The code list is difficult to handle, remains incomprehensible to an outsider, and the different levels of analysis get mixed up. If you use the Code Manager to represent the various levels of your codes instead, the network view function is still at your disposal for higher order conceptual-level analysis.

Most packages I know of offer a tree structure for the code list. Thus, you can immediately sort codes into higher and lower order categories in the tree. Even if a tree structure is available, I recommend starting out with a flat code list – just by having the tree available it is tempting to sort codes into subtrees right from the start. Whether the codes on the main and sublevels are already proper conceptual codes also needs to be worked out when using these programs. Also here the same mistakes in building a proper coding system as explained in Chapter 5 are made. I know it from personal experience teaching MAXQDA once in a while and it is also reflected in the writings of Bazeley and Richards (Bazeley, 2007; Richards (2009); Richards and Richards, 1995). See also the note on p. 156.

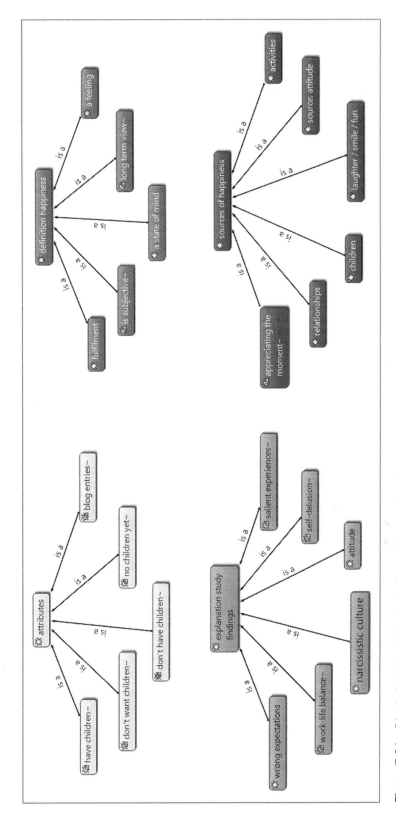

Figure 7.31 Displaying categories in the form of hierarchical trees

Whether a hierarchical tree display of codes is available or a flat code list as in ATLAS.ti, at some point during the analysis most users get to the point where they ask, 'What shall I do next? The data are coded, so what's the next step?' Some programs offering a hierarchical tree display allow you to print out the trees, which are basically the main category codes with their sub-codes. This form of visualizing the coding system gives a false impression that there are already associative links and interesting relations in the data. You can also do it with the aid of the network view function in ATLAS.ti as shown in Figure 7.31.

If you link codes in this way, you can open a tree view for your codes in ATLAS.ti similar to those you may have seen in other packages. This works as long as you only use hierarchical links. In ATLAS.ti this is called the **code forest** (Figure 7.32). To open it, select CODES / MISCELLANEOUS / CODE FOREST from the main menu. The codes shown in Figure 7.31 are all linked via an 'is a' relation. You could also use 'is part of' or another label that you feel suits your data as long as it is a directed relation. As soon as you choose

Figure 7.32   Hierarchical display of codes in the code forest

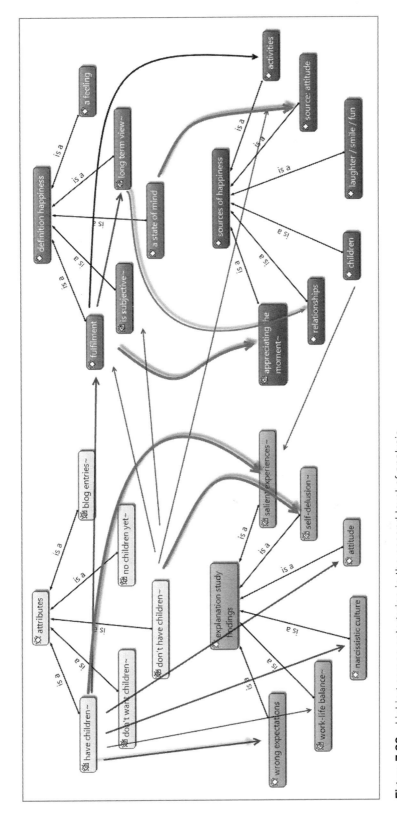

Figure 7.33 Linking across categories in the second level of analysis

a symmetric relation like *code_A is associated with code_B*, then the code forest is no longer hierarchical (see Figure 7.24 for an example).

The tree view has been used quite successfully in team projects where the coding work needed to be allocated to the various team members. When dividing the work into categories, each team member goes through the data applying the codes of one or two main categories, in which case using the code forest works quite well. However, in version 7 the code families in the side panels can be used for this purpose as well. From what I know to date, the code tree and forest will not be developed in the direction of serving as a proper hierarchical display for codes. However, as users including myself do want to sort and order their codes at different levels, version 8 will offer extended functionalities in the Code Manager. Until then, we still need to work with prefixes to build a well-developed and functional coding system.

If you use the network view function to link higher and lower order categories, you visualize first-level descriptive analysis. This also makes it difficult to switch between descriptive- and conceptual-level analysis, to move forward and to look beyond the top-downward view of the categories. Second-level conceptual analysis is about linking data across categories (Figure 7.33). This can be achieved by approaching the data with research questions in mind – querying the data and writing research question memos as explained in Chapter 6.

The aim of using network views for conceptual-level analysis is to illustrate the answers to research questions instead of just displaying the categories. Such network views are likely to contain subcodes of a variety of categories, but only those that are relevant in the context of the research question. For a cleaner methodological approach, I suggest that you define and visualize higher and lower order codes in the Code Manager and reserve the network view function for advanced conceptual-level work, when you begin to find relations between codes and across categories. I have shown a number of conceptual-level network views at the beginning of this chapter, in the sections 'Using network views to present findings' and 'Using network views in publications'.

Hyperlinks in ATLAS.ti

As explained above, hyperlinks are relations between quotations. You can create hyperlinks in network views by applying the various techniques as shown for code–code relations. The practice of using hyperlinks, however, is different. Therefore I have added a further section to this chapter specifically on hyperlinks. I will provide some examples on how to use hyperlinks and show an alternative way of creating them that stays closer to the data than using network views.

Examples of using hyperlinks

Linking repeated occurrences of the same idea

Sometimes an idea or subject is repeated again and again without adding further information. If you code each instance, then the frequency of the code goes up, distorting the code frequency count. The solution is to code only the first segment and connect the repetitive segments via hyperlinks.

Linking different aspects within a document

Take, for instance, an interview situation. The interviewee tells you something and halfway through the interview he or she tells you the exact opposite. Depending on the type of interview you are conducting, you can either query the contradiction on the spot or leave it till later. In order to easily access the contradictory information, you can link the statements via hyperlinks.

Another common issue in interviews is that people don't always stick to chronological order. Hyperlinks can be used to add a chronological structure to an anecdote or statement. Perhaps, while involved in telling a story, your interviewee does not start at the beginning of events but fills in important details later. If this makes it difficult to understand the logic of the argument, one option is to code the section that marks the beginning of the train of thought and link the rest of it via hyperlinks.

As shown in Figure 7.24, hyperlinks can also be used to link various statements that build on each other and that are typical of a particular speaker or illustrate an important line of reasoning.

Linking across documents

Linking across documents is likely to occur when you have several documents on one case, or when using different media types as your primary document. Pictures, for example, can be used to break the ice at the start of an interview. Another data collection procedure may require people to provide visual material themselves and the interview is set up to talk about this material. Drawing diagrams or concept maps can be used as a way of summarizing the main aspects of an interview in agreement with the interviewee. This results in data that contain images as well as the discussion of these images. Hyperlinks can be used to link the verbal and the pictorial aspects of the data.

Furthermore, the possibility of working with geo data using the Google Earth function in ATLAS.ti provides further reasons to create links across data, for example between a quotation in a Google Earth document and the verbal description of the location. Linking across documents has become easier in version 7, where you can open documents side by side.

Skills training 7.7: working with hyperlinks

When linking quotations, you begin by setting one quotation as the source link. Then you select a second quotation as the target. As you continue to link more quotations, you can create a **star** or a **chain**. Creating a star means using the same quotation as the source and linking more target quotations to it. Creating a chain means beginning with one quotation as the source and selecting a quotation as the target; this quotation then becomes the source and you select a new quotation as the target. This is illustrated in Figure 7.34.

You already know how to link quotations within a network view as shown above. Below, I would like to show you how to create hyperlinks while staying close to the data level. Let's try this out using text data. Later you can apply your skills to different types of media.

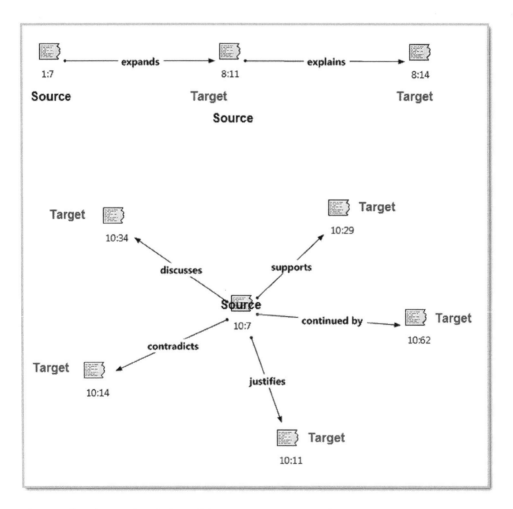

Figure 7.34   Star and chain hyperlink structures

Linking quotations

- Select a data segment that already is a quotation (e.g. by clicking on a code in the margin area). Right click on the highlighted segment.
- Select the option **CREATE LINK SOURCE** from the context menu that pops up. Alternatively you can also select the 'Start Anchor' button in the vertical toolbar after selecting a quotation.

ATLAS.ti marks this quotation as the start anchor. This can be seen in the status bar at the bottom of the screen: it displays the text Start Anchor Defined.

- Select a second quotation as the target. Right click and select the option **CREATE LINK TARGET.** Alternatively you can also select the 'Target Anchor' button in the vertical toolbar.
- A selection of relations will open in a new window. Select one of the relations with a left click.
- Another window will open where you can choose to create either a chain or a star, or whether to quit linking.

The newly created hyperlink becomes visible in the margin area and is shown in the form of a symbol at the beginning of a hyperlinked quotation in the Quotation Manager. The symbol '<' in front of a quotation means that it is a source link; the symbol '>' means that it is a target link. In the margin area, the bitmap image for quotations indicates that a hyperlink exists (see Figure 7.35).

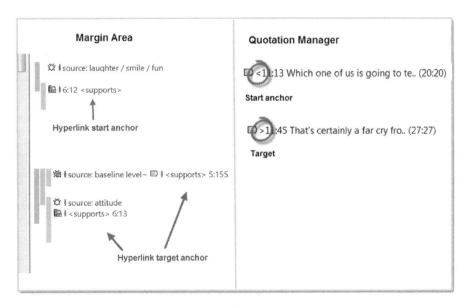

Figure 7.35   Display of hyperlinks in the margin area and in the Quotation Manager

Linking across document regions

- Load two documents side by side (see Chapter 2).
- Left click on a quotation bar in the active region, drag the mouse to a quotation bar in the neighboring region, release the left mouse button and select a relation (see Figure 7.36).

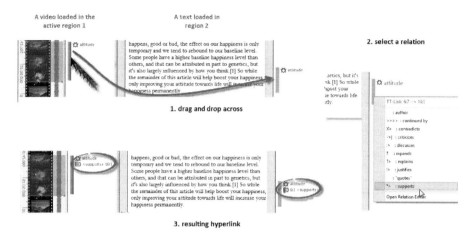

Figure 7.36   Linking across regions

Browsing hyperlinks

- You can display the contents of a hyperlinked quotation by double clicking on the hyperlink icon in the margin area. If the quotation is linked to a text quotation, the content of this quotation is shown in a comment field; if linked to a video or audio quotation, the linked quotation is played (see Figure 7.37).
- You can go directly to the hyperlinked quotation by holding down the CTRL key and then double clicking on the hyperlink in the margin area.

Visualizing hyperlinks in network views

- Right click on a hyperlink and select the option **OPEN NETWORK**.

The network view displays those quotations that are immediately linked. If you have created a chain, then it is possible to expand the network view to show it all:

- Right click on a hyperlink node in the network view, and select the option **IMPORT NEIGHBORS / IMPORT HYPERLINKS**.

Overview of all code–code links and hyperlinks

You can get an overview of all created first-class linkages in the Code Link Manager and Hyperlink Manager (Figure 7.38). You can access these managers

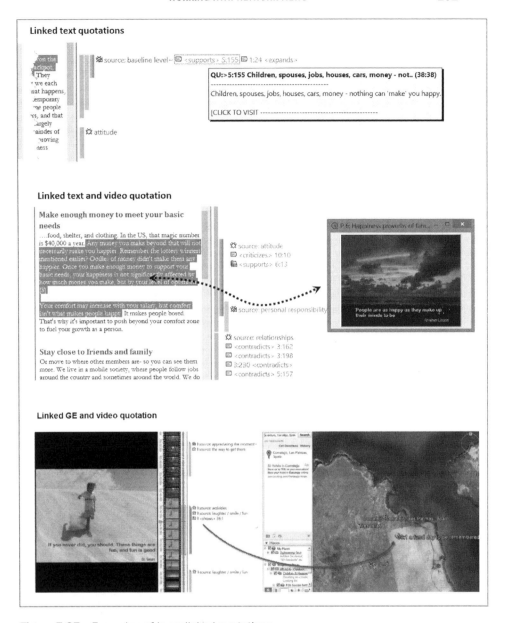

Figure 7.37 Examples of hyperlinked quotations

via the main menu **NETWORKS**. In the managers, you can search for relations, sort them by the column headers, access them in context, open links in network views, and modify, delete and comment links. Starting with version 7.1.7, filter settings also apply to the Code Link and the Hyperlink Manager. This allows you for instance to query the relations of just a particular set of documents, or for a particular set of codes.

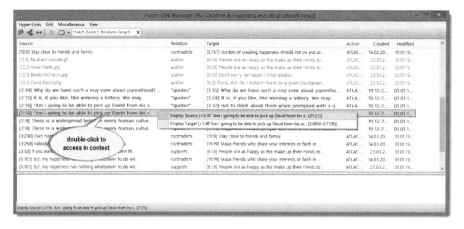

Figure 7.38   Hyperlink Manager

Summary

In working through this chapter, you have learned a number of new technical skills: linking objects within network views, creating new relations, using network views for analytic purposes, using network views to pimp up your code book, inserting network views in reports and presentations, and creating hyperlinks at the data level. Regarding the process of data analysis, the creation of conceptual network views is most likely to occur toward the end of the analytic process, after a deeper exploration of the data material has been made. Hyperlinks and exploratory network views may be created throughout the analysis.

REVIEW QUESTIONS

1   What are network views?
2   What can you do with network views?
3   Which objects can be contained in network views?
4   What is meant by first- and second-class relations?
5   Which objects can be linked via first- and second-class relations?
6   How can you modify existing relations or create new relations?
7   Think of a suitable way to make use of the three alternative link labels.
8   How can you save a network view and when do you need to do so?
9   How can you export network views?
10 In what way and for what purpose can you use the network view function for analytic purposes?
11 Why should network views not be used for organizing your codes into higher and lower order codes?
12 Explain the code forest and why it cannot be used in the same way as a hierarchical tree display of codes.
13 What are hyperlinks?
14 How could you use hyperlinks in your own project to enhance data analysis?

15 What are the steps involved in creating hyperlinks?
16 How can you recognize hyperlinks in the margin area and the Quotation Manager?
17 How can you browse hyperlinks?
18 How do you use the network view function in creating a code book?
19 Where can you see and edit all created first-class linkages?

GLOSSARY OF TERMS

Hyperlinks: These are links between quotations. Quotations can be linked via named relations and thus are first-class relations.

Link: A link is the line that you draw between two objects in a network view.

Network views: These visualize the various ATLAS.ti objects and the links between them. Objects that can be included are: primary document codes, quotations, memos, all object families and the network views as icons themselves. Primary documents can be visualized as thumbnail images.

You can link codes to codes, codes to quotations, codes to memos, memos to memos and quotations to memos. Families can be visualized as well by showing the links between the family name and each member. The family name cannot be linked to other objects. Links between two codes and between two quotations are considered to be first-class relations as the links can be named. All other links are unnamed and therefore 'second class'.

In NCT analysis, network views play a major role in the conceptual level of analysis, when the analyst begins to see relations in the data during the process of writing research question memos.

Nodes: All objects inserted into a network view become nodes. They are visualized as code nodes, memo nodes, quotation nodes, etc., but the generic term applies to all of them. Therefore you need to be careful when deleting a node: you will not just remove the object from the network view, but also delete it from the entire HU.

Relations: These are the names that you can give to a link. This is possible for code–code links and for quotation–quotation links.

Relations Editor: This is the window where you can define new relations or modify existing ones. It can be accessed from within a network view via the menu **Links** or via the main **networks** menu.

Further reading

Attride-Stirling, Jennifer (2001). Thematic networks: an analytic tool for qualitative research, *Qualitative Research*, 1(3), 385–405.

Lewins, Ann and Silver, Christine (2007). *Using Software in Qualitative Research: A Step-by-Step Guide*. London: Sage. Chapter 10.

Miles, Matthew B. and Huberman, Michael (1994). *Qualitative Data Analysis*, 2nd edn. Thousand Oaks, CA: Sage. Chapters 8–13.

Novak, Josef D. and Cañas, Alberto J. (2006). The theory underlying concept maps and how to construct and use them. Institute for Human and Machine Cognition, http://en.wikipedia.org/wiki/Concept_map (accessed 11 December 2010).

Slone, Debra J. (2009). Visualizing qualitative information, *The Qualitative Report*, 14(3), 488–97. Retrieved from www.nova.edu/ssss/QR/QR14-3/slone.pdf.

Bringing it all together: writing your research report

I always find it very exciting to start a project – collecting data, visiting different locations, talking to people, observing, taking notes and pictures, recording audio and video data, and reading about the topic of interest. After having collected some data, of course I am curious to dig deeper and to begin the analytic process, following up on initial hunches, ideas and thoughts. Coding the data can become a bit boring at times, but once this is done another fun phase follows. Based on my coding, document groups and links I have created throughout descriptive-level analysis, I can now query the data in all kinds of different ways and ask all kinds of different questions on the conceptual level. After having found answers, seeing how everything fits together and how the story enfolds, I find it difficult at times to sit down and write it all up. My curiosity is satisfied, I have found out what I wanted to find out and if there were not the external pressure to publish, who knows? The study results might just be stored away in a cupboard. Does this sound familiar to some of you?

I suppose that almost all readers of this book need to write some form of report, be it a student project report, a thesis or dissertation, or a research report. If you followed the suggestion on how to set up a project, how to organize your documents and build up your project, your ATLAS.ti HU already contains lots of elements that you need for your report. When preparing my Master's thesis at Oregon State University in the USA, I was asked to write the first three chapters – introduction, literature review and an outline of the method section – before the first committee meeting was scheduled and the data collection phase began. I found that this was very helpful because it meant that about half of the thesis was already written when it came to writing up the analysis. Also, one had a clearer idea about what one wanted to do in the empirical phase. Based on this positive experience, I always recommend to begin writing the report right at the start of a research project. The introduction is likely to change but it helps you to outline your ideas. The literature review is important to gain an overview of the field and to find the white area in the landscape that has not yet been explored. You can always add to it and modify bits and pieces throughout the course of the project. It helps you to outline and formulate the research question(s) and to find the appropriate methodological approach to study it or them. These can be written up in a draft method chapter before you begin to collect data.

Returning to the metaphor of the journey that I have used in this book, this is all part of the preparatory work, like reading books and articles about the destination, looking at maps and pictures, thinking about the clothes and items to take along, thinking about which means of transportation to use to get there, and packing bags. If well prepared beforehand, a journey is probably more enjoyable, sustainable and prosperous in terms of the overall experience. This also applies to your ATLAS.ti project. Recall Chapters 3 and 5 where I wrote about good data file names and about sorting and organizing your documents. If the overall research questions are not clear and if the direction in which you want to go is vague, it is difficult to come up with meaningful names and document groups. Of course, document names can be changed but it is time consuming. Document groups can be created at all times in ATLAS.ti, but then the initial frame guiding your analysis is missing and it is easier to get or to feel lost. In Chapters 5 and 6 I explained how to make use of the memo function. For example, I suggested writing a project memo after setting up your project so that it contains a list of research questions and ideas. Later I asked you to write research question memos that allow you to approach your analysis in a systematic way. All of this is easier when you prepare your project well in the first place.

How does this relate to writing your report? Assuming you have written a draft method chapter, this can be completed first. Look at the list of documents in the P-Docs Manager and the primary document families. This will help you to describe your sampling and probably also remind you of the data collection phase. If you have interview data and have written interview protocols, reread them in the P-Doc comment field. If you have other types of data, you may have written information on the source file and how you have generated it into the comment field.

Then take a look at your coding system and describe how you have developed it. Rereading your research diary will help you to remember what you did and how it evolved. A good idea is to have saved copy bundle files of the various stages of your project. Keep a copy bundle file of your initial coding before doing lots of sorting and structuring work. It reminds you how you got started. Further, store a copy bundle file at the end of stage-1 coding when you are quite certain about the structure of your coding system. These stages can then be compared to the final version, which allows you to describe the development over time. Select one important category and describe it in detail, including the subcodes and how you have built it up. Add the full code book at the end of your report or in an appendix, so you can refer the interested reader to it. To make it interesting to read, you can add network view images for each category as described in Chapter 7. In the last part of the method section describe how you have approached the next analysis phase, the conceptual level. This can be done by explaining how you set up your research question memos and how quotes from the data are referenced. End the chapter with a list of research questions that you are going to provide an answer for in the results chapter. It might be interesting to compare this list to the initial list of questions in the project memo. This allows you to see whether it was possible to stay with your original ideas or whether the insights you gained from the data during coding moved your research in a different direction.

Writing the results chapter is greatly facilitated by the research question memos. If you set them up as recommended, they are the building blocks for each section of this chapter. Think about a meaningful sequence and copy and paste the content of the memos including the linked quotations into your Word document. Depending on how formally you have written your memos, there is more or less editing to do. You probably have to work on the flow of the text, add a few references, decide which quotes you want to use and integrate them into the text, and so on. As we all know, it is much easier to edit an already existing text than to sit in front of a white piece of paper that waits to be filled with letters. Thus, your research question memos are a good starting point. If you write a paper, you could select two or three memos/research questions and write up your analysis around them. When writing a thesis or dissertation, think about the story that you want to tell, then select the memos you want to include and decide on the sequence.

Other little helpers in scripting your results chapter are the network views that you have created. As appropriate, insert them as images to illustrate your results. You may find it easier to write up your findings by describing the network views. It will also make a nice change for the reader to actually see how the various issues in your data are related.

Thus, it is all in your ATLAS.ti project. You just have to work through it step by step. You can start with the text that is already there in ATLAS.ti, which you have written throughout the course of the analysis. The task that remains is to weave it all together to form a coherent report. When preparing your project and report in this way, the little extra on top is that a third person can trace your analysis; your ATLAS.ti project is the audio trail. The proof is not only in the pudding (your writing). Properly used, software like ATLAS.ti can improve the validity of your research. With this, I would like to end my story. I wish you good luck with your ATLAS.ti projects and with writing up your findings – hopefully resulting in good grades and successful publications.

Epilogue

As Winograd and Flores noted in 1987, 'computers, like every technology, are a vehicle for the transformation of tradition' (p. 179). CAQDAS is transforming our ways of collecting, handling and analyzing qualitative data. Trying to apply traditional manual techniques within a software environment is similar to mounting a dialing plate on a smartphone. I am advocating that qualitative data analysis traditions need to be transformed – not because technology forces us, but because it enhances the research process and allows us to gain insights that otherwise could not have been achieved. Software like ATLAS.ti allows us to analyze qualitative data in a systematic and transparent way without precluding openness. It permits us to query data in ways that are not imaginable with traditional methods. Based on a well-coded project, we can ask questions and find answers that remained hidden in the data before. We don't have to rely on intuitive hunches. We can follow up on ideas without spending three days just finding out they were a dead end. A further advantage is that is is possible for a third person to double-check our findings. All of this improves the quality of qualitative research, thereby enhancing scientific and human knowledge. The requirement is that we teach students and researchers how to work with software to analyze qualitative data. This is no different from using programs like SPSS or STATA. I think there is little disagreement when I state that one needs to be familiar with measurement scales and the requirements of statistical test procedures in order to use these tools properly. The NCT method will help CAQDAS users to understand and learn how to build a coding system in order to prepare qualitative data for further analysis.

Another transformation we are likely to see has to do with the types of data that will be collected, for example induced by mobile devices and apps like ATLAS.ti mobile. Computers will become more and more a hybrid of traditional desktop and Web-based applications with constant access to the Internet and the World Wide Web that you can use for communication and data collection. It is already common practice to send text, image, audio and video messages. If CAQDAS goes mobile, the collection of multimedia data for qualitative analysis can be expected to follow suit. Future versions of the software are likely to become available as both desktop and Web-based applications. The latter will facilitate real-time cooperative work across the globe. Technological advancement will not stand still and after version 7 there will be a version 8 then 9. Apps for tablets and smartphones have just come on the scene and it will be exciting to see how they are adopted and integrated in everyday work routines. In providing user support, software training and project consultation, I will continue to observe how software is used in the qualitative data analysis process, what kinds of data are analyzed and which research topics are investigated. As with this edition, I am certain that the next edition will not just be about modified mouse clicks and menu options. It will be about further possibilities for qualitative data analysis. I am looking forward to an exciting future in the field of computer-assisted qualitative data analysis. Until next time.

Yours faithfully,

References

Alexa, Melina., and Zuell, Corneliy. (2000). 'Text analysis Software: Commonalities, differences and limitations: The results of a review'. *Quality & Quantity*, 34, 299–321.

Araujo, Luis (1995). Designing and refining hierarchical coding frames, in Udo Kelle (ed.), *Computer-Aided Qualitative Data Analysis*. London: Sage. Chapter 7.

Barry, Christine A. (1998). Choosing qualitative data analysis software: Atlas/ti and NUD.IST compared. *Sociological Research Online*, 3(3), http://www.socresonline.org.uk/3/3/4.html (accessed 15 December 2013).

Bazeley, Pat (2007). *Qualitative Data Analysis with NVivo*. London: Sage.

Bazeley, Pat and Richards, Lyn (2000). *The NVivo Qualitative Project Book*. London: Sage.

Bernard, Russel H. and Ryan, Gery W. (2010). *Analysing Qualitative Data: Systematic Approaches*. London: Sage.

Birks, Melanie (2008). Memoing in qualitative research: probing data and processes, *Journal of Research in Nursing*, 13, 68–75.

Blumer, Herbert (1969). *Symbolic Interactionism: Perspective and Method*. Englewood Cliffs, NJ: Prentice Hall.

Bodgan, Robert C. and Biklen, Sari Knopp (2007). *Qualitative Research for Education: An Introduction to Theories and Methods*, 5th edn. Boston, MA: Pearson Education.

Boeije, Hennie R. (2010). *Analysis in Qualitative Research*. London: Sage.

Charmaz, Kathy (2002). Qualitative interviewing and grounded theory analysis, in Jaber F. Gubrium and James A. Holstein (eds), *Handbook of Interview Research: Context & Method*. Thousand Oaks, CA: Sage. pp. 675–84.

Charmaz, Kathy (2006). *Constructing Grounded Theory: A Practical Guide Through Qualitative Analysis*. London: Sage.

Corbin, Juliet and Strauss, Anselm (2008). *Basics of Qualitative Research: Techniques and Procedures for Developing Grounded Theory*, 3rd edn. London: Sage.

Cortazzi, Martin (1993). *Narrative Analysis*. London: Falmer Press.

Creswell, John W. (1998). *Qualitative Inquiry and Research Design: Choosing among Five Traditions*. London: Sage.

Denzin, Norman K. and Lincoln, Yvonne S. (2000). *Handbook of Qualitative Research*, 2nd edn. London: Sage.

Dey, Ian (1993). *Qualitative Data Analysis: A user-friendly guide for social scientists*. London: Routledge.

Di Gregorio, Silvana and Davidson, Judith (2008). *Qualitative Research Design for Software Users*. Maidenhead: Open University Press/McGraw-Hill.

Evers, Jeanine C., Silver, Christina, Mruck, Katja and Peeters, Bart (2011). Introduction to the KWALON experiment: discussions on qualitative data analysis software by developers and users. *Forum Qualitative Sozialforschung/ Forum: Qualitative Social Research*, 12(1), Art. 40, http://nbn-resolving.de/ urn:nbn:de:0114-fqs1101405.

Fielding, Nigel G. and Lee, Raymond M. (1998). *Computer Analysis and Qualitative Research*. London: Sage.

Friese, Susanne (2000). *Self-concept and Identity in a Consumer Society: Aspects of Symbolic Product Meaning*. Marburg: Tectum.

Friese, Susanne (2011). Using ATLAS.ti for analyzing the financial crisis data. Forum *Qualitative Sozialforschung/Forum: Qualitative Social Research*, 12(1), Art. 39, http://nbn-resolving.de/urn:nbn:de:0114-fqs1101397.

Friese, Susanne (2014). On methods and methodologies and other observations, in Friese, Susanne and Ringmayr, Thomas (eds.), *ATLAS.ti User Conference 2013: Fostering Dialog on Qualitative Methods*. University Press, Technical University Berlin. http://nbn-resolving.de/urn:nbn:de:kobv: 83-opus4-44138.

Gable, Robert K. and Wolf, Marian B. (1993). *Instrument Development in the Affective Domain: Meaning Attitudes and Values in Corporate and School Settings*, 2nd edn. Boston, MA: Kluwer Academic.

Gibbs, Graham (2005). Writing as analysis. Online QDA, http://onlineqda. hud.ac.uk./Intro_QDA/writing_analysis.php (accessed 15 December 2013).

Glaser, Barney G. (1978). *Theoretical Sensitivity: Advances in the Methodology of Grounded Theory*. Mill Valley, CA: Sociological Press.

Glaser, Barney G. and Strauss, Anselm L. (1967). *Discovery of Grounded Theory: Strategies for Qualitative Research*. Chicago: Aldine.

Goleman, Daniel (1995). *Emotional Intelligence*. New York: Bantam Books.

Hartmann, Eddie (2011). Strategien des Gegenhandelns: Zur Soziodynamik symbolischer Kämpfe um Zugehörigkeit. Konstanz: UVK.

Hinchliffe, Steve, Crang, Mike, Reimer, Suzanne and Hudson, Alan (1997). Software for qualitative research: 2. Some thoughts on 'aiding' analysis. *Environment and Planning A*, 29, 1109–24.

Hug, Theo (2001). Editorial zur Reihe: 'Wie kommt die Wissenschaft zu Wissen?', in Theo Hug (ed.), *Einführung in die Forschungsmethodik und Forschungspraxis*, Vol. 2. Baltmannsweiler: Schneider-Verlag. pp. 3–10.

Jefferson, G. (1984). Transcript notation, in John Heritage (ed.), *Structures of Social Interaction*. New York: Cambridge University Press.

Kallmeyer, W. and Schütze, F. (1976). Konversationsanalyse, *Studium Linguistik*, 1, 1–28.

Kelle, Udo (ed.) (1995). *Computer-aided Qualitative Data Analysis*. London: Sage.

Kelle, Udo and Kluge, Susann (2010). Vom Einzelfall zum Typus: Fallvergleich und Fallkontrastierung in der qualitativen Sozialforschung. Wiesbaden: VS Verlag.

Khateb, Asaid, Pegna, Alan J., Michel, Christoph M., Landis, Theodor and Annoni, Jean-Marie (2002). Dynamics of brain activation during an explicit word and image recognition task: an electrophysiological study. *Brain Topography*, 14(3), 197–213.

Konopásek, Zdeněk (2007). Making thinking visible with Atlas.ti: computer assisted qualitative analysis as textual practices. Forum Qualitative Sozialforschung/Forum: *Qualitative Social Research*, 9(2), Art. 12, http://nbn-resolving.de/urn:nbn:de:0114-fqs0802124.

Kuckartz, Udo (1995). Case-oriented quantification, in Udo Kelle (ed.), *Computer-Aided Qualitative Data Analysis: Theory, Methods and Practice*. London: Sage. pp. 158–66.

Kuckartz, Udo (2005). Einführung in die computergestützte Analyse qualitativer Daten. Wiesbaden: VS Verlag.

LeCompte, Margarete Diane and Preissle, Judith (1993). *Ethnography and Qualitative Design in Educational Research*, 2nd edn. San Diego, CA: Academic Press.

Legewie, Heiner (2014). ATLAS.ti – How it all began (A grandfather's perspective), in Friese, Susanne and Ringmayr, Thomas (eds.), *ATLAS.ti User Conference 2013: Fostering Dialog on Qualitative Methods*. University Press, Technical University Berlin. http://nbn-resolving.de/urn:nbn:de:kobv:83-opus4-44140.

Lewins, Ann and Silver, Christine (2007). *Using Software in Qualitative Research: A Step-by-Step Guide*. London: Sage.

Mayring, Philipp (2010). *Qualitative Inhaltsanalyse*, 11th edn. Weinheim: Beltz.

Miles, Matthew B. and Huberman, Michael (1994). *Qualitative Data Analysis*, 2nd edn. Thousand Oaks, CA: Sage.

Morrison, Moya and Moir, Jim (1998). The role of computer software in the analysis of qualitative data: efficient clerk, research assistant or Trojan horse? *Journal of Advanced Nursing*, 28(1), 106–16.

Morse, Janice M. (1994). Emerging from the data: the cognitive process of analysis in qualitative inquiry, in Janice M. Morse (ed.), *Critical Issues in Qualitative Research Methods*. Thousand Oaks, CA: Sage. pp. 22–43.

Novak, Josef D. and Cañas, Alberto J. (2006). The theory underlying concept maps and how to construct and use them, Institute for Human and Machine Cognition, http://en.wikipedia.org/wiki/Concept_map (accessed 15 December 2013).

Novak, Josef D. and Gowin, D. Bob (2002). *Learning How to Learn*. New York: Cambridge University Press. (First published in 1984.)

Okeley, Judith (1994). Thinking through fieldwork, in Alan Bryman and Robert G. Burgess (eds), *Analyzing Qualitative Data*. London: Routledge. pp. 111–28.

Paulus, Trena, Woods, Megan, Atkins, David and Rob Macklin, Rob (2014). Current Reporting Practices of ATLAS.ti User in Published Research Studies, in in Friese, Susanne and Ringmayr, Thomas (eds.), *ATLAS.ti User Conference 2013: Fostering Dialog on Qualitative Methods*. University Press, Technical University Berlin. http://nbn-resolving.de/urn:nbn:de:kobv:83-opus4-44295.

Prus, Robert C. (1996). *Symbolic Interaction and Ethnographic Research: Inter-subjectivity and the Study of Human Lived Experience.* Albany, NY: SUNY Press.

Richards, Lyn (2009). *Handling Qualitative Data: A practical guide,* 2nd edn. London: Sage.

Richards, Lyn and Richards, Tom (1994). From filing cabinet to computer, in Alan Bryman and Robert G. Burgess (eds), *Analysing Qualitative Data.* London: Routledge. pp. 146–72.

Richards, Tom and Richards, Lyn (1995). Using hierarchical categories in qualitative data analysis, in Udo Kelle (ed.), *Computer-Aided Qualitative Data Analysis.* London: Sage. Chapter 6.

Riessman, Catherine K. (2008). *Narrative Methods for the Human Sciences.* Thousand Oaks, CA: Sage.

Saillard, Elif Kus (2011). Systematic versus interpretive analysis with two CAQDAS packages: NVivo and MAXQDA. *Forum Qualitative Sozialforschung/Forum: Qualitative Social Research,* 12(1), Art. 34, http://nbn-resolving.de/urn:nbn:de:0114-fqs1101345.

Saldaña, Jonny (2003). *Longitudinal Qualitative Research: Analyzing Change through Time.* Walnut Creek, CA: AltaMira Press.

Saldaña, Jonny (2009). *The Coding Manual for Qualitative Researchers.* London: Sage.

Seale, Clive (1999). *The Quality of Qualitative Research.* London: Sage.

Seidel, John (1991). Methods and madness in the application of computer technology to qualitative data analysis, in Nigel G. Fielding and Raymond M. Lee (eds), *Using Computers in Qualitative Research.* London: Sage. pp. 107–16.

Seidel, John V., (1998). Qualitative Data Analysis, http://www.qualisresearch.com/qda_paper.htm (originally published as Qualitative Data Analysis, in *The Ethnograph v5.0: A User's Guide,* Appendix E, 1998, Colorado Springs, Colorado: Qualis Research).

Seidel, John and Kelle, Udo. (1995). Different functions of coding in the analysis of textual data, in Udo Kelle (ed.), *Computer-Aided Qualitative Data Analysis.* London: Sage. Chapter 4.

Silver, Christina and Lewins, Ann (2010). Computer Assisted Qualitative Data Analysis, in Barry McGaw, Penelope Peterson and Eva Baker, (eds.) *The International Encyclopedia of Education,* 3rd edn. Oxford: Elsevier.

Silver, Christine and Rivers, Christine (2014). Learning from the Learners: the role of technology acceptance and adoption theories in understanding researchers' early experiences with CAQDAS packages, in Friese, Susanne and Ringmayr, Thomas (eds.), *ATLAS.ti User Conference 2013: Fostering Dialog on Qualitative Methods.* University Press, Technical University Berlin. http://nbn-resolving.de/urn:nbn:de:kobv:83-opus4-44300.

Silverman, David (2000). *Doing Qualitative Research: A Practical Handbook.* London: Sage.

Silverman, David (2006). *Interpreting Qualitative Data: Methods for Analysing Talk, Text and Interaction.* London: Sage.

Smith, Beverly A. and Hesse-Biber, Sharlene (1996). Users' experiences with qualitative data analysis software: neither Frankenstein's monster nor muse. *Social Science Computer Review*, 14(4), 423–32.

Strauss, Anselm L. and Corbin, Juliet (1998). *Basics of Qualitative Research: Techniques and Procedures for Developing Grounded Theory*, 2nd edn. London: Sage.

Strübing, Jörg and Schnettler, Bernt (2004). Klassische Grundlagentexte zur Methodologie interpretativer Sozialforschung, in Jörg Strübing and Bernt Schnettler (eds), *Methodologie interpretativer Sozialforschung: Klassische Grundlagentexte*. Konstanz: UVK. pp. 9–18.

Welsh, Elaine (2002). Dealing with data: using NVivo in the qualitative data analysis process. *Forum Qualitative Sozialforschung/Forum: Qualitative Social Research*, 3(2), Art. 26, http://nbn-resolving.de/urn:nbn:de:0114-fqs0202260.

Winograd, Terry and Flores, Fernando (1987). *Understanding Computers and Cognition*. Reading, MA: Addison-Wesley.

Wolcott, Harry F. (1994). *Transforming Qualitative Data: Description, Analysis, and Interpretation*. Thousand Oaks, CA: Sage.

Wolcott, Harry E. (2009). *Writing Up Qualitative Research*, 3rd edn. London: Sage.

Woolf, Nick (2014). Analytic strategies and analytic tactics, in Friese, Susanne and Ringmayr, Thomas (eds.), *ATLAS.ti User Conference 2013: Fostering Dialog on Qualitative Methods*. University Press, Technical University Berlin. http://nbn-resolving.de/urn:nbn:de:kobv:83-opus4-44159.

Index

Figures and Tables are indicated by page numbers in bold.